STUDIES IN IRISH HISTORY, SECOND SERIES

edited by

T. W. MOODY
Professor of Modern History
University of Dublin

J. C. BECKETT
Professor of Irish History
Queen's University, Belfast

T. D. WILLIAMS
Professor of Modern History
National University of Ireland

VOLUME VIII

RURAL DISORDER AND POLICE REFORM
IN IRELAND 1812–36

STUDIES IN IRISH HISTORY, SECOND SERIES

RURAL DISORDER AND POLICE REFORM IN IRELAND, 1812–36

by
GALEN BROEKER

LONDON: Routledge & Kegan Paul
TORONTO: University of Toronto Press
1970

14431

First published in Great Britain in 1970
by Routledge and Kegan Paul Ltd
and in Canada and the United States of America
by University of Toronto Press
Printed in Great Britain by
Cox & Wyman Ltd
London, Fakenham and Reading

SBN 7100 6801 8
UTP ISBN 0 8020 1719 3

CONTENTS

v

Contents

PREFACE

THE PRIMARY PURPOSE of this work is twofold: to investigate organized peasant opposition to the existing economic and religious systems in Ireland between 1812 and 1836, and to examine the methods developed by the authorities to deal with the violence used by the peasants to make this opposition known. In addition, the work fills certain gaps in the knowledge of the early career of Robert Peel, and makes some contribution to the history of the catholic emancipation crisis of 1828–9.

Since it was rural violence that made it difficult for the governing classes to ignore the poverty of the majority of the Irish people, and that convinced some of the more perceptive politicians that the traditional coercive instruments alone would never 'civilize' Ireland, this work is not concerned with the cities and larger towns. In comparison with the countryside, the cities and towns presented only minor problems for those responsible for law and order during this period.

Throughout, the word *banditti* is used to identify members of the agrarian secret societies. It is an honourable word, meaning 'one who is proscribed', and was used by the officers of the Irish military establishment, who found it very difficult to identify the secret societies by their chosen titles.

I wish to acknowledge the assistance given me by the staffs of the libraries and record offices in England and Ireland in which I did much of the research for this work. I am grateful to the American Council of Learned Societies for a grant in the early stages of my research, and to the University of Tennessee for a leave of absence to complete the research and for a generous grant in aid of publication. Special thanks are due Professor T. W. Moody of Trinity College, Dublin, for his valuable editorial advice. Finally, mention must be made of the invaluable advice and assistance provided by my wife.

A portion of the material in the early chapters of this work appeared in an article of mine in the *Journal of Modern History* in 1961, and is used with permission of the editor.

The University of Tennessee   GALEN BROEKER

ABBREVIATIONS

B.M., Add. MSS	British Museum, Additional Manuscripts.
Hansard 1	*Hansard's parliamentary debates,* 1812–20.
Hansard 2	*Hansard's parliamentary debates,* new series, 1820–30.
Hansard 3	*Hansard's parliamentary debates,* third series, 1830–36.
H.C.	House of commons.
H.L.	House of lords.
H.O.	Home Office.
n.d.	no date.
N.L.I.	National Library of Ireland.
P.R.O.	Public Record Office of England.
S.P.O., C.S.O.	State Paper Office of Ireland (Dublin Castle), Chief Secretary's Office.
W.O.	War Office.

Note: For other abbreviations used in footnotes see 'Rules for contributors to *Irish Historical Studies*', second edition, by T. W. Moody, in *Irish Historical Studies,* supplement I (Jan. 1968).

I

THE TORIES AND IRELAND,
1812-30

~~~~~~

IRELAND FROM 1812 to 1830 was the despair of the governing
and the governed – threatening, gloomy, stubborn, too disturbed to respond effectively to civil government, not disturbed
enough to justify full-scale military occupation. The act of
union which combined the parliaments of Ireland and England
had not united the peoples. To the Irish peasants, the economic,
religious, and political system inflicted by an alien, protestant
minority seemed to threaten their very existence. To many
Englishmen, the Irish were clearly inferior beings and potential
traitors, automatically suspect on grounds of religion and history. The politicians and administrators who governed Ireland,
confronted by the baffling intricacies of the 'Irish problem',
faced a situation imperfectly understood by all concerned. Year
after year a procession of men considered capable, even brilliant,
in other areas of government found themselves determining
policy and administering Irish affairs in an atmosphere of anger,
fear, and perpetual frustration.

Lord Liverpool, tory prime minister from 1812 to 1827,
described Ireland as 'a political phenomenon – not influenced by
the same feelings as appear to affect mankind in other countries'.[1] Robert Peel, closely associated with Irish affairs during

<hr>

[1] Lord Liverpool to Robert Peel, 28 Jan. 1816 (Peel papers, B.M., Add.
MS 40181).

these years, determined the cause of continual disturbance in Ireland to be 'that natural predilection for outrage and a lawless life which I believe nothing can control'.[2] Such exasperation is understandable. Both Liverpool and Peel were able and conscientious leaders in the tory government that successfully guided England through the difficulties of 1812–27; both sincerely desired a peaceful and prosperous Ireland, and gave their best efforts to achieving it. But the policies they supported in England – efficient and economical government, the firm maintenance of public order, moderate reforms – failed dramatically when applied in Ireland.

The Irish peasants did not settle down to cultivate their very modest gardens. Bound together by oaths, armed with stolen weapons, sometimes decked out in crude uniforms, a considerable portion of the population continued to accept 'agrarian outrage' as a legitimate weapon in the continuing struggle against those who represented authority – landlords, magistrates, policemen, and soldiers. In 1829 the tories approached the end of their long period of domination still seeking 'a system of measures for the permanent civilization' of Ireland.[3]

The basic cause of agrarian unrest was the abject poverty of the great number of Irishmen who tried to make a living from the soil. Irish agriculture was backward and wasteful, thwarting progress and fostering dissension. Irish industry, concentrated in the north-east, had little significance in the total Irish economy. As the nineteenth century progressed, the number of people who looked to the soil for their livelihood increased. In spite of sporadic famine, disease, and emigration, the population rose from not quite five and a half million in 1804 to over eight million in 1841. In most areas, about 75 per cent of the families depended on agriculture.[4]

Were there less abundant evidence of the state of the Irish in these years, it would be difficult to believe the traditional description of the stark misery of rural Ireland. The potato, which allowed the peasant to feed his family from a small

[2] Peel to Liverpool, 15 Oct. 1813 (Liverpool papers, B.M., Add. MS 38195).

[3] Peel to Lord Francis Leveson Gower, 30 July 1829 (Peel papers, B.M., Add. MS 40337)

[4] Black, *Econ. thought & Ir. question*, p. 3.

acreage, provided the means of bare subsistence, but a crop failure, a rise in rent, or an economic fluctuation that lessened chances of employment could mean beggary and starvation. Population pressure and a lack of alternative employment created a desperate demand for land, which in turn raised rents and made tenure uncertain. High rents encouraged subdivision by the landlords and subletting by the tenants: between the landlord and the man who actually cultivated the soil, there could exist a hierarchy of agents, middlemen and under-tenants. By the 1840s, the average square mile of improved land was occupied by sixty families.[5]

Over the years, witness after witness arrived at Westminster from Ireland to testify before parliamentary commissions and committees on Irish social and economic problems. These experts were not particularly successful in suggesting viable solutions for the problems under investigation, but their testimony did help to reveal the extent and depth of rural poverty and to create the image of a class of villains – the landlords and their agents. Holdings were fragmented in an effort to squeeze as much rent as possible from every estate; tenants were evicted in order to extract a higher rent from others; estates were packed with forty-shilling freeholders who, under threat of eviction, voted in county elections as the landlord directed. These and similar practices form part of the historical record of early nineteenth-century rural life. But Ireland's faulty economic structure and expanding population were not the exclusive creations of landlords and agents. The major contribution of these men to the conditions of the time lay in the intensification, by their actions, of an already existing situation.

The province of Ulster provided an exception to the dreary pattern of Irish agrarian misery. Domestic linen manufacture gave many rural families a higher and more certain income than farming alone could do. Tenant right, which meant that a tenant could not be evicted without compensation for his interest in the farm, made tenure more secure and encouraged better farming. Over a large area of the province, landlords and tenants alike were protestants of British ancestry, so that common religion and a shared dislike for the native Irish may

[5] T. W. Freeman, *Pre-famine Ireland, a study in historical geography* (Manchester, 1957), p. 35.

have made for better relations between classes. Not all of Ulster, however, shared in the relative prosperity, and the areas along the boundaries were at best marginal.[6] Bad relations between landlords and tenants were far from unknown and hostility between the catholic and the protestant populations was an established fact of the Ulster way of life. But beyond doubt better social and economic conditions prevailed in Ulster than in the other three provinces.

The religious division of Ireland into protestant 'conquerors' and catholic 'savages' deepened and aggravated the bitterness stemming from the economic plight of the peasants, and accentuated the differences between the governing class and the governed. The great majority of landlords, magistrates, and office-holders were protestant, as were the clergymen who received the tithe paid by all Irishmen, protestant and catholic, towards the maintenance of the clergy of the established church. Prior to the 1830s, opposition to the tithe appeared most frequently as but one item in the programme of the disaffected. But an overly zealous incumbent could trigger a local tithe 'war'. For example, around 1823 the Rev. Mr Morett of Castleowen attempted to 'screw up the natives' by increasing the income of his benefice. Those who protested were charged with 'Whiteboyism' and imprisoned. Only the 'vigilance of the gentry and the admonitions of the clergy' prevented serious trouble. It is worth noting that banditti programmes occasionally included opposition to the payments requested of the peasants by the catholic clergy.[7] The tithe as a cause of agrarian discontent appears to have been basically more economic than religious, but by its very nature the tithe problem when it arose assumed a religious character.

To the peasants, the religious aspect of the Irish problem was quite elementary; to them, there was no distinction to be made between protestant and 'Saxon oppressor'. Before the 1820s, the long, often emotional catholic emancipation controversy meant little to the average Irishman, who was too concerned with his more immediate problems to worry much about the question of

[6] Ibid., p. 270.
[7] M. Collins to Brigade-major Mahoney, 26 July 1823 (Surrey Record Office, Goulburn papers, II/14); Richard Willcocks to Peel, 23 Mar. 1814 (P.R.O., H.O. 100/177).

catholic parliamentary representation. During the early decades of the century, there were scattered 'revolts' against candidates of the landlords, perhaps triggered by politically conscious priests, but it was not until about 1824, when O'Connell and the catholic clergy began to teach the peasant to oppose the disabilities, that the struggle for catholic emancipation became in itself a threat to the authority of the government.

The controversy over catholic emancipation did, however, have an influence on the Irish countryside prior to 1824. An extended debate on any controversial topic involving Ireland would sooner or later reach the rural areas. In places where both catholics and protestants lived, the emancipation debates might provide for a triumphal parade or a show of strength by one of the two religious groups, and the opposing group could always be relied upon to take exception. In 1815, an 'information centre' was established in Armagh, where religious factions posted resolutions containing a list of fairs where catholics and protestants might meet to fight it out.[8] Year after year, reports of these sectarian clashes arrived at the seat of the Irish administration, Dublin Castle, and were conscientiously forwarded to London, there to become part of the home office records. Some of the more diligent magistrates tried to prevent the outbreaks, but unless the temper of the area involved seemed to threaten more than a purely local affray, the clashes were often allowed to run their course. Few participants were arrested, and the usual attitude of the local authorities was that indicated in a report from a magistrate in Maghera, Londonderry. Somewhat whimsically, he had set about determining responsibility for a riot following a fair by counting the number of broken window-panes. Evidently the responsibility was almost evenly divided, for 605 'protestant windows' and 615 'catholic windows' had been smashed.[9] Not only did these outbursts strengthen and perpetuate local hatreds, but since protestantism and the government of Ireland were so closely connected, they also helped to extend and intensify resentment against the government itself, thus sustaining the habit of violent opposition to the protestant ascendancy.

[8] State of the country, Aug. 1815 (P.R.O., H.O. 100/184).
[9] Enclosure in William Gregory to Henry Hobhouse, 3 July 1823 (P.R.O., H.O. 100/209).

Over the centuries, rebellion had played a prominent role in the history of Anglo-Irish relations. The pattern was familiar to the men of Westminster and Dublin Castle: England, involved in a war of sufficient magnitude and duration, would find its leading adversary working with Irish malcontents to add another front to the conflict. It was also part of the pattern for foreign aid to be tardy and insufficient, leaving the Irish rebels to do most of the fighting and to bear the consequences of defeat. Britain's success in dealing with Irish insurrections caused certain officials to view the prospect of rebellion with limited approval, as a means of clearing the air, of forcing the disaffected out into the open where they could be more readily dealt with. As the lord lieutenant of Ireland observed in 1813, another revolution might be good for Ireland. It would lead to an unfortunate loss of life, 'but the results would be favourable to the tranquillity of the country'.[10]

In the early years of the nineteenth century, however, certain changes began to appear in the traditional pattern of opposition to British rule. The necessary conditions for revolution seemed to be present: an economic situation that threatened the existence of a majority of the people; a governing class alienated from the same majority and unwilling or unable to help them; and, until 1815, England's involvement in a Continental war. From 1800 to 1823, there were altogether only about five years free from serious agrarian disturbances in various sections of the country. But open rebellion did not materialize. The memory of the bloody suppression of the rebellion of 1798 and the might of British sea power, which made further French intervention unlikely, no doubt contributed to the absence of open revolt. But of equal importance was the dearth of leadership capable of moulding an effective revolutionary force. The radical movement, which had sought to unite the discontented during the second half of the eighteenth century, had all but disappeared. The small but growing Irish catholic middle class was still seeking its place in society and was widely separated from the masses by income, education, and interest. Leadership of a sort was provided by the catholic clergy in their efforts to check the growing tendency towards rural violence, but with very

[10] Lord Whitworth to Peel, 18 Nov. 1813 (Peel papers, B.M., Add. MS 40187).

limited success. Thus during the early decades of the nineteenth century, until Daniel O'Connell gained prominence, the Irish peasant was left alone to work out his own economic and social salvation. The result was the rise of agrarian secret societies and the spread of terrorism, designed to enforce peasant-made law over the law of the state. The activities of the peasant organizations presented the Irish government with a problem that demanded a major portion of its time and kept the authorities in a state of nervous apprehension for many years. All too frequently the arrival of autumn brought a fresh series of outbreaks of rural violence which Dublin Castle anxiously investigated for signs of 'insurrectionary activity of a political nature' or evidence of 'leadership by respectable people' which might indicate, not the usual agrarian disturbance, but the beginning of a revolution.

It is difficult, probably impossible, to separate and identify the many peasant organizations – Whiteboys, Carders, Rockites, Caravats, and others – which helped to create the rural chaos of this period. Different local officials in the same area might designate a single organization by several names. A degree of order can be introduced by ignoring problems of regional distribution and identification by name and attempting instead to classify the groups by organization and purpose. So classified, they fall into three categories: agrarian secret societies, religious societies, and local factions. The categories, however, tend to overlap. On occasion the Ribbon society, a catholic protection organization, might turn away from its major concern and pursue economic goals similar to those of the agrarian secret societies. Local factions, formed to perpetuate peasant feuds by gang-fighting at markets and fairs, often resembled the Ribbonmen in their enthusiasm for clashes with protestants. Where both agrarian secret societies and local factions existed in the same area, it is quite possible that the former drew part of their members from the latter. Nevertheless, the separate groups that comprise any one of the three major categories were committed to certain basic and long-established purposes that make classification relatively easy: the agrarian secret societies were most concerned with the economic problems of the peasants, the religious societies with the protection of those of one faith from the depredations of those of another, and local factions with whatever residual sources of violence the countryside might contain.

The agrarian secret societies had originated around 1760 among the peasants of Munster, when an organization known as the 'Whiteboys' started a campaign of violent opposition to eviction, low wages, and the tithe. Similar organizations then appeared in other provinces, and quickly developed the structure, policies, and tactics that were to characterize them for decades to come. The period of rebellion and repression at the end of the eighteenth century destroyed the secret societies or drove them underground, but by 1806 they had reappeared, stronger and more militant than before. Cornewall Lewis, writing in the 1830s, describes the secret societies as a 'vast trades union for the protection of the Irish peasantry'.[11] A present-day authority characterizes their efforts as 'a crude form of politics, by which the will of the community was enforced and evils ignored by the legislature redressed'.[12] An Irish landlord in 1815 designated them more succinctly as 'midnight legislators',[13] and the harassed authorities lumped the societies together as organizations of an 'insurrectionary nature'. To the officers of the Irish military establishment, despairing of identification of the societies by their chosen titles, they were the 'banditti'. To the general public, they remained the 'Whiteboys'.

The agrarian secret societies formed the 'standing army' of the disaffected, and seem to have had a continuous existence in Tipperary, Limerick, Westmeath, and Kildare from around 1806 to the 1840s. The names changed, but the same or similar organizations continued to make their presence known to the authorities.[14] There is no way to determine the size of any of these societies at all accurately, for numbers varied as local conditions changed. During quiet periods, active membership was probably limited to a small leadership group who served as the collective conscience of the peasant community and as custodians of the few firearms that had escaped seizure by the

---

[11] Sir G. C. Lewis, *Local disturbances in Ireland* (London, 1836), p. 99.
[12] McDowell, *Public opinion & govt policy*, p. 59.
[13] Arthur Vesey to Lord Norbury, 15 Sept. 1815 (P.R.O., H.O. 100/185).
[14] See *Returns respecting crimes and outrages in Co. Limerick*, H.L. 1841. (40), xviii.

authorities. Most surprising is the speed with which the societies could be reactivated if rents were raised, a zealous tithe-proctor appeared, outsiders were hired as labourers, or other evils seemed to threaten the peasants. The state of the country report for October 1817 showed Ireland to be for the first time in years free of disorder; yet by November secret societies were active throughout Sligo and were beginning to appear in Mayo, after landlords had begun an attempt to raise the already high rent-level in these counties.[15]

This ability to disappear and reappear suddenly was implicit in the organization of these societies. The members were drawn from the local peasantry, men who were farmers by day and banditti by night. They were bound together by an oath, which was the most potent weapon they possessed. The oath not only insured the obedience of the active members, but also was used to enlarge and strengthen the society. It could be imposed by threats of force upon reluctant members of the community, who would then become subject to the terrible punishment meted out to the oath-breaker. Thus a considerable portion of the community, by choice or by coercion, either belonged to secret societies or were neutralized by the oath to prevent their assisting the authorities in any way. An oath, even one extorted by fear, was not taken lightly by the Irish peasant.

From the earliest appearance of the agrarian secret societies in the eighteenth century, their operations tended to conform to a recognizable pattern. The announcement that, for example, rents were to be raised might be followed by the posting of a proclamation, written in a kind of pseudo-legal jargon and signed 'Captain Rock' or a similarly fanciful name, ordering the peasants not to take land under the new terms. The banditti programme might be rounded out with a warning against paying the tithe and hiring outside labourers and, on several occasions prior to the end of the Napoleonic wars, with some kind of pro-French statement. There is no evidence of ties between the peasants and the French, but the mere mention of the emperor's name could cause near hysteria in ascendancy circles. As late as September 1815 a magistrate solemnly informed the Castle that he had received information that there were French officers in Tipperary, that some of the banditti now

[15] State of the country, Oct. and Nov. 1817 (P.R.O., H.O. 100/193).

wore 'Napoleonic' uniforms, and that their French associates were in contact with St Helena.[16]

Aside from opposition to the tithe for primarily economic reasons, the role of religion in formulating banditti goals seems to have been minor. Local protestants might be threatened, protestant merchants might be boycotted (tradition required it), but the protestant who was visited by the banditti was usually marked for attention by his failure to honour the demands of the secret society rather than for religious considerations. The homes of the landlords were relatively immune from attack. Cattle might be maimed, pasture turned up, and crops destroyed, but well-armed servants with policemen and soldiers in reserve were more than a match for peasants armed with rocks, farm tools, and perhaps a few worn-out guns. Thus most of the victims of rural terrorism were Irish catholic peasants. Those who failed to heed the warnings of the society were visited by its members and threatened with terrible reprisals unless they yielded. If opposition continued, the rather pathetic efforts of the banditti to preserve elements of dignity and respectability faded away as torture, murder, rape, and the destruction of property were used to enforce the orders of the leaders. When the inevitable counter-attack developed, the banditti might take to the hills and wage guerrilla warfare against the soldiers and policemen sent against them. Not infrequently, the efforts of these partisans were rather surprisingly successful. Between 1813 and 1816, and between 1819 and 1823, considerable portions of the south and west were under the domination of peasant 'armies'. Landlords fled, magistrates abandoned their posts, dispatch riders and mail coaches had to be provided with escorts, and armed policemen might be forced to operate under the protection of soldiers. In 1820, an officer writing from the village of Hampstead near Kilconnel in Galway described the tenuous position of the army in that area:

. . . we occupied a slate house belonging to Mr Evans which had been very much injured, while the proprietor was assisting in the defence of Hampstead . . . about a month ago. The house . . . is situated about a quarter of a mile from town upon a gentle declivity, there is no ground near it that can have been built up and I have ordered

---

[16] Thomas Westropp to Gregory, 17 Sept. 1815 (P.R.O., H.O. 100/185).

loopholes to be made and other steps taken which will completely cover it from any attack. . . . It is perfectly adequate to contain Captain Mill and his party, but they have no bedding, nor do I see how it can be procured.[17]

To the men responsible for Irish affairs, a source of understandable concern was the possibility of local secret societies combining with similar organizations in other parts of Ireland. But despite reports of banditti 'emissaries' operating in parts of the country, it seems that efforts to form effective larger combinations, including more than a handful of agrarian secret societies, proved futile during this period. On several occasions, the Castle claimed to have uncovered headquarters of conspiracies involving numbers of societies, but on examination these claims appear to have been false or exaggerated.[18] When the relative calm of a province was disrupted by widespread outbreaks of violence, all taking place during a brief period of time, it was logical for the authorities to assume that co-operation between the societies was involved. However logical, evidence of such co-operation is unconvincing, and once a society 'came out' it pursued its own destiny with little apparent concern with what was happening elsewhere. Apparently there were few local leaders capable of creating and then keeping together the larger organizations. Suspicion of all outsiders, even those bearing the credentials of other societies, was a normal attitude among the banditti.

From union to the famine, Tipperary and Limerick were the most consistently disturbed counties in all Ireland, but just why this area should have become a kind of banditti epicentre is uncertain. A long history of bad relations between landlord and peasant did exist in parts of the two counties; on a number of occasions the Castle criticized the treatment of peasants on the Courteney estate in Limerick. Poverty and land-hunger were causes of much hostility, but the two counties were not the most poverty-stricken or overpopulated parts of the country. According to Cornewall Lewis, agrarian secret societies had greater continuity and were most active in areas where the soil was fertile, the population relatively dense, and the peasantry 'one

[17] Col. George Grey to the lord lieutenant, 3 Mar. 1820 (P.R.O., H.O. 100/198).
[18] See pp 63–4 below.

degree removed above the lowest poverty'.[19] It would seem that such conditions prevailed in both counties.[20] Well-established traditions of peasant violence, land-hunger, population pressure, a level of poverty which allowed the peasant to concentrate less on his stomach and more on hatred of his 'betters' – all were present and provide an interim explanation for the consistently disturbed condition of Tipperary and Limerick.

The second group of peasant organizations, the religious societies, are the most difficult of all to categorize. Little reliable information exists about the leading catholic organization, the Ribbon society: it was a secret organization, the authorities were wildly indiscriminate in the use of the terms 'Ribbon' and 'Ribbonmen', and it sought somewhat different aims in different areas. In Ulster, where membership was concentrated, the society was a catholic protection organization, a counter-force against the ultra-protestant Orange order. Its immediate concern was the protection of the catholic peasant against economic abuse by protestant landlords and physical attack by Orangemen. During periods of 'tranquillity' the members might amuse themselves by faction-fighting, preferably against protestants, and by attacking Orange processions. But during periods of deep unrest, Ribbonmen activities might become indistinguishable from those of the banditti in other parts of the country. In Dublin, Ribbonism was both religious and political, and apparently was associated with trade unionism. In other parts of Ireland, Ribbon influence was limited to the years around 1820 during which the leadership may have attempted to make the organization country-wide. In other instances, reports of Ribbonism occurring outside of Ulster and its environs probably represented a misuse of the term by the authorities.

At least as early as 1814, attempts were made to exercise some control over local Ribbon groups by committee,[21] and around 1820 the Ribbonmen of Dublin and the rural areas were apparently tenuously connected in 'a kind of proletarian underground'.[22] At this time, Ribbonism grew rapidly in a

[19] Lewis, *Local disturbances*, p. 90.
[20] Freeman, *Pre-famine Ireland*, pp. 211–24.
[21] See Peel to Sir George Hill, 16 Jan. 1814 (P.R.O., H.O. 100/176).
[22] McDowell, *Public opinion & govt policy*, p. 63.

considerable portion of rural Ireland, and may have been associated with outbreaks of violence in the central, western, and south-western parts of the country. Early in 1821, 'swearing' was reported in all parts of the country. The centre of activity seemed to be at Kilbeggan in Westmeath, and the disaffected may have had ties with Dublin Ribbonmen. The purpose of the plotters (described by the authorities as 'indefinite') was far more sophisticated than that of the average agrarian secret society: the exclusion of foreign produce, in order to provide ample work for the population and stop emigration.[23] But attempts at centralization were not successful. Quarrels were common, local groups failed to obey orders, and beyond general agreement on the desirability of revolution and the hatred of protestants, policy seems to have been vague and uncertain. And while the men of Dublin might strive to co-ordinate the activities of all the disaffected in preparation for England's next involvement in a war,[24] the peasants remained most concerned with tithes, land tenure, and other immediate threats to their existence. Perhaps the relatively elaborate structure of the Ribbon society helps to explain its frequent penetration by the authorities, which in turn led to arrests, spread suspicion, and may have made the peasant leaders reluctant to accept Ribbon leadership. For example, in 1813, a man named Toland was able to join the 'headquarters' of a Ribbon group. He marked the mail sent from there so that it could be opened and read at the post office, learned where the organization was purchasing guns, and marked each weapon for future identification.[25] When the central organizations were broken by the authorities, the ties between them and the local societies proved so weak that little effect could be noted on the activities of local groups, which apparently continued to function as before.

The leading protestant society, the Orange order, was both political and religious. Founded in 1795, it remained exclusively and militantly protestant and politically ultra-conservative in its opposition to any measure which might lessen the favoured protestant position. Just how many Orangemen there were

[23] Ibid., pp 63–5; Charles Grant to Lord Sidmouth, 2 Jan. 1821 (P.R.O., H.O. 100/200).
[24] Lord Talbot to Sidmouth, 9 Jan. 1821 (P.R.O., H.O. 100/200).
[25] Gregory to Heyland, 11 Dec. 1813 (P.R.O., H.O. 100/175).

during the early nineteenth century remains uncertain: the movement was a secret one, and both the leadership and the opposition seem to have claimed a far greater membership for the lodges than actually existed.[26] But at any time during the first twenty-five years following union, total Orange membership in Ireland would have been in the tens of thousands. Most of the lodges were in Ulster, but a number could be found wherever there were concentrations of protestants, and the organization could make itself felt in almost every level of society. The Castle, the magistracy, the military, the courts, the landlords, the clergy, and the peasantry were represented in the order. It is not surprising that to the catholic peasant of the north, 'Orangeism', 'protestantism', and 'authority' seemed synonymous.

The very existence of Orangeism was certain to promote bad feeling. Not only did it tend to make Ribbonism seem necessary to the catholic minority of rural Ulster, but also the insistence by the rank and file of the lodges that any sign of overt catholic activity called for an Orange reaction occasionally had tragic results. An example of the troublemaking potential of the lodges, even outside Ulster, is provided by the results of an investigation conducted by Dublin Castle in 1814 into the outbreak of agrarian violence which had spread over part of Ireland during the winter of 1813–14. It appeared (though proof was lacking) that the disturbances in Meath and Dublin counties had been precipitated by the appearance of anti-catholic handbills distributed by the local Orange lodges. Rumour among the catholic peasantry interpreted the handbills as an attempt to goad them into violence, thereby giving the government an excuse to 'conquer' the area and destroy them. The peasants evidently felt that their hopes lay in an association with disaffected groups in other counties, and in this way they were caught up in the violence of that winter.[27] Year after year, reports arrived at Dublin Castle of attacks by one religious faction and retaliation by the other. In 1815 the Orangemen were driven from a fairground in Derry, only to return with firearms and in turn drive out the Ribbonmen. This affray was

[26] See Senior, *Orangeism, 1795–1836*, pp 162, 230–31.
[27] Lt.-col. T. Marlay to Gregory, 15 June 1814 (P.R.O., H.O. 100/176).

the culmination of a series of fights which had gone against the catholics, who now determined on revenge. Emissaries were sent throughout Londonderry, Tyrone, and Donegal, and 'ten thousand' Ribbonmen prepared to meet at the Dunnemanagh fair. The Orangemen were more than willing to meet them, and only after the more level-headed protestants of the area asked the military authorities for protection did a strong military force arrive to close the fair and disperse the 'multitudes' on the surrounding hills.[28]

During the Wellesley administration of the 1820s, there was a flurry of anti-Orange activity, leading to the suppression of the movement between 1825 and 1828, but, with this exception, open hostility between government and Orangeism was kept in check until the 1830s. The Castle was fully aware of the dangerous part the lodges played in keeping a sizeable portion of the country in ferment. But, supported by powerful interests in England and Ireland, dedicated to the maintenance of the protestant constitution, the order could not be labelled 'insurrectionary', nor did most members of the Irish government wish to place it in that category. The consensus was to applaud the 'loyalty' of the Orangemen and to condemn their traditional methods of expressing it. Thus despite the temporary success of the Wellesley administration, and other attempts to limit Orange activity by proclamation, legislation, and occasional threats of more drastic action, about all the Castle did was to keep Orangeism at a minimum in the government and the military, and to forbid some of its more deliberately provocative activities.

The third group of peasant organizations, the local factions, can perhaps best be characterized as social organizations. Factions were formed to meet similar groups at fairs and market towns, where the contending parties could make a test of strength; motive, beyond the desire for a fight, was seldom important, though quarrels over the occupancy of land seem to have provided added incentive. In some areas, the selection of opponents was made easier by already-existing family feuds, and some of the factions – like the Ryans and Dwyers of Tipperary – were formed on a family basis. Other factions were apparently organized on a geographical basis, while still others drew on

28 Hill to Peel, 2 Sept. 1815 (P.R.O., H.O. 100/185).

several areas – the famous Caravat and Shanavest factions, for example, were scattered throughout five counties of south-west Ireland.[29] Again, the attitude of authority towards these faction affrays seems to have varied. It was quite common to ignore them as long as the participants confined their activities to fighting with one another and did no damage to the 'better class' elements of the neighbourhood.[30] It was not uncommon to withdraw police and military detachments from fairs to avoid clashes with the rioters, and it was not until 1836 that any instructions were given to the local authorities on the course to follow in such circumstances. There were occasions when conscientious magistrates attempted to stop the incidents, but the usual procedure was to 'let them fight it out'.[31]

Like the religious riots, these factional fights provided training in violence and contempt for the law. But their existence provided an even greater problem for the Irish government in another way, for during periods of extensive agrarian disturbances these local factions either provided men for the agrarian secret societies or operated as groups in loose co-operation with them. In this way a relatively small secret society could conceivably double its strength when the need arose. This is what happened in Tipperary in 1815, when the Ryans and Dwyers forgot their differences and joined their efforts with those of the 'Whiteboys' against the tithe proctors. In 1811 the Caravats and Shanavests in Tipperary, Waterford, Kilkenny, and Limerick agreed to forget years of bitter feuding and joined their efforts in an attempt to stop tenants from paying higher rents or the tithe. But their hatred for each other proved stronger than their hatred for the landlord or the tithe proctor, and the attempt at joint action collapsed.[32] The pursuit of essentially economic goals by co-operating factions marked such a departure from normal behaviour that banditti involvement seems likely.

In its efforts to cope with rural violence, the Castle was severely handicapped by a lack of reliable information from the

[29] Report, Whitworth to Sidmouth, 5 June 1816 (P.R.O., H.O. 100/189).
[30] Thomas Davenport to Gregory, 4 Sept. 1815 (P.R.O., H.O. 100/185).
[31] Testimony of Thomas Drummond, *State of Ireland in respect of crime, part iii,* H.L. 1839 (20), xx, 967.
[32] Report, Whitworth to Sidmouth, 5 June 1816 (P.R.O., H.O. 100/189).

countryside. Attempts to buy or extort information from the peasantry were seldom successful since fear of the peasant societies and the vengeance they could inflict was usually greater than greed or fear of the law. But paid informers abounded – 'I have very little scruple in the encouragement of treachery of this nature,' wrote Peel.[33] The Castle had little direct contact with these faceless men; instead local police officials and magistrates recruited their own informers and forwarded the information to the proper authorities. The future of the informer was at best uncertain. In 1815 a police official reported that he had found a possible informer, but that the man refused to talk until he had collected all money owed him. After talking, he planned to leave the area in a hurry.[34]

The intelligence provided by these 'villains' was recognized by castle authorities as having little worth,[35] but tales of French agents, seditious priests, and imminent uprisings all had to be investigated. Under-secretary William Gregory wrote to Peel in 1814,

A most absurd report was brought yesterday evening from some of the alarmed magistrates in the town of Naas that a rising was certainly to take place during the night in the county of Kildare. This was sent to commander of the forces . . . in consequence of which strong patrols were sent forward and every precaution used as if the story had been believed. . . . Tho' I attached no credit to the story, yet I remembered Emmet and the Castle caught napping.[36]

The considerable number of anonymous letters reaching the civil and military authorities during periods of unrest added to official confusion. Incompetent police and military officials and corrupt magistrates were favourite subjects of the letter-writers: '. . . do not consider from the appearance of this letter that it is written by a person moving in a low situation, the writer having disguised his hand and stile', wrote a 'constitutional and loyal subject' in his attack on the 'most corrupt and

---

[33] Peel to Hill, 16 Jan. 1814 (P.R.O., H.O. 100/176).

[34] Edward Wilson to Peel, 4 Nov. 1815 (P.R.O., H.O. 100/187).

[35] See Gregory to Henry Goulburn, 13 June 1822 (Surrey Record Office, Goulburn papers, box C, part 1).

[36] Gregory to Peel, June 1814, in *Mr Gregory's letter-box, 1813–1830*, ed. Lady A. Gregory (London, 1898), p. 50.

unfit' magistrates of Limerick.[37] Since the authorities were aware of flaws in the instruments at their disposal, considerable effort was expended investigating anonymous letters that might conceivably have been founded on fact.

As long as the peasant organizations were strong, they were seldom penetrated at the local level. It was next to impossible for outsiders to enter an organization whose members were all known to one another. And when individual members were arrested and brought to trial, most of them remained silent, or apparently gave false information to their interrogators. Thus reports and letters from police officials, army officers, magistrates, and others associated with the ascendancy were the major sources of intelligence. Over the years, a seemingly endless number of documents relating to Irish disorder were deposited in the official repositories of London and Dublin. Much of the material still exists; collectively it constitutes the history of a war compiled from the records of only one of the combatants.

In fairness to the ministers, members of parliament, and administrators responsible for Irish affairs from 1812 to 1830, one must ask just what they could have done towards measurably improving the condition of Ireland. It is completely unrealistic to blame the tory leadership for failing to launch a major overhaul of the land-tenure system. Its evils were so deeply entrenched that it was vulnerable only to full-scale assault, and the mere suggestion that government might attack the fundamentals of property rights would have aroused only horror and disbelief in the governing classes. It is equally unrealistic to fault a nineteenth-century government for its failure to provide the massive infusion of capital needed to provide alternative employment.

The tories of the Liverpool-Wellington era were not indifferent to Ireland's plight. Between 1812 and 1830, they effected a series of reforms: they further improved the administrative system, tried to eliminate corrupt and inefficient local government and to make the tithe less iniquitous, strengthened the administration of justice, and established a countrywide police organization, operating under a degree of government control.

[37] Anonymous, n.d. (S.P.O., C.S.O., Official papers, ser. 2, 581/534/15).

In the tradition of the toryism of the period, these 'improvements' were attempts to make existing institutions more efficient, and timid and inadequate as they may seem they represented part of the growing realization that Ireland was different from England, almost colonial in status, and that the magnitude and complexity of its problems justified the more extensive use of government resources. A case in point is the sub-letting act of 1826, a rather drastic item of legislation which went appreciably beyond the level of government interference acceptable in England.

It seems obvious, nevertheless, that the tories could have given Ireland better than it got. The separation between the Irish people and the English executive resulted in a notable lack of understanding and an atmosphere of continuing suspicion and dislike. At best, the average Irishman was treated with an amused, almost Kiplingesque toleration; at worst, he was treated as a member of an inferior and suspect race – dirty, ignorant, and prone to violence. Furthermore, Liverpool and his colleagues made major contributions to the prolongation of the catholic emancipation controversy, a dreary debate that exacerbated feelings in both islands and eventually brought Ireland to the brink of rebellion. And if the tories can hardly be blamed for their failure to halt the march of Malthusian mathematics, the tory ministers might stand in higher repute today had they shown a greater willingness to deal even with the periphery of basic problems. All too often, areas that might have been improved by legislation (primary education and the need for a poor law, to mention two of the more obvious) were tentatively considered, only to be shelved or dropped completely: prejudice, tradition, current economic dogma, and considerations of practical politics provided cogent arguments against new ideas and methods. And in Ireland, even more than in England, tory government could become severe and occasionally brutal when confronted with problems beyond its understanding.

II

THE PROBLEM OF LAW-ENFORCEMENT, 1812-13

~~~~~~

THE IRISH GOVERNMENT[1] in the early nineteenth century was similar to other Irish institutions – simple in theory but clumsy and perplexing in operation. At its head was the lord lieutenant, a peer of sufficient prestige to hold such an important position and to exercise the considerable powers granted the viceroy by statute and patent. He was assisted by an Irish privy council and a 'cabinet' consisting of the Irish lord chancellor, attorney-general, and solicitor-general. While the home secretary exercised a vague supervision over Irish affairs, matters of importance were frequently settled by correspondence between the lord lieutenant, residing in Ireland, and the prime minister. The lord lieutenant's assistant, the chief secretary, was a key figure in both the executive and the administrative branches of the Irish government. A member of parliament, he was the leading exponent of official Irish policy and worked in close association with the cabinet; an able chief secretary at Westminster during the parliamentary session could exercise an influence on policy at least equal to that of his absent superior. During the parliamentary recess, he managed the domestic affairs of the Irish government from Dublin Castle, aided by a civil and a military under-secretary. In 1819, the military

[1] On departments of government in Ireland, see McDowell, *Ir. administration.*

under-secretaryship fell vacant and was not filled, its few remaining duties going to the civil under-secretary.

The complexities of Ireland's many problems made the chief secretaryship an ideal testing ground for an aspiring young politician. In parliament, debates involving Ireland were certain to cause varying degrees of acrimony and criticism of the government. As William Gregory, civil under-secretary from 1812 to 1830, observed, 'The house of commons may, if game is scarce this season, amuse themselves by unbagging an under-secretary, Ireland being the principal scene for parliamentary sport.'[2] And the chief secretary had still to keep a close supervision over a wide range of domestic affairs, even during parliamentary sessions ('I would not on any account be made responsible for withholding a water-closet from the head magistrate of police', wrote Peel in 1814).[3] At Dublin Castle during the recess, the process was reversed. The chief secretary conferred with the lord lieutenant and other officials, compiled information from various sources, dealt with the backlog of problems requiring his direct attention, and attempted to keep the prime minister and home secretary *au courant* by correspondence.

In September 1812, Robert Peel arrived in Dublin to assume the office of chief secretary for Ireland – the first important appointment for the young tory member for Cashel. From the beginning of his tenure as chief secretary, the high level of ability shown by Peel at Westminster and Dublin Castle increased the prestige of both the incumbent and the office: one of his biographers was guilty of only slight exaggeration when he wrote that 'successive lords lieutenant reigned, Mr Peel governed'.[4]

Professor Gash, surveying Peel's long political career, observes that 'his lifework was to fashion a viable compromise between the system he inherited and the pressing necessities of the changing world in which he found himself'.[5] The chief

---

[2] Gregory to Goulburn, 28 Feb. 1824 (Surrey Record Office, Goulburn papers, box C, part 2).

[3] Peel to Gregory, 20 Apr. 1814 (Peel papers, B.M., Add. MS 40286).

[4] *Sir Robert Peel from his private papers*, ed. C. S. Parker (London, 1899), i, 35 (hereafter cited as Peel, *Private papers*).

[5] N. Gash, *Mr Secretary Peel* (Cambridge, 1961), p. 13.

secretaryship made important contributions to Peel's preparation for that great accomplishment, for it was in Ireland that the comfortable assumptions of his brand of conservatism were given their first serious test. His industrialist father, the first Sir Robert Peel, had schooled him in the toryism of the younger Pitt, with its respect for established institutions combined with acceptance of the need for cautious, careful adjustment of these institutions to meet changing circumstances. But with the young Peel of 1812, respect for established institutions came close to veneration. Sensitive, rather shy, apparently somewhat embarrassed by his family's mercantile background, he had been fashionably educated at Harrow and Christ Church, Oxford, then plunged into the heady atmosphere of parliament. The result was that Peel, anxious to identify with the old-established leadership group, adopted a rather romanticized view of the worth of British institutions and the 'natural order' of society.

If Peel can be said to have had an Irish policy during his years as chief secretary, beyond a desire for good, resolute government, it was founded on the belief that in Ireland the traditional system of local leadership had broken down. The 'country gentlemen' who were expected to provide magistrates and grand jurors from their ranks and thus dominate the machinery of local government, were failing to perform what Peel and others considered the functions of their class. The result of this failure was the crime, agrarian outrage and near-revolution that made government by ordinary processes almost impossible. As Peel saw the situation, the leaders of Irish society had to be persuaded, if necessary coerced, into the proper performance of their traditional duties, after which much of the Irish problem would solve itself. From this belief originated Peel's angry feud with the Irish magistrates, which provided one of the major themes of his period as chief secretary and led directly to the first of his police reforms. That Peel had undertaken no easy task was noted in 1814 by Abbot, the speaker of the house, who cautioned:

. . . we must not flatter ourselves that such a work can be speedily accomplished. Putting down the turbulent and encouraging the well-affected are the first and indispensable steps towards a durable system, which perhaps can only be established beneficially and effectually by an improvement in the habits of the country gentlemen, a work in itself beyond all legislative reach, and attainable only by an increase of their intercourse with other persons and parts of the United Kingdom.[6]

The struggle between the Castle and the Irish magistracy was to continue in some form for the next twenty-two years, and prove to the Irish government that the traditional system of maintaining order, centred on the magistrates and their constables and reinforced by the military, could no longer function effectively. In its place there gradually emerged a system based on a new concept of police, which after years of trial and error could in its final shape be characterized as 'the most valuable boon conferred by imperial legislation upon Ireland'.[7]

Whether at Westminster or at Dublin Castle, two facets of Irish domestic affairs dominated all others and made inordinate demands upon the time and patience of those responsible for the direction of the government: the administration of patronage, by which the support of the influential was 'bought', and the always present and always exasperating problem of public order.

From the time of the union, there had been a series of rather feeble public attacks on patronage. The number of jobs at the disposal of the government had been somewhat reduced, but the practice of placing county and borough patronage at the disposal of pro-ministry members of parliament remained. Thus even the remote outposts of government were part of the system of political bribery. The system was generally deplored by those charged with its administration; as the lord lieutenant observed in 1813, 'I quite agree with the French minister who expressed his dislike at having a place to bestow, as the only effect it produced was to make six discontents and an ingrate'.[8] Frequent attempts were made to control the worst abuses of the system, but as another lord lieutenant wrote in 1829, 'Favours must be conferred, solicitation must be yielded to, influence must prevail. This is the natural course of things and we must submit to it.'[9]

[6] The Speaker to Peel, 17 Oct. 1814, in Peel, *Private papers*, i, 157.

[7] Lecky, *Eng.*, viii, 501.

[8] Duke of Richmond to Peel, 5 June 1813 (N.L.I., Richmond papers, vol. 14).

[9] Duke of Northumberland to Peel, May 1829 (Peel papers, B.M., Add. MS 40327).

As for the problem of public order, Lord Lieutenant Whitworth informed Peel in 1813 that this was 'a brand of warfare' to which he was 'not yet accustomed',[10] and placed the task of tranquillizing Ireland into the hands of the chief secretary.

Peel had arrived in Ireland during a period of 'peace', one of the brief and increasingly less frequent lulls, relatively free from agrarian outrage. Perhaps 'truce' would be the better term, for although no signal fires burned on the hills of southern Ireland and no banditti emerged from the darkness to terrorize the countryside, the atmosphere in Dublin Castle was tense and uneasy. Throughout 1811 and early 1812, Tipperary, Waterford, Kilkenny and Limerick had been terrorized by the local Caravat and Shanavest factions bent alternately on forcibly lowering rents and regulating tithes and on destroying each other. The outbreaks had followed a pattern Peel would soon know all too well: murder or mutilation of those who took lands at higher rent or paid the tithe, use of the secret oath, and night raids for arms. Arrests had been made, followed by the inevitable executions and sentences of transportation, but the example thus offered to the lawless apparently had produced only a temporary effect. Now the government was anxiously awaiting the onset of winter and an almost certain renewal of trouble.[11] Nor was the tension in Dublin Castle created by agrarian disorder alone. The first months of 1812 had witnessed a series of alarms growing largely out of rumours reaching the cabinet late in 1811, concerning a French scheme to invade Ireland.[12] But by June, when Napoleon turned his armies against Russia, fear of invasion by a French army had evaporated. Now concern came from rumours of increased activity of French agents in Ireland. The Irish government was convinced that, while no insurrection could possibly succeed without foreign aid, any outside assistance to the disaffected could easily spark an uprising, which even if abortive would cause the government serious trouble.[13]

[10] Whitworth to Peel, 12 Sept. 1813 (Peel papers, B.M., Add. MS 40187).

[11] See above, p. 16; Report, Whitworth to Sidmouth, 5 June 1816 (P.R.O., H.O. 100/189).

[12] W. W. Pole to R. Ryder, 22 Nov. 1811 (P.R.O., H.O. 100/165).

[13] See Gregory to Peel, 10 Mar. 1813 (Peel papers, B.M., Add. MS 41195).

Entangled with these potential threats to the peace and surpassing them in the minds of castle officials, was the ever-present issue of catholic emancipation. In June 1812, Canning's motion to place the catholic question under consideration in the ensuing session had been passed by a respectable majority, and the Liverpool cabinet had decided to treat the matter as an open question; it appeared that remaining restrictions on His Majesty's catholic subjects soon would be considerably weakened, if not entirely removed. Such a course was strongly opposed in the upper echelons of the Irish government, for the lord lieutenant, the duke of Richmond; William Saurin, the attorney-general; and William Gregory, the under-secretary, were staunch opponents of emancipation. Thus to the attorney-general, 'resistance to the catholic claims is not only essential to the stability of the present administration, but what is of far greater importance, to the safety of our establishments, and to the connection of Great Britain and Ireland'.[14] And the duke of Richmond wrote in March 1813, '. . . we shall probably have a little fighting, but that is not of much consequence. We shall lose a few valuable lives, and hang a good many that richly deserve it'.[15] Peel heeded the anti-catholic sentiments of his superior, Richmond, and endorsed the views of Saurin. In 1816 the chief secretary was able to write:

It is quite impossible for anyone to witness the remorselessness with which crimes are committed here, the almost total annihilation of the agency of conscience as a preventive of crime, and the universal contempt in which the obligation of any but an illegal oath is held by the mass of the people, without being satisfied that the prevailing religion of Ireland operates as an impediment rather than an aid to the ends of the civil government.[16]

Grattan's emancipation bill of 1813 was dropped in May, after the clause allowing catholics to sit in parliament had been rejected in the commons by the narrow margin of 251 to 247. But the margin of victory was too slight to bring more than momentary relief to Dublin Castle.

Thus the first months of Peel's chief secretaryship were plagued by anxiety over renewal of agrarian disturbances and

[14] Saurin to Peel, 30 Sept. 1812 (Peel papers, B.M., Add. MS 40211).
[15] Richmond to Peel, 3 Mar. 1813, in Peel, *Private papers*, i, 75.
[16] Peel to Abbot, 25 Dec. 1816, in Peel, *Private papers*, i, 236.

possible French encouragement to the disaffected, and by the catholic emancipation struggle in parliament. The first indication of renewed trouble appeared in Westmeath in February, 1813. This time the raiders, styling themselves the 'Carders', were intent on forcing a policy of controlling rents, protecting tenants from eviction, and regulating the fees payable to the catholic clergy. Within less than a month, raids were reported in Waterford, Roscommon, King's, Tipperary, Limerick and Kilkenny. As disturbances increased in number and intensity, the general programme of the disaffected was soon replaced by a more specific one, and this time the banditti concentrated their efforts against those who took leases at rents higher than those paid by the previous tenants, and against those who gave information to the authorities. The disturbances of early 1813 provided one of the rare instances of the small farmers and other members of the 'lower orders' combining to resist the threats and attacks of the banditti. Aided by the exertions of local magistrates and a strong reinforcement of troops, their efforts were successful, and the raids were momentarily halted.[17] But the following month brought a tragic demonstration of the futility of peasant resistance against groups of organized terrorists. One Gahagan, a farmer who had successfully defended his home against arms raiders, was shot and killed as he stood talking with friends in a crowded churchyard on Palm Sunday. None of the people present attempted to stop the assassin, and later no one remembered who he was. The priest denounced the crime from the altar, only to have his own life threatened, and vengeance promised against anyone who attended his church.[18]

By the end of March, the banditti had recovered the initiative to such an extent that it was impossible to persuade victims to testify against their attackers. Informers' reports reaching Dublin told of a 'mature organization', complete with 'signs of fraternity' and an oath of allegiance to Bonaparte, sending delegates from Dublin, Kildare, Wicklow and King's counties to a meeting in Westmeath. Under-secretary Gregory (who had held his position only since October 1812) discounted the reports

[17] Willcocks to Peel, 23 Mar. 1814 (P.R.O., H.O. 100/177); Report, Whitworth to Sidmouth, 5 June 1816 (P.R.O., H.O. 100/189); Gregory to Peel, 13 Feb. 1813 (Peel papers, B.M., Add. MS 40195).
[18] Gregory to Peel, 17 Apr. 1813 (Peel papers, B.M., Add. MS 40195).

of organization, deputations, and oaths to Bonaparte, but had to admit that the situation was potentially dangerous.[19]

As was often the case, the number of disturbances lessened with the approach of summer and wider opportunities for employment. But by October, the areas disturbed during the spring of 1813 were once again in turmoil. This time 'midnight legislation' to redress agricultural grievances was noticeably absent, and the emphasis seemed to be almost entirely on arms raids. In Limerick, the Palatine yeomanry corps were left 'without arms' following a series of quick raids by banditti, and the Kerry yeomanry corps lost an unspecified number of guns. In November, a detachment of regulars at Ballymahon was robbed, and Lord Granard's yeomanry lost twenty 'stands' of arms within a few days.[20] A prominent Kilkenny magistrate warned the government that the disaffected were 'in possession of every musket, fowling piece, pistol, etc., that were held by farmers, poachers, and servants' and Peel was cautioned that 'if something is not speedily done, you will have the country completely disciplined – the law as it now stands is not equal to meet the evil'.[21]

Notices appeared in Armagh, Sligo, and Westmeath forbidding catholics from dealing with protestants, and a magistrate in Sligo reported that a local faction was offering a twenty-pound reward for an 'Orangeman or protestant' delivered into its hands.[22] The Irish government was completely unable to determine the causes of the rapidly spreading discontent. Richard Willcocks, the Castle's leading investigator, gave his views a few months later on the situation in Westmeath, reporting that the entire lower class, including some of the better farmers, had been put under oath by the banditti, many

---

[19] Report, Whitworth to Sidmouth, 5 June 1816 (P.R.O., H.O. 100/189); Gregory to Peel, 23 Mar. 1813 (Peel papers, B.M., Add. MS 40195).

[20] General Darby to Peel, 13 Oct. 1813, and William Hull to Peel, 18 Oct. 1813 (P.R.O., H.O. 100/173); Major D'Arcy to Peel and Lord Granard to Peel, 7 Nov. 1813 (P.R.O., H.O. 100/174).

[21] Gustavus Rochfort to Gregory, 7 Nov. 1813 (P.R.O., H.O. 100/174); Lord Castlemaine to Peel, 25 Oct. 1813 (P.R.O., H.O. 100/173).

[22] Reports of the brigade-majors of the yeomanry, 15 Oct. 1813; Wilson to Gregory, 3 Oct. 1813; G. Atkinson to Peel, 9 Oct. 1813 (P.R.O., H.O. 100/173).

of them by coercion. To Willcocks, it could not be coincidence that the identical problem was appearing in many different areas. Some of his informants had blamed French influence and cited an oath 'to be true to Bonaparte' to underline their point. Although he did not give too much credence to the reports, Willcocks did not deny the possibility of such a link.[23] By November, the raiders were no longer waiting for darkness, but were attacking the houses of 'respectable individuals' in daylight.[24] The magistrates of Westmeath saw in the depredations of the Carders part of a

scheme long laid and artfully conducted by men capable of combining and arranging their plans with art, regularity, and secrecy. Captivating the favourable regards of the lower orders by insidiously pretending that the object of their association was to lower rents and serve the poor.

The real goal of the Carders, the magistrates seemed to believe, was contained in a clause added to the secret oath, 'to assist the French and Bonaparte, and to plant the tree of liberty in the centre of Ireland'.[25] The lord lieutenant, Lord Whitworth, in a letter to the home secretary, commented on the mounting frequency of the outrages with considerable insight:

They afford a proof of a very general disposition among the lower orders to attempt by force and intimidation, the redress of what they consider to be their grievances, they excite the utmost alarm among the peaceful and well disposed, for the safety of their persons and property, and if suffered to gain a degree of strength and consistency, they become engines which the designing and disaffected can readily employ in the furtherance of their political views.

But the only immediate measures he could suggest were 'a vigorous exertion of our present powers and ... the co-operation of the military force'.[26]

During Peel's first year as chief secretary, his duties in parliament had kept him in England for all but a few months, and it was to this apparently dangerous state of affairs in Ireland that

[23] Willcocks to Peel, 23 Mar. 1814 (P.R.O., H.O. 100/177).
[24] Report, Whitworth to Sidmouth, 5 June 1813 (P.R.O., H.O. 100/189).
[25] Magistrates of Westmeath to Whitworth, 29 Nov. 1813 (P.R.O., H.O. 100/174).
[26] Whitworth to Sidmouth, 15 Jan. 1814 (P.R.O., H.O. 100/176).

he returned late in 1813. In August, the duke of Richmond had resigned the lord lieutenancy and had been replaced by Viscount Whitworth. Ex-soldier, diplomat, a relative by marriage of the prime minister, Whitworth has been characterized as a 'not unpopular' lord lieutenant, dominated by his wife, a woman of great vanity and greater ambition.[27] Whitworth and Peel were able to work together quite effectively. They held similar views on the catholic question and shared a common suspicion of things Irish. The new lord lieutenant also possessed a willingness to experiment and to take an occasional chance which made him receptive to his subordinate's occasional departure from accepted practice. But Whitworth, 'past sixty and somewhat bored',[28] was quite content to place the major burden of governing Ireland upon the shoulders of his chief secretary. When he returned to Ireland, Peel turned his attention to those institutions traditionally responsible for maintaining order, in the hope of discovering the causes of their failure and the means of strengthening them.

By the beginning of the nineteenth century, each county had its own police force, or baronial constabulary. The 'barnies' were appointed by the grand jury, took orders from the magistrates, and as an organization were considered so inefficient as to be generally worthless: the onset of trouble was often signalled by the departure of the 'barnies' from the scene. Apparently it was not uncommon for influential landowners to 'retire' employees by having the grand jurors provide them with jobs as sub-constables, and the pay was so poor that most of them held other jobs as well. During the troubled years following 1812, the baronial constabulary was generally ignored by the government in its attempts to muster forces to aid in the pacification of the rural areas.

Most pressing were the problems connected with the Irish military establishment, consisting of regiments of the British army stationed in Ireland and, until 1816, various militia units on 'actual' service. Traditionally the Castle's major weapon against rural violence, the military establishment was headed by the commander of forces who took his orders from London and,

---

[27] C. O'Mahoney, *The Viceroys of Ireland* (London, 1912), pp 217–18.
[28] Ibid., p. 217. For a more favourable view of Whitworth, see Gash, *Peel*, pp 130–3.

at least in theory, was required to co-operate with the lord lieutenant in the defence of Ireland. The number of men at the disposal of the commander of the forces varied, but from 1800 to 1805 it seems that the establishment's strength averaged around 50,000 effectives, of whom an estimated 20,000 were members of the militia.[29] As Britain's military participation in the Napoleonic wars increased, heavy demands were made on the Irish establishment. More and more regular regiments were withdrawn until at the end of 1813 the strength of the establishment had diminished to around 35,000 men, of whom only about 11,000 were regulars.[30] Nor does the total figure present an accurate indication of actual military strength, for as regulars were withdrawn for duty on the Continent they were replaced (when possible) with militia units, and it was assumed that the efficiency of the establishment had been weakened by an increase in the number of inferior men. As early as August 1813, Richmond warned the home office that the Irish establishment was growing too weak to 'afford the military assistance that is called for in various quarters in aid of the civil power'. And by December, Peel was protesting against the 'stripping of the forces from Ireland'. But the only help forthcoming was a promise of additional militiamen (from England) and an expression of considerable official sympathy.[31]

By late 1813, it was obvious that unless something were done to strengthen the government's forces for maintaining order, large sections of the countryside would have to be abandoned to the banditti. As the situation in Ireland grew more critical, the military authorities in London became increasingly concerned over the possible destruction of the weakened Irish establishment if a fully developed uprising should occur. For in an attempt to provide some protection for a wide area of the Irish countryside, much of the establishment had been divided into small units which, in the event of a serious disturbance, might

[29] Return of the effective men in the British army stationed in Ireland to 1806, n.d. (P.R.O., H.O. 100/176). In 1803, the militia numbered 18,315, and in 1809, 21,000. See Sir H. McAnally, *The Irish militia, 1793–1816* (Dublin, 1949), pp 176, 230.

[30] Regulars in Ireland in 1813, 14 Jan. 1814; Statement respecting the military force in Ireland, n.d. (P.R.O., H.O. 100/176).

[31] Richmond to Sidmouth, 24 Aug. 1813 (P.R.O., H.O. 100/171); Sidmouth to Whitworth, 9 Dec. 1813 (P.R.O., H.O. 100/175).

be destroyed piecemeal. The use of the army in a police capacity in Ireland had long been an accepted practice, but seldom had so few troops been scattered over so large an area. One gentleman, living in a town that had had a regimental headquarters for twenty-three years, complained in 1815 that a detachment of militia recruits were the only soldiers around: two were on leave, two were sick, and four were guarding the barracks.[32] Regular and militia units were stationed in the larger towns, and magistrates applied to these centres for troops to assist them in maintaining order. The result was division and subdivision of militia and regular units, until in at least one instance (at Castletown) a corporal and two privates were sent to answer the request of a magistrate.[33] Peel admitted his intention of turning these military detachments into police groups, 'to appropriate them to the objects of the civil government and to convert them from a military body to a body of police (for from the numberless detachments into which they are divided they can hardly be considered in any other point of view)'.[34]

Given the war with France and the existing belief that an Irish insurrection was possible, it is easy to understand the opposition from the military and the cabinet to such a plan. By December 1813, Peel and Whitworth were under strong pressure to withdraw the small units and combine them into groups capable of defending themselves. Sidmouth, the home secretary, wrote to Peel that he had been particularly charged by the cabinet 'that the measure of dividing the army . . . into small detachments for the purpose of police will never be resorted to except under the pressure of an undisputed and urgent necessity'.[35] But criticism by the military of the practice of using regulars as police went beyond the issues of the current controversy. The job of harrying ragged peasants around the countryside was considered beneath the dignity of the British army and interfered with its main duty, the defence of Ireland. The officers and men of the regular units must have resented operating under civilian orders when performing police duties; in most instances, police functions were carried out under the supervision of a

[32] P. Lloyd to the chief baron, 6 Sept. 1815 (P.R.O., H.O. 100/185).
[33] Langton to Gregory, 16 Oct. 1813 (P.R.O., H.O. 100/173).
[34] Peel to Sidmouth, 5 Jan. 1815 (P.R.O., H.O. 100/176).
[35] Sidmouth to Peel, 19 Jan. 1814 (P.R.O., H.O. 100/176).

magistrate. Furthermore, too deep an involvement in Irish affairs might have a deleterious effect on discipline. A sizeable percentage of the regulars were Irish catholics, and there was a danger that the soldiers might become infected with the 'insurrectionary' habits of the peasants. On several occasions during the 1820s, this fear seemed justified; official concern was expressed over the 'possible influence of bigotry and religious feuds upon our Roman catholic soldiers', and several regiments did become involved in the great debate on catholic emancipation.[36] But despite the concern of its leaders, the army remained basically reliable, and in 1832 the adjutant-general could write that 'barring individual instances of irregularity and violence occasioned . . . by the effect of whiskey and abetted by that spirit of party which pervades the whole country and eagerly enlists every drunken soldier in its cause, I have . . . the firmest reliance on their loyalty and devotion'.[37]

Another aspect of the problem was created by traditions of hostility existing between the regulars and the lower classes in certain parts of Ireland. It seems that the mere appearance of troops in some areas might lead to an explosive situation. And it was widely held by both military and civil authorities that many of the requests by local officials for soldier-policemen were not justified. As a member of Sir George Murray's staff observed, 'too frequent use of the military where the police is sufficient . . . may create a degree of alarm . . . and give an idea of disturbance which the circumstances do not justify'.[38]

But in 1813, to follow the wishes of the cabinet and the military would have been to abandon portions of the disturbed areas to the marauders, and Peel stubbornly refused to yield, insisting that, while he admitted to certain objections, his stand must be justified on the ground of necessity.[39] The cabinet and the military yielded, but the chief secretary had learned one of the more obvious hazards in using regulars as policemen. The British army was controlled from London, not Dublin, and

[36] Sir Herbert Taylor to General George Murray, 24 Dec. 1826 (P.R.O., W.O. 80/1).
[37] General D'Ajuilar to General George Murray, 14 Oct. 1832 (P.R.O., W.O. 35/26).
[38] Wedderburn to Doyle, 7 Sept. 1826 (P.R.O., W.O. 80/6).
[39] Peel to Sidmouth, 28 Jan. 1814 (P.R.O., H.O. 100/176).

whenever the interests of Westminster failed to coincide with those of Dublin Castle, the former (if of sufficient importance) were almost certain to prevail. Peel's 'conversion' of the British army in Ireland 'from a military body to a body of police' was a temporary and uncertain arrangement.

While Peel had successfully opposed attempts to limit the dispersal of the military establishment, however, the problem of raising and maintaining its strength remained unsolved. Castle officials had decided that the minimum force necessary to maintain order in Ireland was 40,000.[40] But by 1813, the establishment had dwindled to about 24,000 militiamen and 11,000 regulars. While the militia troops were considered inferior to the regulars in discipline and training, they did have one significant advantage which increased their value to the Irish government: they were not likely to be sent abroad. And since by late 1813 it was abundantly clear that few regulars were to be obtained for Ireland, Peel and Whitworth turned to the militia as the best possible means of strengthening the establishment.

The Irish militia, created in 1793, had been intended to follow the pattern of its English counterpart.[41] The units were to be raised and maintained by counties and cities. Officers were required to meet certain property qualifications; the ranks were to be filled by volunteers or men selected by ballot. The act of 1793 provided for an annual training period of twenty-eight days in peacetime and for 'actual' service of unspecified duration. Initially, it was intended that the Irish militia would serve only in Ireland, but in 1811 an interchange act was passed, allowing one-fourth of the English militia to serve in Ireland and one-third of the Irish militia in Great Britain for two-year tours of duty. Apparently it was hoped that the exchange would 'civilize' the Irish units and at the same time provide Ireland with troops not closely connected with the people and therefore more reliable in quelling disturbances or possible revolution.

Almost from the moment of its creation, the Irish militia had acquired a character of its own. With the exception of a brief period in 1802–3 it was on active service from the year of origin until it was disembodied in 1816. No serious effort was made to exclude catholics, who seem to have 'predominated in the ranks

---

[40] Peel to Sidmouth, 18 May 1814 (P.R.O., H.O. 100/178).
[41] See McAnally, *Irish militia*, pp 15 ff.

in at least the proportion of catholics in the population generally',[42] and there were an undetermined but probably small number of catholic officers. In part because of official suspicion of the trustworthiness of the militia, units were moved frequently from one part of the country to another, a practice which helped diminish the ties with districts the units nominally represented. The ballot was used infrequently, property qualifications for officers were relaxed, and the Irish militia became little more than a professional army 'of limited function however'.[43] Following 1803, the militia's two most important functions were the training of men for transfer to the regulars and the suppression of rural crime. But the government refused to accept the militia units, Irish and English, as being truly reliable, and perhaps with some justification. An Orange lodge was discovered in the Westmorland militia, operating with the 'concurrence and apparently the encouragement of Major Scott, the commanding officer'. An 'association for mutinous purposes', led by a 'committee of delegates', was reported to exist in the militia units of Dublin, and disaffection in the Limerick County militia became so pronounced that it had to be transferred to a less troubled area.[44]

The militia units in Ireland during the fall of 1813 consisted of 11,050 British and 12,901 Irishmen on active duty.[45] For several years, part of the units had been badly under strength; in late 1812, the twenty-three Irish units stationed in Ireland had a deficiency of 3,885 men from an authorized establishment of 16,435.[46] Although such a contingency had been anticipated by the ballot provisions of the militia act, Richmond felt that it would be impossible to fill the ranks by balloting because of 'difficulties which might be found in carrying it into effect in many parts of the country, in consequence of the defective state of civil arrangements necessary for that purpose'.[47] A recruiting campaign was launched, but by mid-1813 the supply of recruits had diminished to the point that the militia threatened to

[42] Ibid., p. 58.
[43] Ibid., p. 288.
[44] Hay to General Brereton, 5 Mar. 1813; General Aylmer to General Meyrick, 18 Apr. 1815; Hay to——, 18 Dec. 1813 (P.R.O., W.O. 35/25).
[45] Militia force in Ireland, n.d. (P.R.O., H.O. 100/176).
[46] Peel to Sidmouth, 12 Dec. 1812 (P.R.O., H.O. 100/168).
[47] Richmond to Sidmouth, 20 Jan. 1813 (P.R.O., H.O. 100/169).

disappear unless something were done. Yearly losses through death, injury, enlistment in the regular army, and desertion were extremely high. A possible further setback was administered by the British government in November 1813, when an act was passed allowing militia units either by blocks or as a whole to transfer to the line for foreign service. Initially, the act brought little response, and in December Whitworth informed the home secretary that no regiment had lost more than eighty men by volunteering and that some had lost as few as seven or eight. Even as a failure, however, this act cost the British and Irish militia units several thousand men.[48]

Thus the only immediate possibility for strengthening the military establishment in Ireland lay in obtaining more English militia units. The obstacle in the way of such an arrangement was the militia interchange act, but on 6 December 1813 the conditions of interchange were suspended, and the way was opened to employ more English militia units in Ireland. The actual success of the expedient is difficult to determine. On 9 December, Sidmouth promised to send 'with all possible dispatch' 3,000 English militia, but in January, Peel complained that only 1,400 had arrived. Additional units were promised, but in March 1814 Whitworth complained that if a scheduled departure of regulars took place and if all the promised militia units arrived, the establishment would be increased by only 3,365 men.[49]

During these attempts to prop up the sagging Irish military establishment, Castle officials seem to have given relatively little consideration to what had become, in effect, a third line of defence, the yeomanry corps. This group, not considered a part of the military establishment, was a volunteer force similar in organization to the home-guard units of more recent times. Formed in 1796, it had become almost from the beginning an ultra-protestant organization, concentrated largely in the north; during the troubled years at the end of the eighteenth century, it had gained a reputation for brutal, undisciplined

[48] Whitworth to Sidmouth, 8 Dec. 1813 (P.R.O., H.O. 100/175); Whitworth to Sidmouth, 12 Jan. 1814 (P.R.O., H.O. 100/176).

[49] Sidmouth to Whitworth, 9 Dec. 1813 (P.R.O., H.O. 100/175); Peel to Sidmouth, 5 Jan. 1814 (P.R.O., H.O. 100/176); Whitworth to Sidmouth, 26 Mar. 1814 (P.R.O., H.O. 100/177).

behaviour. Provisions of the act which had established the yeomanry in 1796 were few and unclear. Under the act, the corps offered arms, equipment, uniforms and pay to volunteers who would submit to discipline and place themselves under officers holding commissions from the crown or the lord lieutenant. The act went no further, and it has been suggested that the government had wished to avoid creating a force which might either compete with the militia or develop into a body similar to Lord Charlemont's Irish Volunteers of the pre-1793 period. The underlying purpose in the creation of the yeomanry seems to have been to provide forces for local defence if it became necessary to concentrate the regulars and militia to deal with a real or apprehended invasion.[50] As the nineteenth century progressed, the organization of the yeomanry was improved and a body of regulations evolved, but the organization retained its local character and ascendancy connections.[51] Corps were usually based on towns and when called to active duty by the lord lieutenant could function only in their own 'districts'. For administrative purposes, the corps were formed into divisions, and for every two divisions there was a brigade-major who was required to inspect each local unit every two months. Although concentrated largely in Ulster, the corps existed in the other provinces as well: in 1831, for example, there were 340 corps containing a total of around 29,000 men – 19,000 in Ulster, 5,500 in Leinster, 2,000 in Munster, and 2,200 in Connaught.[52] In some areas the corps were so closely associated with the Orange lodges that separation was difficult.

In 1814 the peacetime strength of the yeomanry was established at 40,000 men.[53] However, Dublin Castle saw the organization as a very inferior third line of defence – in many respects even a liability to the government, since yeomanry units were poorly disciplined and frequently became involved in the riots they were sent to suppress. The Orange connection and the dark reputation which the yeomanry had gained in the past made their presence in an area much more likely to cause trouble than

[50] McAnally, *Irish militia*, pp 92–3.
[51] Ibid., p. 126 n.
[52] Stanley's memorandum on the yeomanry, 1831 (Durham University, Grey papers, box 65, file 3).
[53] Whitworth to Sidmouth, 11 July 1814 (P.R.O., H.O. 100/179).

to quell it. A brigade-major wrote in 1813 that he regretted that 'magistrates should resort to yeomanry for assistance, as it too often leads rather to increase . . . than prevent disturbance'.[54] Although the government understood the dangers inherent in the use of the yeomanry in local disturbances, apparently it also realized that such a group would be of some value in the event of actual revolution or invasion and that it might be politically unwise to disband such a loyal body. Whitworth hoped that the units could eventually be purged of their questionable members and reorganized into an efficient, disciplined corps. But for the moment, he was bound to conclude, 'I am afraid it can scarcely be deemed an efficient force. The numbers although large on paper, are small in point of fact; the expense enormous. . . .' At a later date, Peel observed that such men, if placed under strict discipline, might be less troublesome than if they were 'left to themselves with arms in their hands for their individual protection'.[55]

As the problem of maintaining the military establishment became more acute, the Irish government was forced to use the yeomanry. In some instances, it worked reasonably well, especially in the north and in the larger cities, where it was possible to withdraw the regular or militia units and to place the responsibility for maintaining order in the hands of the yeomanry. Nor is there reason to doubt that some of the units in the south performed their duties with at least a degree of success, although all too often the government's distrust proved well-founded.

The most serious threat from the yeomanry in late 1813 lay in their role as unwilling sources of arms for the disaffected. Since members of the yeomanry normally lived at home, they kept their arms and equipment with them and were thus logical targets for the arms raider. Perhaps because of carelessness and poor discipline, even detachments on active duty lost arms through theft or in raids by gangs. All this was too much for Whitworth, and the government acted immediately, with little regard for the sensitivities of the yeomanry or their friends. A yeomanry unit which 'lost' arms would have the rest confiscated,

[54] State of the country, Apr. 1815 (P.R.O., H.O. 100/183).
[55] Whitworth to Sidmouth, 18 Jan. 1814 (P.R.O., H.O. 100/175); Peel to Goulburn, 6 Dec. 1824 (Surrey Record Office, Goulburn papers, II/13).

and in a very short period a number of units were disarmed by the government.[56] Evidently it was felt that the threat of guns going into the hands of the banditti was not offset by the value of the yeomanry units, for, once disarmed, they ceased for all practical purposes to exist.

When Peel had arrived in 1812, he had found the atmosphere in Dublin Castle merely tense and uneasy; by the end of 1813, the precarious military situation and the increasing frequency of outrages in rural Ireland had changed that atmosphere to one of near despair. As outrages increased, the means of coping with them weakened, and it seemed for the moment quite impossible to maintain an efficient, reliable military force to control the disturbances. The existing establishment was a makeshift affair, maintained by unsatisfactory expedients. The Irish government was responsible for maintaining order in Ireland with a force not completely under its control. Peel and others began to wonder if the solution to the problem of order in the rural areas might lie, not in the military establishment, but in some different method. The archbishop of Cashel, writing to Peel in 1813, stated:

I know not that even an increase of military, if in the present circumstances it could be spared, would lessen it – it has taken deep root in the country, and nothing I believe but a radical reform of the police and the most vigorous measures in connection with it will subdue the spirit.[57]

While considering the possibility of creating a rural *gendarmerie*, the chief secretary had also been giving considerable attention to another institution closely associated with maintaining order, the Irish magistracy. Peel was convinced of the basic importance of the magistrates, the 'natural leaders' of rural society, to any plan for controlling agrarian outrage, but in his association with the Irish magistracy so far he had found it sadly wanting.

[56] Whitworth to Peel, 10 Nov. 1813 (Peel papers, B.M., Add. MS 40187); Gregory to Granard, 15 Nov. 1813 (P.R.O., H.O. 100/174).
[57] Cashel to Peel, 30 Dec. 1813 (P.R.O., H.O. 100/175).

III

THE FAILURE OF THE
MAGISTRACY, 1812-13

~~~~~~~~~~~~~~~~~~~~~~~~~~~~~~~~~~~~~

IRELAND'S CREAKY LEGAL machinery was a continuing source of embarrassment to the Liverpool administration. The 'anachronistic confusion' of the system itself and the frequent charges of maladministration of justice in the local courts led to criticism in parliament and added to the problems of those responsible for the conduct of Irish affairs. When Peel arrived in 1812, there were six superior courts, concerned with civil, criminal, and ecclesiastical matters. There were also courts of assize, which convened twice annually in each county, appellate courts, and a confusing array of local courts established by the charters of cities and boroughs. In response to whig pressures, a commission was appointed in 1815 to investigate the Irish courts and gradually the administration of justice was somewhat improved.[1] The courts of assize, when dealing with criminal cases, seem to have functioned somewhat more humanely than their English counterparts. But the main tory effort at juridical improvement took the form of a long, involved, and bitter struggle to better the enforcement and administration of law in the rural areas by improving the quality of the men directly responsible for these vital functions – the justices of the peace, or magistrates.

The Irish magistracy was often corrupt, partisan, and in-

[1] See McDowell, *Ir. administration*, pp 104 ff.

D   39

competent. As in England, it was intended that the local magistrate should be a person whose social standing and means gave him authority and influence over his neighbours. Traditionally a sense of duty and an interest in public affairs motivated those who accepted the commission of the peace, and there undoubtedly were Irish magistrates who met these qualifications. But the commission went all too often to men who considered that they had merely been given a job, profitable both financially and politically.

It has been suggested that if the magistrates of Ireland were less effective than their English counterparts, it was in part because the Irish 'country gentlemen' who manned the magisterial bench tended not to be gentlemen.[2] In 1822, when a general revision of the magistracy was under consideration, the lord lieutenant admitted that appointments were frequently made 'more with reference to local or temporary exigencies than to personal merit or qualification',[3] and the surviving reports of officials who surveyed the magistracy in their districts at this time tend to support the contention. In Roscommon, eighteen were deemed 'eligible' and ten 'ineligible'. In King's County, a majority were 'fit and proper' and there seemed to be no 'corrupt or trading magistrates', but one was a 'man of small property but no discretion', one was a 'lunatic', another was 'old and inactive'. In the town and neighbourhood of Clara, 'dissension and party feeling' prevailed because three of the eight magistrates there were catholic and the curate was a 'man of no property and . . . too violent to be a discreet magistrate'. A third official forwarded a list of those he felt should be removed from office: one was 'not considered in the light of a gentleman', another was 'scarcely ever sober', Daniel O'Connell was a 'very corrupt man and of very disaffected principles', another was 'at times insane', and one was a 'most besotted man and was recently fined £100 for possessing illicit whiskey'.[4]

Instances of corruption among the magistracy before 1822

---

[2] McDowell, *Public opinion & govt policy*, pp 80–1.

[3] Wellesley to Peel, 27 Sept. 1822 (S.P.O., C.S.O., Private and official correspondence books, vol. 3).

[4] Wellesley to Goulburn, Dec. 1822; Powell to Goulburn, 3 Dec. 1822; Warburton to Goulburn, 7 Dec. 1822 (S.P.O., C.S.O., Official papers, ser. 2, 581/534/15).

were so often recorded that there can be no doubt that they were frequent and widespread. These instances ranged from bribes taken to influence the decision of the magistrate down to the practice of having a minor culprit work out his punishment in the magistrate's garden. The commission of the peace was also valuable to the holder in another way. The magistrates, as members of the local élite, could influence the appointment of the 'barnies' and some used this influence to reward those who had been of service to them.[5] Nor were accusations of corruption and jobbery limited to the local magistrates, for as late as 1829 the lord chancellor of Ireland, Sir Anthony Hart, was accused of accepting bribes in return for appointments to the magistracy. The lord lieutenant defended him against this charge, but admitted that considerations of patronage rather than qualifications for the position often determined the selection of magistrates.[6] Perhaps it was only natural that magistrates selected in such a system, and often motivated only by self-interest, should be viewed with suspicion and dislike by the lower classes. A catholic priest stated in 1825 that the administration of justice in Cork had left the 'impression upon the minds of the common people, that there was no law for them but the will of the magistrates; and there was no law from which they could derive redress, no *fixed law* of the land except through the interest or favour they may happen to possess with magistrates'.[7]

Undoubtedly religious considerations influenced some of the Irish magistrates in the performance of their duties.[8] Particularly in the north, and to a lesser extent throughout Ireland, members of the Orange order appeared on the magisterial bench, and their allegiance to that organization could outweigh their

[5] See Testimony of Richard Willcocks, Testimony of Maxwell Blacker, *Second report from the select committee on the subject of the disturbed districts in Ireland*, H.C. 1825 (35), xiii, 84, 138.

[6] Duke of Northumberland to Peel, May 1829 (Peel papers, B.M., Add. MS 40327).

[7] Testimony of the Reverend Michael Collins, *Third report from the select committee on the subject of the disturbed districts in Ireland*, H.C. 1825 (36), xi, 335.

[8] It is difficult to determine how many catholic magistrates there were at this time. One source guessed in 1825 that were 'many' in southern Ireland; another believed that all the catholic gentry of the south who were qualified were magistrates. *Second report . . . disturbed districts in Ireland*, H.C. 1825 (35), xiii, 95, 129.

obligations as magistrates. The Orangeman might escape punishment for infraction of the law, while the catholic offender might not receive the same consideration. An example of pro-Orange bias can be seen in an 1815 case concerning a Dutchman beaten by a group of catholics in County Armagh for wearing an Orange cockade on his hat. The men were arrested and appeared before the local magistrates sitting in quarter sessions, where the chairman treated the offenders to a violent tirade:

Who are the Orangemen of whom you are afraid? Loyal men, true to their king and country, and to their protestant religion. They are lawful societies – they have had the approbation of His Majesty's government and parliament. . . .

A second magistrate objected to this statement, regretting that it had been made, and denied that the Orange order had the legal sanction of the government. But the third magistrate came to the aid of the first: 'It is an old custom to wear an orange cockade on the first of July, and I trust God it will long be worn.'[9]

Successive Irish governments of the early nineteenth century must be credited with a considerable share of responsibility for the condition of the magistracy. They were responsible not only for allowing its continuance as part of the patronage system, but also for general neglect of the institution itself. The results of the government's belated 1815 investigation of the magistracy must have been somewhat embarrassing. The rolls listed the names of 4,175 magistrates for all Ireland. Of these 557 were dead, 1,355 were no longer resident in Ireland, and 311 were no longer acting as magistrates. This left 1,952 magistrates for the whole country.[10] But while the numerical decline brought expressions of anxiety from the government, a greater concern was the quality of the men serving as magistrates. The problem was beginning to appear as one more of Ireland's insolubles. In 1816, Peel was evidently ready to support a 'general revision and reform' of this institution,[11] but Saurin, the Irish attorney-general, opposed such a move as 'damaging to the feelings of the

[9] Dublin *Evening Post*, 7 Feb. 1815.

[10] The magistracy of Ireland, Nov. 1815 (P.R.O., H.O. 100/187).

[11] Peel to the attorney-general, 29 Mar. 1816, in Peel, *Private papers*, i, 218.

many loyal and good ones' and entailing 'tremendous difficulty in deciding whom to reform'.[12] Apparently Saurin's opinion was shared by others who exercised influence over Peel, who now admitted, 'I wish to God it was possible to revise the magistracy, for half our disorders and disturbances arise from the negligence of some and corruption and party spirit of others. But what other local authorities can you trust to?'[13] Throughout his years in Ireland Peel steadfastly maintained that it was impossible to find even a small number of 'persons free from local connections, accustomed to perform magisterial duties, and of the high character demanded by the great powers of the job'.[14] At the same time, he could not abandon the potential effectiveness of the institution itself:

I am satisfied that ten good magistrates in any county of Ireland – combining together steadily to administer the law – determined to enforce it – to represent to the government the misconduct of the magistrates – if other magistrates sought to counteract them by improper exercise of their authority – would succeed against the united influence of mobs and priests and demagogues.[15]

Political considerations presumably entered into the government's hesitancy in attempting an effective reform of the magistracy. Such an undertaking would have involved an attack on patronage, which in turn affected to some extent most of the important Irish political figures. It had long been the practice to give the patronage of a constituency to the member representing it at Westminster in return for his support,[16] and to tamper with this arrangement could have been politically dangerous. Thus while Peel and his associates were damning the magistrates at one level, they were most considerate of them at another. For example, while Peel in his private correspondence could refer to Lord Castlemaine as 'that grand alarmist',[17] and Gregory could write that 'whenever Field-Marshal Funck commands, the enemy is sure of appearing formidable',[18] no

[12] Saurin to Peel, 4 Apr. 1816 (Peel papers, B.M., Add. MS 40211).
[13] Peel to Saurin, 8 Apr. 1816 (Peel papers, B.M., Add. MS 40211).
[14] Peel to Wellesley, 12 Apr. 1822 (Peel papers, B.M., Add MS 40324).
[15] Peel to Leveson Gower, 14 Aug. 1829 (Peel papers, B.M., Add. MS 40337).
[16] McDowell, *Public opinion & govt policy*, p. 46.
[17] Peel to Whitworth, 1 Dec. 1813, in Peel, *Private papers*, i, 125.
[18] Gregory, *Letter-box*, p. 49.

indication of this contempt appeared in their correspondence with Castlemaine himself. When he wrote to Peel complaining of the inadequacy of the existing laws for keeping the peace, Peel replied, '. . . if they are found to be so, the government will not attribute this failure to any want of vigour on your part in carrying them out'.[19] And in 1816, Peel opposed the general revision of the magistracy proposed in parliament as 'productive of great injustice', while in his correspondence with Saurin he was blaming the magistrates for 'half our disorders and disturbances'.[20]

But corruption and partisanship were not at the bottom of the bitter controversy of 1813 between Dublin Castle and the magistrates of the disturbed areas. Though it is conceivable that a corrupt and partisan magistrate could provide effective and courageous leadership for his district when it was threatened by agrarian outrage, such leadership was all too infrequent, and to the list of faults were now added charges of timidity towards, and even connivance with, the banditti. In October 1813, Peel castigated the magistrates of the disturbed areas for being 'supine from timidity',[21] and to the prime minister he wrote concerning the prevalent disorders, 'Party spirit and a timid magistracy have their full share in continuing their existence.'[22] Somewhat later he stated that agrarian outrage arose 'out of sheer wickedness, encouraged by the apathy of one set of magistrates, and the half connivance of another'.[23] If this was true, the situation was indeed serious, for the magistrate was the cornerstone of the law-enforcement system, whose first duty was to keep the peace.[24] He was expected to intervene personally to quell disturbances, and the baronial constabulary was under his control. It was the magistrate who requested military assistance to help in maintaining order, and in most cases a magistrate personally directed the operation of the military

[19] Peel to Castlemaine, 25 Oct. 1813 (P.R.O., H.O. 100/173).
[20] *The speeches of the late right honourable Sir Robert Peel, Bart.* (London, 1855), i, 61 (hereafter cited as Peel, *Speeches*); Peel to Saurin, 8 Apr. 1816 (Peel papers, B.M., Add. MS 40211).
[21] Peel to Darby, 7 Oct. 1813 (P.R.O., H.O. 100/173).
[22] Peel to Liverpool, 15 Oct. 1813 (Liverpool papers, B.M., Add. MS 38195).
[23] Peel to Lord Desart, 10 Feb. 1814 (Peel papers, B.M., Add. MS 40285).
[24] F. W. Maitland, *Justice and police* (London, 1885), p. 91.

when used for police purposes. In Ireland, the magistrate had increased powers of arrest under the provisions of the Whiteboy act, which provided that if a magistrate and his party encountered a group of armed men, an arrest could be made without suspicion of felony. If the men resisted arrest or fled, the magistrate and his party could use any force necessary to take them into custody.[25] Police or soldiers acting without the supervision of a magistrate might be charged with murder if a suspect was killed while attempting to evade arrest. A quorum of the magistrates in a given county constituted the court of quarter sessions, a court with broad criminal jurisdiction; to improve the quality of justice administered by the 'country gentlemen', a trained professional, the assistant barrister, was assigned to quarter sessions as a consultant.[26] A breakdown of the magistracy in a disturbed area, then, could mean the collapse of the normal processes of the law, and this is precisely what was happening in much of southern Ireland in 1813. The primary reason for the breakdown had little to do with corruption; the magistrates were simply afraid to move.

The baronial constabulary was so inefficient as to make it usually worthless; military assistance was often uncertain and temporary. Yet the magistrates were expected to lead the attack upon the agrarian secret societies, to convict the offenders, and then to live among the hostile population after the area had been tranquillized. Logically the banditti viewed the magistrate who performed his duties not as an instrument of the government but as a personal enemy. The least that such a magistrate might expect was to have his crops destroyed, his trees cut down, his fences levelled; the worst was death for himself and perhaps for his family.[27] Fear is undoubtedly the explanation for the refusal of some of the magistrates to prosecute apprehended terrorists in 1813, a refusal which earned them Castle accusations of duplicity.[28]

[25] 15–16 Geo. III Ser. 6, c. 21.

[26] For the civil functions of the assistant barrister, see McDowell, *Ir. administration*, p. 113.

[27] An example is provided in the report on the assassination of one Mr Baker in 1815 and its effects on the other magistrates. Report, Whitworth to Sidmouth, 5 June 1816 (P.R.O., H.O. 100/189); Moore to Littlehales, 4 Dec. 1815; Willcocks to Gregory, 14 Dec. 1815 (P.R.O., H.O. 100/188).

[28] Gregory to Peel, 29 Mar. 1813 (Peel papers, B.M., Add. MS 40195).

There were, of course, exceptions among the magistrates, conscientious men who continued to perform their duties without regard for personal safety. Nor did all the others respond in an identical way to the dangerous situation which confronted them. They tended to fall into two groups, which the Castle termed 'timid' and 'alarmist'.

The 'timid' magistrates, evidently from fear of reprisals, often disappeared at signs of trouble, perhaps moving into the nearest city to wait out the storm. If they remained in their areas, they were careful not to offend the disaffected, secure in the realization that, if they chose to do nothing, the government was powerless to force them to act. If a magistrate just was not there when needed, there was nothing the government could do.[29] This group, the magistrates functioning half-heartedly or not at all, received the earliest attention from the Irish government. In January 1813, a meeting of the Tipperary magistracy was called at Fethard to work out a plan of common action to handle the current disturbances. But the meeting was thinly attended and accomplished virtually nothing. Peel expressed the regrets of the Castle at this lack of attendance, and reminded the magistrates that the state of the country called for 'the active and zealous exertion of those whose duty and interest it is to co-operate in the maintenance of public tranquillity'.[30]

In spite of the weakness of the military establishment, the Irish government encouraged the magistrates to request military assistance when it was obviously needed. Gregory wrote to one of them, promising 'every aid which is in our power to afford consistent with the present circumstances of the military stationed in the kingdom'.[31] In some cases such an offer was accepted and properly used; in others aid was accepted and wasted by using it to guard the homes of prominent individuals, while the appeals of others for troops went unanswered.[32] There are indications that some of the magistrates actually feared the presence of soldiers, preferring to attempt to maintain order with

---

[29] See Testimony of Thomas Drummond, *State of Ireland in respect of crime, part iii*, H.L. 1839 (20), xx, 989.

[30] Peel to B. Bradshaw, 27 Jan. 1813 (P.R.O., H.O. 100/169).

[31] Gregory to Rochfort, 23 Mar. 1813 (P.R.O., H.O. 100/169).

[32] Peel to F. Woodly, 27 Jan. 1814 (P.R.O., H.O. 100/176).

the small body of local police, because soldiers would 'attract the attention of the banditti, and lead to further trouble'.[33]

The second group, the 'alarmist' magistrates, represented a type of problem that would plague the Irish government for many years. As dissatisfaction increased in the various areas and more of the lower classes were absorbed into the disaffected groups, less information was available and rumour replaced fact. It is astonishing that many of these rumours could have been believed and even passed on to the government. A by no means exceptional report early in 1814 solemnly described an attack by a force of one hundred armed men on a military dispatch rider, in which the rider was robbed of his papers, beaten, and left for dead. One of the judges on circuit conducted a brief investigation of his own, and found that the dispatch rider had simply been drunk, fallen from his horse, and lost his documents.[34]

Lacking a qualified body of observers capable of evaluating rumours, Castle officials were likely to view most reports with suspicion, and the phrase 'you have omitted to supply particulars' became a common one in Peel's correspondence with the magistrates.[35] The unreliable nature of the information received by the Castle greatly complicated the problems of maintaining order. At times the government discounted genuine reports of serious disturbances;[36] at others it rushed troops into areas where they were not needed.

By early winter of 1813, relations between the Castle and the magistrates in the disturbed areas were dominated by mutual distrust. The Castle continued to insist that 'local magistrates are the properest authorities for putting down local disturbances – no intimidation or unjust aspersion of partiality should deter men from stepping forward and the faithful discharge of public duty'.[37] It undoubtedly appeared to the magistrates that the government was determined to meet the rising problem of agrarian outrage by conventional methods, a course of action which the magistrates were now determined to oppose, for they began to press for special legislation as the solution to their

---

[33] Brigade-major Sankey to Peel, 21 Oct. 1813 (P.R.O., H.O. 100/173).
[34] Gregory to Peel, 31 Mar. 1814 (Peel papers, B.M., Add. MS 40195).
[35] See Peel to Arthur Usher, 14 Jan. 1814 (P.R.O., H.O. 100/176).
[36] Gregory to Peel, 23 Mar. 1813 (Peel papers, B.M., Add. MS 40195).
[37] Gregory to Sir George Hill, 17 Nov. 1813 (P.R.O., H.O. 100/172).

problem. In November, a group of King's County magistrates petitioned the Irish government: '. . . they consider strong measures to be absolutely necessary, and that nothing short of the insurrection act will enable them to restore the tranquillity of the county'.[38] Within a few weeks there followed similar petitions from magistrates in Westmeath and Waterford.[39]

The insurrection act[40] for which the magistrates clamoured had been repealed in 1810, shortly before it was due to expire. It was such a severe measure that, although never actually applied, it had been regarded as a success: the Castle chose to believe that the marked decline in agrarian outrage coincident with its enactment in 1807 was due to the ominous threat of the act.[41] Its repeal had been an obvious attempt to gain favour with the members who were opposed to such 'unconstitutional' legislation. The act provided that seven magistrates in special session could inform the lord lieutenant that their county was in a disturbed state. The lord lieutenant, acting on the advice of the Irish privy council, could proclaim the county or any part of it to be in a disturbed condition. All people living in the proclaimed area were required to remain in their homes from sunset to sunrise, under penalty of seven years' transportation. All who demanded arms or administered illegal oaths (without the use of violence), or who possessed weapons and refused to give them to the authorities, were liable to the seven-years' transportation penalty. When the act was finally applied, after its re-enactment in 1814, the most important provision proved to be that authorizing the suspension of trial by jury in the proclaimed area. Persons arrested under the act were tried before a court of general sessions, presided over by an assistant barrister, who was assisted by as many magistrates as could be persuaded to attend. Apparently crimes of a capital nature were reserved for the courts of criminal assize. The assistant barrister usually attempted to get as many magistrates as possible to sit with him; one

[38] Magistrates of King's County to Gregory, 17 Nov. 1813 (P.R.O., H.O. 100/174).

[39] Report, Whitworth to Sidmouth, 5 June 1816 (P.R.O., H.O. 100/189).

[40] For the provisions of the insurrection acts of 1807 and 1814, see 54 Geo. III, c. 180, 30 July 1814.

[41] Report, Whitworth to Sidmouth, 5 June 1816 (P.R.O., H.O. 100/189).

assistant barrister stated that he refused to try a serious case with fewer than six magistrates present.[42] The assistant barrister usually guided the deliberations of the magistrates, and a convicted man could apply to the court for a review, after which the court would decide whether or not to request a pardon from the lord lieutenant.[43]

The insurrection act was strong legislation designed to meet a serious challenge to the authority of the government, and its use could be justified only by extreme necessity and most careful application. An area proclaimed under its provisions was 'frozen' between sunset and sunrise. It was unnecessary to obtain proof against a person suspected of being involved in agrarian outrage beyond the fact that he had been out of doors after sunset. He might actually be apprehended or he might merely be absent from home when the authorities called. Judgment was swift, and there can be little doubt that circumstantial evidence and the reputation of the accused strongly influenced the decisions of the court.[44] In the actual operation of the insurrection act, the assistant barristers apparently lessened the severity of the punitive provisions of the measure whenever possible. Assistant Barrister Maxwell Blacker, commenting on a provision of the act that anyone found in a public house after 9 p.m. was liable to transportation, stated, 'I have never applied [this provision of] the act, not giving up, however, the right to put the act in force where there was evidence of the assembling being for the purpose of carrying into effect any of their [the disaffected's] plans.'[45] The majority of those apprehended for being outside their homes after dark were never brought to trial, for in practice such offenders were released after showing 'just cause'.[46]

[42] Testimony of Maxwell Blacker, *Second report . . . disturbed districts in Ireland*, H.C. 1825 (35), xiii, 120.

[43] Ibid.

[44] George Bennett admitted in 1825 that no person sentenced by him under the provisions of the act had actually been proved to have committed the outrage. Testimony of George Bennett, *Second report . . . disturbed districts in Ireland*, H.C. 1825 (35), xiii, 53.

[45] Testimony of Maxwell Blacker, *Third report . . . disturbed districts in Ireland*, H.C. 1825 (36), xi, 22.

[46] Testimony of Francis Blackburne, *Second report . . . disturbed districts in Ireland*, H.C. 1825 (35), xiii, 7.

When the conscientious magistrates joined the timid and the alarmist magistrates in petitioning Dublin Castle at the end of 1813 to solve their problems by a re-enactment of the insurrection act,[47] the Irish government refused to request such legislation. Undoubtedly Whitworth, the lord lieutenant, was strongly influenced by the problem of pushing such legislation through parliament, where it was certain to encounter strong opposition; but also he wished 'to see if it is possible to govern without recourse to the insurrection act'. He was encouraged in this attitude by a belief that a scheduled reinforcement of English miltia units would provide sufficient troops to conduct his 'experiment' without any real danger to the country. In a rather lofty vein, he informed Sidmouth, 'It is not good to get into the habit of suspending the constitution, and it weakens the effect of such suspension.'[48] Shortly before, he had thanked Peel for not recommending to the cabinet that the act be restored, for while he realized that he might lose popularity in Ireland, '. . . I certainly should very much regret marking the outset of my government by such a proceeding unless called for by irresistible necessity'.[49] Whatever Sidmouth may have thought of Whitworth's reasons, he was obviously relieved to know that the cabinet would not be forced to sponsor such a bill. With a promise for such legislation should the future demand it, he wrote, 'The authority of a government which is not forward in seeking an enlargement of its powers will always be adequately re-enforced in a moment of actual danger.'[50]

Peel and Gregory seem to have had little faith in the 'experiment' of their superior. Gregory, usually quick to echo the ideas of the men above him, wrote in December 1813,

The repeal of the insurrection act was a measure . . . as unaccountable as the conduct of the Westmeath insurgents. No one I think conversant with the country but must be satisfied of the necessity of always leaving in the hands of the executive a strong and efficient power to be called out when urging and discretion require.[51]

---

[47] See Rochfort to Gregory, 19 Nov. 1813; Magistrates of Westmeath to Whitworth, 29 Nov. 1813; Magistrates of King's County to Gregory, 17 Nov. 1813 (P.R.O., H.O. 100/174).

[48] Whitworth to Sidmouth, 13 Dec. 1813 (P.R.O., H.O. 100/175).

[49] Whitworth to Peel, 27 Nov. 1813 (Peel papers, B.M., Add. MS 40187).

[50] Sidmouth to Whitworth, 18 Dec. 1813 (P.R.O., H.O. 100/175).

[51] Gregory to R. S. Tighe, 3 Dec. 1813 (P.R.O., H.O. 100/175).

Writing to Whitworth in the following summer, Peel presented an even stronger case for the act:

What is there unreasonable in this in the present state of Ireland? Supposing it an evil, compare it with that for which it is intended as a remedy, with the cardings and burnings and murders, which are committed by men who leave their homes at nights, and who escape detection because you cannot make them at present account for their absence.[52]

But Peel's support of such legislation was a qualified one. Most of those pressing for re-enactment of the insurrection act viewed it as an efficient means of suppressing agrarian outrage at the county or even at the baronial level, and therefore as a measure which should be put freely into operation by the government whenever requested. Peel thought differently, and in this he was again in agreement with Saurin. The attorney-general insisted that while it was desirable to have the legislation available for emergency use, such an extreme measure should be invoked only when an actual insurrection threatened.[53] Peel held to this view throughout his tenure as chief secretary. Writing to Gregory in 1815, he requested that the magistrates be informed of the government's

fixed determination not to put the insurrection act in force unless called upon by urgent and imperious necessity, by a much stronger case of necessity it must be observed than at present exists . . . it can only be such a case which can warrant the executive government in confining within their houses during the night the inhabitants of a whole district upon penalty of transportation and introducing a form of trial unknown to the ordinary law.[54]

While supporting the use of such legislation in instances of 'imperious necessity', Peel also realized that, if misused, the act could work to the detriment of forces of law and order. For by strengthening the powers of the magistracy, the act made it possible for a handful of magistrates to perform the necessary duties in a disturbed area, a situation which the Castle earnestly wished to avoid. The form of trial established by the act made it easy for the timid magistrates to shirk their judicial duties, and the provisions of the act made less necessary the magistrate's

[52] Peel to Whitworth, 7 July 1814, in Peel, *Private papers*, i, 147.
[53] Saurin to Peel, 14 June 1814 (Peel papers, B.M., Add. MS 40211).
[54] Peel to Gregory, 17 May 1815 (Peel papers, B.M., Add. MS 40288).

accompanying any military detachments used for police purposes. Under the normal operation of the law, soldier-policemen
had to be 'employed solely under the personal direction of the
magistrate' who required their services. Under the insurrection
act, military detachments might be led by policemen who had
been certified by the lord lieutenant as qualified to lead soldiers
on police duties if such an arrangement had the approval of two
magistrates.[55]

Of greatest importance to the government was the fear that
the act would encourage the magistrates to neglect their most
important duty, the prevention of crime. If trouble-makers were
arrested, if 'loose and disorderly persons' were kept under
surveillance, and if the agrarian secret societies were broken up,
serious agrarian outrage would never develop, and there would
be no need for large military establishments and special
legislation. The magistrates, the designated leaders of the
people, thus had it in their power to solve the problem of
agrarian crime. But by 1813 it was clear that the magistrates
were not carrying out their duties in the disturbed areas, and the
government believed that the act would only encourage the
inefficient magistrates in their laxness. For they could then rely
on this measure to correct the situation they had themselves
helped to create. At a later date, Peel wrote to the lord lieutenant:

The possession of the enormous power which it gives spoils the
magistracy for ordinary exertions and after all, the power, great as
it is, liable unless incessantly watched and controlled to be much
abused, is not very efficacious; it leaves the country just where it
found it; the disaffected unreclaimed.[56]

At the same time that the majority of the magistrates in the
disturbed areas seemed to be failing in their duties, the magistrates of Kilkenny were proving to the satisfaction of the Irish
government that its view of the proper role of the magistracy
was correct. In Kilkenny, the magistrates met, and instead of
asking for the insurrection act, publicly expressed in a series of
resolutions their desire to co-operate with one another for the

[55] Littlehales to Hewett, 20 June 1814; Peel to Desart, 24 Jan. 1817
(S.P.O., C.S.O., General private correspondence books, 2).
[56] Peel to Northumberland, 5 Oct. 1829 (Peel papers, B.M., Add. MS
40327).

preservation of the peace. They divided the entire county into districts and assigned one magistrate to supervise each. The military command of the district assigned every magistrate a body of troops with which to patrol his district at 'unexpected' hours. These exertions appear to have been successful, for Peel was able to report later that 'since this system has been acted upon, no outrage has been committed'.[57]

The system in operation in Kilkenny was part of a general plan of co-operation worked out by Castle officials and some of the more conscientous magistrates as a substitute for the insurrection act. It called for the close co-operation of the magistrates with one another and with the military commanders of their districts, a general and simultaneous search for arms in each district of the disturbed area, and the immediate notification of any serious trouble.[58] This attempt by Castle officials to provide a plan of action for the magistrates, however, met with little success outside Kilkenny. The patrol system was tried out in several places, evidently with some positive results,[59] and extensive plans were made in Dublin for a co-ordinated general search for arms.[60] An elaborate scheme was worked out under which all the magistrates in the disturbed areas were to be sent search warrants, but not informed when they would be used, and 'covering' parties of troops were to be brought in from adjacent areas;[61] but there is no indication that this ambitious plan was ever tried. Evidently it had proved to be as difficult to lead the magistrates as it was to push them, and by the end of 1813 a stalemate had been reached between the Castle and the magistrates of the disturbed areas. Those in Kilkenny, and the few others who were performing their duties as the government felt they should, were exceptions; others continued to press for legislation which would free them of many of their responsibilities as magistrates.

Thus another of Ireland's institutions had been found want-

[57] Peel to Bagwell, 8 Jan. 1814 (P.R.O., H.O. 100/176).
[58] Peel to archbishop of Cashel, 12 Jan. 1814 (P.R.O., H.O. 100/176).
[59] Gregory to Thomas Shea, 10 Dec. 1813 (P.R.O., H.O. 100/175).
[60] The arms act (53 Geo. III, 78, signed 2 July 1813) limited the possession of arms to 'responsible' people who could show need for them, permission being granted by the local magistrates. Being a protestant was often considered sufficient proof of responsibility.
[61] Rochfort to Gregory, 14 Nov. 1813 (P.R.O., H.O. 100/176).

ing: the magistracy, like the military establishment, was not functioning as it should. However, while it was unlikely that the Irish government could stop the decline in the effectiveness of the military establishment, there did appear a possibility of correcting some of the defects of the magistracy. By late 1813, Peel was working on a plan centring on a disciplined police force under Castle control, commanded by a stipendiary magistrate, which could be used to replace the local magistrates who were failing in their duties, and could thus stop agrarian outrage before it developed into a serious threat. If such a plan could be put into operation, there would be no need for an insurrection act or a powerful military establishment; and, of more importance to the Castle at this time, it would cost the government nothing, for the residents of the area in which it operated were to pay for its services. Peel's was an ambitious plan, typical in many ways of the intelligence and administrative genius of its originator, but it proved to have several serious flaws.

IV

THE PEACE PRESERVATION
FORCE, 1813-14

~~~~~~

THE LEGISLATION GOVERNING the baronial police was due
to expire on 1 March 1814, and Peel hoped to introduce a bill
for an improved system of police during the session of 1813–14.[1]
By June 1813 his plans for the bill were well under way.[2] Other
matters occupied him over the summer, but in October he was
again considering police legislation, writing, 'I should be very
unwilling to resign my share of distinction which it will confer.'[3]
Recent clashes between groups of protestants and catholics,[4]
the problems of the military establishment, the possibility of an
insurrection, and the weakness of the magistracy all cautioned
against further delay, and by February 1814 he had completed
the rough outline of a new police system.[5]

The police force envisioned by Peel differed in organization
and purpose from the existing rural police in Ireland. At the
centre was a stipendiary magistrate – a paid, full-time police
official with the powers of a magistrate, appointed by and

[1] Peel to Desart, 15 Oct. 1813 (Peel papers, B.M., Add. MS 40285).
[2] See proposal headed 'Constables' (Peel papers, B.M., Add. MS
40226).
[3] Peel to Desart, 15 Oct. 1813 (Peel papers, B.M., Add. MS 40285).
[4] Peel to Liverpool, 15 Oct. 1813 (Liverpool papers, B.M., Add. MS
38195).
[5] Peel to Desart, 24 Feb. 1814; Peel to Sir Edward Crofton, 28 Feb. 1814
(Peel papers, B.M., Add. MS 40285).

responsible to the Irish government. The stipendiary magistrate had under his exclusive control a body of special constables, also selected by the government. This Peace Preservation Force, as it came to be called, was sent to a disturbed area after a specified number of the local magistrates had requested the lord lieutenant to proclaim the area in a state of disturbance. While the force was operating, the stipendiary or chief magistrate was superior to the other magistrates of the area, who functioned under his direction. The cost of the operation was paid by the area involved, and when tranquillity was restored the Force was either withdrawn or disbanded. Thus, during periods of serious disorder, the traditional machinery of rural law enforcement was to be augmented by trained policemen in mobile units under the authority of the central government.[6]

The Peace Preservation Force was planned with a definite purpose beyond the mere strengthening of the instruments already at the disposal of the Irish government: from the beginning, the new police system was designed to restore the magistrate to a position of leadership in his community, by either helping him or forcing him to perform his duties. As Peel said in a letter to Lord Desart,

We have a right to call on country gentlemen for the performance of the ordinary duties of a magistrate, but in the event of a commotion and general disposition to acts of outrage, we can scarcely expect from them, at least we can only find in rare instances that degree of activity and vigilance which is necessary for their suppression.[7]

He then asked Desart whether the 'active' magistrates in his area would object to a stipendiary magistrate being placed over them? Peel felt that objections from active magistrates should receive consideration, but that in other areas, where the failure of the magistrates was more complete, such objections should not influence government action:

But I could name other counties – Co. Wexford, for instance, where I should wish to put the magistracy to shame and make them contribute to the expense of their own disgrace by paying the man who performed their duty.[8]

---

[6] Ibid.
[7] Peel to Desart, 24 Feb. 1814 (Peel papers, B.M., Add. MS 40285).
[8] Ibid.

As plans for the new police progressed, the punitive side of the new system increased in importance. The cost of the entire operation of the Peace Preservation Force in a disturbed area, including the salaries of the stipendiary and his constables and their equipment, was to be borne by the district. As finally established, the punitive provisions went beyond making the magistrates 'contribute to the expense of their own disgrace', and imposed a burden upon a much more extensive section of the population of the area involved. Writing to Abbot in September 1814, Peel stated:

You are aware that the expense of this extraordinary establishment of police, the salary of the chief magistrates, the rent of his house, the cost of horses and accoutrements for the constables, is to be borne by the disturbed district. It falls upon the occupying tenant . . . every peasant has his half acre, and thus every peasant has a direct pecuniary interest in . . . preventing it from being proclaimed . . . the most effectual way, I am confident, of keeping the country tranquil, is by making the inhabitants pay for the luxury of disturbance.[9]

Thus if agrarian crime appeared to be threatening an area to an extent beyond the control of the magistrates, they had only to request assistance from the government, and a detachment of the Peace Preservation Force would be sent. Since the cost of such an operation was to be borne by all levels of the community, co-operation to free themselves from this expensive burden could be expected from the 'lower orders'. Through the combined efforts of the magistrates, the populace, and the Peace Preservation Force, the area would be speedily tranquillized, and the Force would be withdrawn. The costs would end, and the magistrates would resume control. But if speedy tranquillization did not occur, if the magistrates did not exert themselves to the utmost, if they continued in their inefficient ways and thus became responsible for the continuation of outrage, they were to be put to shame and disgraced 'by paying the man who performed their duty', and, along with all other levels of the population in the proclaimed area, 'fined' by being forced to continue payment of the Force until the Castle was convinced that they were performing their duties. Here it is important to note that while the magistrates acted with the lord lieutenant in

---

[9] *The diary and correspondence of Charles Abbot, Lord Colchester,* ed. Charles, Lord Colchester (London, 1861), ii, 517.

installing the new system, only the lord lieutenant could stop its operation.[10] Thus, according to Peel's plan, the Irish government, if it wished to do so, could keep the Peace Preservation Force in operation in a proclaimed area indefinitely, against the wishes of the residents and at a considerable expense to them.

Perhaps to make the punishment really effective, it was decided to make the cost of the Force relatively high. Not only were the costs of houses, horses, and accoutrements to be paid by the proclaimed areas, but it was also proposed that the 'petty' constables of the Peace Preservation Force be paid the rather surprising sum of £80 a year,[11] as contrasted with the meagre salaries paid to the baronial police. Yet punishment was not the only reason for the proposed high rate of pay: Peel was determined to avoid an error common to most of the inefficient English police systems of the time. He realized that if his new force was to induce a 'better description' of persons to take the position of constable, the salary must make the position worth having,[12] though he also knew that in Ireland high salaries alone would not guarantee capable men. Thus in July 1816 he wrote:

... in the appointment of the chief magistrate and special constables all considerations of parliamentary or local interests should be overlooked, and I believe that the less previous connection they have had with the county in which they are employed, the more effectual will their exertions be.[13]

And after it was certain that his new system would be sanctioned by parliament, he warned: 'If the present or any other government make a job of it, they will most grossly betray the confidence which parliament has placed in them, and shamefully sacrifice the best interests of the country to the worst.'[14] It was also established that catholics were not to be excluded from the Force.[15]

Aside from its punitive aspects, there was little original in

[10] Peel to Crofton, 28 Feb. 1814 (Peel papers, B.M., Add. MS 40285).
[11] Ibid.
[12] Ibid.
[13] Peel to Crofton, 3 July 1814, in Peel, *Private papers*, i, 151.
[14] Peel to Saurin, 5 July 1814 (Peel papers, B.M., Add. MS 40287).
[15] Peel to R. S. Tighe, 27 June 1814 (Peel papers, B.M., Add. MS 40287).

Peel's proposal; stipendiary magistrates and specialized police forces had been used in England for some time, and since 1808 the Dublin police had been under a chief magistrate appointed by the lord lieutenant. It is also probable that the chief secretary had some knowledge of recent police developments in France.[16] And since at least the fall of 1813 the effectiveness of the stipendiary in rural Ireland had been undergoing tests. Men armed with a magistrate's commission, and responsible to the Castle alone, had been sent into the disturbed areas to act in conjunction with the military commanders and any magistrates who desired to co-operate with them.[17] These government agents – Wilson, Willcocks, and Wills – were given authority 'to make such arrangements as they think necessary to be of service in restoring tranquillity to the country', and the magistrates were instructed to give them all possible information and assistance.[18] These Castle magistrates were not the superiors of the local magistrates, but were to work with them to devise measures to handle outrages.[19] They were sent into Roscommon, Limerick, and Westmeath, and evidently achieved some success, for early in 1814 Peel wrote, '. . . we have admitted the principle, why not . . . extend its operation'.[20] But if the use of government agents as magistrates provided an example, it also provided a warning that such an innovation would not be unopposed. As early as October 1813 the bishop of Elphin had written to Peel warning him that some of the magistrates of Roscommon were going to exert pressure to remove Wills from their area. Peel had been disturbed that 'an example so worthy of imitation is so little followed by them'.[21]

The expiration of statutes regulating the Irish police came on March 1814, before Peel's new system was completed. There was placed before Parliament a stop-gap measure designed to keep the old system in operation and giving notice in very general terms that new plans for the preservation of the peace

[16] On several occasions the chief secretary assured his associates that he had no intention of creating a *gendarmarie*.

[17] Peel to General Darby, 7 Oct. 1813 (P.R.O., H.O. 100/173).

[18] Gregory to Wilson, 15 Dec. 1813 (P.R.O., H.O. 100/175).

[19] Gregory to Rochfort, 3 Dec. 1813 (P.R.O., H.O. 100/175).

[20] Peel to Desart, 24 Feb. 1814 (Peel papers, B.M., Add. MS 40285).

[21] Peel to bishop of Elphin, 15 Jan. 1814 (Peel papers, B.M., Add. MS 40285).

in Ireland were to be introduced. Peel, with the support of Whitworth, turned to the problem of selling his new system to the cabinet. In January 1814 the lord lieutenant had taken steps to prepare the way, pointing out that the failure of the government in the area of public peace resulted from the state of the existing law. The possibility of extending the powers of the Irish government and the magistracy should be considered before the next session of parliament convened.[22] Initially Whitworth had questioned 'whether it would be practicable to make the disturbed districts pay for the rods which are used for their correction',[23] but by April he was earnestly supporting Peel's proposal. Writing to Sidmouth, and perhaps anticipating the objections of some of the cabinet, he maintained that Ireland could not be governed as if it were England, for there was a difference in the character and spirit of the governed. He emphasized that 'it is only by a protecting force that the magistrates can be encouraged to do their duty, and by an imposing one that the lower orders can be kept down'.[24]

But Whitworth's preparation of the cabinet had not removed two truly formidable opponents of the proposed measure, the prime minister and the leader of the house of commons. Both Liverpool and Castlereagh opposed Peel's reforms on constitutional grounds, perhaps seeing in them an interference with the traditional duties of the venerable institution of the magistracy. Liverpool characterized the proposed bill as 'not English', an argument which made little impression on Whitworth, who told Peel that since the reforms were intended for Ireland, there was no need for them to be 'English', and implied that the proposed bill might be too good for the Irish.[25] Castlereagh's opposition appeared preposterous to the lord lieutenant, for as an Irishman, Castlereagh 'ought to know his own countrymen, and that they cannot be governed by the ordinary means'.[26]

---

[22] Whitworth to Sidmouth, 15 Jan. 1814 (P.R.O., H.O. 100/176).

[23] Whitworth to Peel, Feb. 1814(?) (Peel papers, B.M., Add. MS 40187).

[24] Whitworth to Sidmouth, 21 Apr. 1814 (P.R.O., H.O. 100/177).

[25] Whitworth to Peel, 30 Apr. 1814 (Peel papers, B.M., Add. MS 40188).

[26] Whitworth to Peel, 20 Apr. 1814 (Peel papers, B.M., Add. MS 40188).

Whether or not the efforts of the lord lieutenant and his chief secretary could have overcome such formidable opposition is not known, for at this point a series of events in Ireland and on the Continent intervened to remove the opposition and give the Irish government a much stronger measure than they had hoped to achieve.

While Peel had been working out his new system, the situation in the disturbed areas had become more alarming. Aided by a winter described by Whitworth as 'such as I have scarcely seen exceeded in Russia',[27] the strength of the groups of disaffected grew until they were described as 'better organized, better armed and more desperately inclined than they were in 1798'.[28] The Irish government flooded the disturbed areas with all available troops, leaving the north almost completely without military force, but the outrages, oath-swearings, and arms raids continued.[29] In March, a leading Irish whig, Sir Henry Parnell, told Peel that in the worst areas of Queen's County the protestants were leaving their homes and moving into the towns. The banditti had cleared Queen's County of arms, and were now extracting twenty to thirty-shilling contributions from the remaining farmers.[30] Further to complicate matters, religious strife now reappeared in the north. In Kilkeel, County Down, catholics and protestants clashed, and the catholics chased their opponents to cover. Protestant reinforcements poured into town, and when the fighting was over it was reported that over forty homes had been destroyed.[31] Although evidently unconnected with the troubles in the rest of Ireland, it was potentially dangerous for such strife to appear since it was apt to spread rapidly in an area with, at the moment, very few troops.

It was not the situation in Ireland alone, however, that finally overcame cabinet opposition. By mid-March 1814, both Westminster and Dublin Castle were aware that the war in Europe would be over in a matter of weeks,[32] but evidently no

[27] Whitworth to Sidmouth, 18 Jan. 1814 (P.R.O., H.O. 100/176).
[28] John Fallisen to John Bagwell, 4 Jan. 1814 (P.R.O., H.O. 100/176).
[29] Peel to archbishop of Cashel, 12 Jan. 1814 (P.R.O., H.O. 100/176).
[30] Sir Henry Parnell to Peel, Mar. 1814 (P.R.O., H.O. 100/177).
[31] Peel to Sidmouth, 13 Apr. 1814 (P.R.O., H.O. 100/177).
[32] Whitworth to Sidmouth, 19 Mar. 1814 (P.R.O., H.O. 100/177).

one had paused to consider the possible effects on the military establishment in Ireland. There could be no doubt that the British government, influenced by a need for rigid economy, would cut the British army to the lowest possible figure. From the remainder, the demands of the Irish establishment would be forced to compete against the demands of the army of occupation in France and British commitments elsewhere in the world. Napoleon abdicated in April, and by the first week in May London had decided to limit the peacetime military establishment in Ireland to fewer than 30,000 men.[33] Whitworth was stunned by the news. The lord lieutenant found it hard to believe that he was expected to keep Ireland tranquil with such a meagre force, and declared once more that an establishment of 40,000 men was the lowest possible figure, adding that 'a peace establishment may do in England. But here we are not at peace'.[34] Peel agreed that a force of 40,000 men was the absolute minimum needed, and he was greatly disturbed by the further news that plans were under way to disembody the militia. The possibility that the Irish countryside would soon receive thousands of men, many of them unemployed and all with military training, caused Peel to warn Sidmouth that good soldiers could become bad citizens.[35]

To emphasize the seriousness of this proposed reduction of the military establishment, the commander of the forces in Ireland, Sir George Hewett, went to London to lay the problem before his superior, the duke of York. He hoped that by promising rigid economy and by reducing his staff, he might persuade his superiors to raise the figure to 40,000 men.[36] In spite of the combined efforts of Whitworth, Peel, and Hewett, no increase in the number could be obtained, but these efforts to underline the dangers resulting from an under-garrisoned Ireland bore fruit in another direction. Evidently it was the need for economy coupled with the awareness of the dangerous situation in Ireland that weakened cabinet opposition to Peel's police system.[37] The

[33] Whitworth to Peel, 8 May 1814 (Peel papers, B.M., Add. MS 40188).
[34] Ibid.
[35] Peel to Sidmouth, 18 May 1814 (P.R.O., H.O. 100/178).
[36] Whitworth to Peel, 14 May 1814 (Peel papers, B.M., Add. MS 40188).
[37] Sidmouth to Peel, 19 May 1814 (P.R.O., H.O. 100/178).

proposed force, working with the magistrates, could stop agrarian outrage before it developed to dangerous proportions, and in unco-operative areas, could coerce the population into greater efforts to tranquillize their districts. The need for a strong military establishment would be lessened, and the tranquillizing process could be accomplished at limited cost to the government. Although it would be performing the duties traditionally assigned to military detachments, the Peace Preservation Force was never considered as a substitute for the army. Both Peel and Whitworth realized that the proposed force alone could not suppress an extensive, fully-developed campaign of agrarian outrage like that existing in Ireland at this time. But the force could stop the spread of disturbances into uninfected areas, and enable the government to concentrate the weakened military establishment in areas where it was most needed: 'A strong and active police and a commanding military establishment' would assure a peaceful Ireland.[38]

The proposal to diminish the military establishment by 10,000 men was not the only shock administered to the Irish government in late May and early June 1814. Over the strong objections of Whitworth and Peel, it was officially announced that the militia would be disembodied,[39] and a few days later reports reached the Castle warning of an uprising scheduled for 16 June 1814. According to the reports, informers had infiltrated the 'headquarters' of a conspiracy and had uncovered an organization extending into Dublin County, Longford, Meath, Westmeath, Kildare, Wicklow, Wexford, and Carlow, under the leadership of 'Mr Executive Secretary'. The purpose of the projected uprising was to end the connection with England, abolish the tithe and taxes, and lower the price of land. It was feared that only a portion of a larger conspiracy had been uncovered, one based on the general dissatisfaction of much of south Ireland, and waiting only for the militia to be disembodied before making its full strength known to the Irish government.[40]

[38] Whitworth to Peel, 20 Apr. 1814 (Peel papers, B.M., Add. MS 40188).
[39] Whitworth to Sidmouth, 3 June 1814 (P.R.O., H.O. 100/178).
[40] Peel to ——, 11 June 1814; General Dana to Lt.-general Meyrick, 16 June 1814; 'Representation of certain magistrates . . .', June 1814; Peel to Sidmouth, 18 June 1814; Whitworth to Sidmouth, 27 June 1814 (P.R.O., H.O. 100/178).

The circumstances surrounding the 'Kildare conspiracy' are obscure to say the least. A raid on the headquarters in the town of Kildare took place on 5 June, and two days later a local official complained that it had failed because the soldiers had been drunk. On the 10th, Whitworth warned Peel of an expected uprising in Kildare, but by the 17th the lord lieutenant seemed to be treating the matter as a bad joke. Nevertheless, on 27 June he sent a lengthy report to the home secretary of a 'systematic plan of insurrection' revealed by papers seized during the raid.[41] At a later date, it was suggested that these papers never existed, and the lack of reliable evidence led to the release of those arrested.[42] The loss of important papers was not unknown in Irish government circles, but it is possible that the 'vast conspiracy' existed only in the minds of informers and over-zealous magistrates. It seems unlikely that the conspiracy had been fabricated to assist the Castle in getting what was wanted from parliament. Instead, the magistrates may have been guilty of accepting the grandiose schemes of a local group at face value. But the Dublin authorities, usually suspicious of 'plots' uncovered by the magistrates, wasted little time in rushing the 'evidence' to London. Actual or imagined, the news of the conspiracy came at a most opportune moment.

In the light of this series of events, Peel was no longer certain by 11 June that his proposed police measure was strong enough to meet so critical a situation. Writing to Gregory, he said, 'I am decidedly of opinion that we ought to have a very strong law. Shall that law be the revived insurrection act or the police act as I have it now prepared?' He proceeded to answer his own question, informing Gregory that he thought

the police are hardly strong enough. I think the insurrection act very strong, but it has a sort of strength which is not precisely that which we require. The police act would be more effectual, though infinitely more moderate in its provisions. I think the police act should be the permanent law of the land, but I should like to have for the next three years some additional powers in the proclaimed districts

[41] Letter from Fenton Aylmer, 7 June 1814 (P.R.O., H.O. 100/178); Whitworth to Peel, 10 June 1814 (Peel papers, B.M., Add. MS 40188); Whitworth to Sidmouth, 27 June 1814 (P.R.O., H.O. 100/178).
[42] See Cash, *Peel*, pp 169–70; Peel to Gregory, 12 July 1814, in Peel, *Private papers*, i, 148–9.

beyond those which it gives. If I could include these permanent and temporary provisions in the same act . . . I should get what I believe would be much more effectual than the old insurrection act.[43]

It is not clear how a decision was reached to try to gain permission from the cabinet to introduce both the police bill and a bill re-enacting the insurrection act. It is possible that Attorney-general Saurin was responsible. In a letter to Peel of 14 June 1814, he argued for the police bill as a better measure than the insurrection act, pointing out that the police bill made no alteration in the existing law, but provided only for its more effectual execution. Unlike the insurrection act, the police bill would be available whenever needed, and would apply only as long as necessary; the government need have no scruples about invoking it. He did admit that the insurrection act might be necessary for emergency use, but he insisted that the bills must be completely separate. To combine the measures or even to identify them too closely with each other might make it difficult to pass the police bill (the more important of the two proposals) and make the government hesitate to use the new police.[44] On the following day, the lord lieutenant repeated the same arguments in simplified form, suggesting that the new police were needed for 'everyday use' and the insurrection act 'if you can get it' for emergency use.[45]

Almost at once, this new course of action ran into strong opposition from Castlereagh, who told Peel that he could not have both acts, for, while he was willing to support the police bill, Castlereagh refused to sanction renewal of the insurrection act. In refusing Peel's request, however, he made a suggestion of his own, a modified police bill that would incorporate some of the strength of the insurrection act.[46] Unfortunately, there is no information available on the exact nature of Castlereagh's modifications, but in the police bill as introduced to the house of commons on 23 June 1814 there appears one significant change which may incorporate one of Castlereagh's suggestions. This change made it possible for the lord lieutenant to proclaim

[43] Peel to Gregory, 11 June 1814, in Peel, *Private papers*, i, 143–4.
[44] Saurin to Peel, 14 June 1814 (Peel papers, B.M., Add. MS 40211).
[45] Whitworth to Peel, 15 June 1814 (Peel papers, B.M., Add. MS 40188).
[46] Peel to Saurin, 18 June 1814 (Peel papers, B.M., Add. MS 40287).

an area and install a detachment of the Peace Preservation Force without first receiving a request from the magistrates – making this draft of the bill a much stronger measure than Peel's original plan. Other changes may have restored certain provisions that had been modified in an attempt to make the bill more acceptable to the Irish members at Westminster.[47]

The provisions of the bill as finally passed[48] were as follows: The lord lieutenant, acting with the advice of the Irish privy council, could proclaim any county, county of a city or town, barony or half-barony, or any combination of these, to be in a state of disturbance requiring a chief magistrate and an 'extraordinary' establishment of police. In practice, the Castle proved reluctant to apply the act against the wishes of the magistrates of the area involved, and bitter argument often preceded the appearance of the Force in a disturbed area. A chief magistrate of police was to be appointed for each barony or half-barony within a proclaimed area 'as shall seem best', and might be removed or replaced by the government at any time. The chief magistrate was to have the powers of a justice of the peace in his district and for a seven-mile radius beyond. He had to reside in his assigned area, and could leave only in the course of duty or with permission from the lord lieutenant. All magistrates within his district were to be under his jurisdiction and were required to assist him in all ways. The lord lieutenant would appoint for the 'aid and support of such chief magistrates', a clerk, a chief constable, and sub-constables up to fifty in number, all of whom were to be under the control of the chief magistrate with specific orders to obey no other magistrate unless ordered to do so.

The chief magistrate was to receive £700 per year and a suitable house, his clerk £150, the chief constable £150, and each sub-constable £50. All of these salaries were 'rateable', meaning that if order were restored in less than twelve months the force would be paid in accordance with the amount of time served. All costs of operation, even for horses, arms, and equipment, were to be defrayed by presentment, and, to forestall any possible financial delays, the lord lieutenant was authorized to

[47] See Peel to Gregory, 3 June 1814 (Peel papers, B.M., Add. MS 40286); Peel to Saurin, 27 June 1814 (Peel papers, B.M., Add. MS 40287).
[48] 54 Geo. III, c. 131, 25 July 1814.

pay these expenses from the consolidated fund and then to collect from the proclaimed area. Considering that it was possible for a half-barony to be billed for £3,500 in wages alone in a year's time under the provisions of this bill, Peel's 'pecuniary fine' provided a real incentive for an area to avoid a need to be subjected to its provisions.

The baronial police received only slight attention in Peel's bill, and continued to function as before. An added opportunity for the magistrates and the respectable citizens of a disturbed area to prove their zeal was afforded by a provision in the bill that quarter sessions were allowed to appoint an unlimited number of unsalaried special constables for a twelve-month period.

The lord lieutenant and Irish privy council were empowered under the bill to proclaim peace restored in either a part or all of the designated area, at which time the office of chief magistrate and his force ceased to function. Since costs were high, the separate detachments of the Force were disbanded when not actively employed; the officers and men were paid a percentage of the remainder of their yearly salaries and discharged to await possible future re-employment. When a detachment was disbanded, the arms and equipment remained the property of the Irish government, a provision designed to keep them from falling into the hands of the disaffected. A sub-constable was subject to a £10 fine for failure to deliver up his arms at the end of his period of service.

It is difficult to say why this bill, which was to be strongly opposed after its enactment into law, met so little criticism in parliament. Certainly one reason was Peel's very capable handling of the bill in the house of commons. As Peel presented it, the bill was designed not to meet a sudden emergency, but rather to aid the solution of a long-standing problem with which the existing laws could not cope. Now that Bonaparte had been defeated, Peel 'did not wish that, at a season of general happiness and rejoicing for the restoration of tranquillity, Ireland alone should form an exemption'. He presented carefully documented details of outrages and descriptions of the various 'combinations', and even produced and read the oath of the members of a recently discovered conspiracy. This unfortunate situation, he said, had developed in spite of the 'great exertions . . . used on the part of the magistracy to check and subdue them'. Summarizing the provisions of the bill, he emphasized that the chief magistrate would be 'called upon for those exertions which could not be required from ordinary magistrates, who could not be expected to devote the whole of their time to the public service'. Without going into details, Peel explained that the new constables were to be paid good salaries and selected from among 'farmers' sons and persons of that class . . . to make them keep a kind of watch and ward in the disturbed area'. Again he insisted that while many magistrates in Ireland were willing to devote their time to public service, 'putting down disturbances in Ireland was often a full-time job'.[49]

In introducing the police bill, Peel steered carefully away from any accusations of incompetence in the Irish magistracy. His description of the conditions in Ireland that made such legislation necessary was based entirely on documents and specific cases, all selected to prove that the existing powers of the Irish magistracy were not sufficient to maintain tranquillity. The proposed solution of the government was presented as an offer to take over duties which were too much for the ordinary magistrates. Clearly Peel left much unsaid. There was no recorded opposition to the bill in the discussion which followed its initial presentation, and none on its first reading on 27 June.[50] At the committee stage, Sir Francis Flood seems to have recognized that the bill would supersede the ordinary magistrates, and would be costly, and while he approved of the general idea he opposed the bill as it then stood.[51] Another member protested that the proposed measure was not strong enough,[52] but the opposition which Peel had feared might greet his earlier version failed to materialize when the much stronger bill was presented.

Neither Peel nor Witworth was willing to accept without comment Castlereagh's decision against the insurrection act. In early July, the rumour that parliament might not meet again until the first of the next year, along with the scheduled disembodiment of the militia, made Peel determined to try again for cabinet permission to introduce the act:

[49] Peel, *Speeches*, i, 25–30.
[50] *Hansard 1*, xxvii, 163–74, 259–62.
[51] *Hansard 1*, xxvii, 523–3.
[52] Ibid.

It can do no harm to have the power, though I firmly believe it would lie dormant, and if there should be a 'dispute in Thomas Street' as Emmet's rebellion is called, we might reproach ourselves hereafter for not being better provided for the emergency.[53]

Sidmouth was easily convinced of the need for the act as an emergency measure,[54] and a meeting was arranged for Peel, Sidmouth, Liverpool, and Castlereagh to discuss the matter. Peel wrote:

The first question I asked was, whether there was reason to believe that parliament would meet in November. I was told that there was every probability that it would not. . . . I observed that in that case I was decidedly of the opinion that the Irish government should be prepared for a possible emergency by the extension of their powers. I did not wish to overstate the danger, but it is impossible to conceal from ourselves the probability that there may be some partial rising which . . . may, unless effectively and speedily controlled, spread into something more formidable. . . .

Castlereagh now felt that 'it would have a bad effect on the negotiations [in Vienna] to create an impression that Ireland is in a state of great agitation and disturbance'; Liverpool felt that 'it was very inconvenient to have violent debates and angry discussions at so late a period of the year'. Thus the objections of the party leaders were now of a purely practical nature, and Castlereagh and Liverpool gave way.[55]

On 8 July 1814, Peel introduced a bill for the re-enactment of the insurrection act, and it was soon apparent that the only serious obstacle to its revival had been surmounted when Castlereagh and Liverpool gave their consent. Of the Irish members, only Sir Henry Parnell offered strong objections. Sir Samuel Romilly and Francis Horner both questioned the need for such legislation, and Horner accused the tories of waiting to introduce the bill until the end of the session when most of the Irish members were absent. But there seemed little doubt from the start that the measure would pass; it received its final reading late in July,[56] and became law to be effective for three

[53] Peel to Whitworth, 2 July 1814, in Peel, *Private papers*, i, 145.
[54] Sidmouth to Whitworth, 4 July 1814 (P.R.O., H.O. 100/179).
[55] Peel to Whitworth, 7 July, 13 July 1814, in Peel, *Private papers*, i, 146–8, 149–50.
[56] *Hansard 1*, xxviii, 686–96, 803–9.

years.[57] Thus by the end of the session, Peel possessed in the Peace Preservation Force and the insurrection act two additional measures to help in restoring order in Ireland.

From the start, the Peace Preservation Force was planned as a civil force organized on military lines. As early as May, Whitworth had suggested that the chief magistrates be selected from militia officers with experience as magistrates. Such magistrates would have the requisites of both civil and military experience, and could manage not only the ordinary duties of their office but any 'military situation' as well.[58] The first two chief magistrates, however, were not militia officers, but Castle magistrates, Wilson and Willcocks. Both were experienced policemen and as Castle magistrates had been involved in efforts to cope with agrarian disorder. The chief constables and sub-constables were to be drawn from discharged militia men and regulars 'of the better description',[59] for Peel's suggestion to the house of commons that the new constables be drawn from farmers' sons had been dismissed by Whitworth with the comment, 'I have no great opinion of farmers.'[60] Their military experience was the first reason for using discharged soldiers. They were accustomed to discipline and capable of acting in formation – both absolutely essential in handling banditti groups of superior strength. A lesser consideration was found in the fact that as ex-militiamen they were better qualified to watch the disbanded militiamen who would soon be returning to their homes and might join the disaffected.[61]

---

[57] 54 Geo. III, c. 180, 30 July 1814. Peel had asked that the act be valid for only two years, but a clerical error made it three instead. Sir Charles Flint to Peel, 20 Oct. 1814 (Peel papers, B.M., Add. MS 40215).

[58] Whitworth to Peel, 26 May 1814 (Peel papers, B.M., Add. MS 40188).

[59] Peel to Sir John Newport, 14 July 1814, in Peel, *Private papers*, i, 150.

[60] Whitworth to Peel, 29 June 1814 (Peel papers, B.M., Add. MS 40188).

[61] Whitworth to Peel, 18 July 1814 (Peel papers, B.M., Add. MS 40189).

V

THE FORCE AND
INSURRECTION ACT, 1814-15

~~~~~~

THE PASSAGE OF the peace preservation act and the insurrection act seemed to have little immediate effect. Outrage diminished, but this frequently happened with the arrival of summer. Only Westmeath was seriously disturbed: canal-building attracted a deluge of job-seekers, and in a series of clashes the residents drove the outsiders from the county.[1] The Castle continued to accuse the magistrates of failure to perform their duties, and to show concern over the diminution of the military establishment. In an effort to keep the militia embodied, Irish officials bombarded the home office with information uncovered during the 5 June raid in Kildare: while some of the plotters had been dispersed or arrested, the situation remained dangerous; the plot might easily be revived; 'secret information' had disclosed that an uprising was planned to coincide with the disbanding of the Irish militia. The Castle claimed that the disaffected looked forward to this date with 'the greatest hope and exultation', and that it would see not only the drastic reduction of the military establishment, but also the release to the insurgents of recruits with military training.[2]

By the end of June, the dire warnings emanating from the

[1] Gregory to Peel, 24 July 1814 (P.R.O., H.O. 100/179).
[2] Peel to Sidmouth, 18 June 1814; Whitworth to Sidmouth, 27 June 1814 (P.R.O., H.O. 100/178).

Irish government had their desired effect, and Sidmouth joined Whitworth and Peel in advocating a strong military establishment. Writing to the duke of York, he said, 'it is necessary, under the present circumstances, to keep a larger military establishment in Ireland than was thought necessary during the latter period of the war', and he proposed that no militia regiments should be disbanded and no military forces withdrawn from Ireland until replacements were available.[3] But in spite of all efforts, at the end of July the size of the planned peacetime establishment remained at about 30,000 men.[4]

The disbanding of the militia began in August, with units of the lowest strength disbanded first, to be followed by the rest.[5] As they were disbanded, the militia units were replaced by regulars. Thus the numerical weakness of the military establishment would be offset somewhat by its increased reliability, for the government remained suspicious of the loyalty of the Irish militia. The process continued until November, when it was suddenly halted. Nine of the strongest Irish militia units – Armagh, North Cork, Donegal, Londonderry, North Mayo, Roscommon, Tyrone, Tipperary, and Wexford – were kept embodied and it was announced that eighteen of the remaining English militia units in Ireland were to remain.[6] The only information available to help explain this abrupt reversal is a letter from Sidmouth to Whitworth, dated 15 October 1814, in which Sidmouth says that Peel had suggested to the duke of York that the remaining British units be kept during the winter.[7] And perhaps the increasing pressure of the British government's economic problems and the continuance of the war with the United States made it impossible to continue replacing the militia units with regulars. The decision to keep the English and Irish units still embodied on active duty aroused considerable opposition,[8] and could be justified only for the duration of the war with the United States. The move was at best another attempt to maintain the Irish military

[3] Sidmouth to the commander-in-chief, 3 July 1814 (P.R.O., H.O. 100/179).

[4] Sir George Hewett to Gregory, 29 July 1814 (P.R.O., H.O. 100/179).

[5] Whitworth to Sidmouth, 6 Oct. 1814 (P.R.O., H.O. 100/181).

[6] McAnally, *Irish militia*, pp 256–7.

[7] Sidmouth to Whitworth, 15 Oct. 1814 (P.R.O., H.O. 100/181).

[8] See *Annual Reg., 1814*, 206–10.

establishment by the use of temporary expedients, perhaps further motivated by the belief that 'good soldiers may be worse civilians when they get among their friends'.[9]

Thus by the last half of 1814 there could be no doubt that the Irish government would have to get along with a military establishment much smaller than any available since the union. This was to be underlined in the following February, when the budget introduced by Vansittart called for the expenditure of £29,000,000 for maintaining the army and navy on a peacetime footing, a proposal which, along with his plan to continue the wartime income tax to help finance it, 'provoked an explosion of general discontent'.[10] The problem of maintaining public order in Ireland since Peel's arrival in 1812 had tended to emphasize the uncertainty of depending on the military establishment and to increase the importance of an alternative force such as that outlined in the peace preservation act. Circumstances were steadily forcing the Irish government to attempt a civil solution to the problem of a disordered land.

The first attempt to apply the peace preservation act got off to an inauspicious start. Tipperary in the spring of 1814 had been the scene of a series of exceptionally violent outrages, culminating in the assassination of one of the more active magistrates, identified only as 'Mr Long'. This naturally frightened the other magistrates of the county, and after deliberating among themselves they decided to ask the government to apply the peace preservation act to the most troublesome portion of the county, the barony of Middlethird. To the embarrassment of the Castle, it was necessary to inform the magistrates that although the peace preservation act had been passed by parliament, it had not yet received the royal assent. The lord lieutenant assured the magistrates that in the meantime he 'relied upon their exertions to bring the offenders to punishment'.[11] It was not until September that all the obstacles had been cleared and the government was able to act. In the interim, the causes of the original request had vanished in one of those strange cessations of violence which seemed to have no

[9] Peel to Sidmouth, 18 May 1814 (P.R.O., H.O. 100/178).
[10] Elie Halevy, *The liberal awakening* (Loddon, 1926), pp 6–7.
[11] Report, Whitworth to Sidmouth, 5 June 1816 (P.R.O., H.O. 100/189).

explanation, but occasionally occurred in the midst of periods of disorder. Rather naïvely, Peel felt that the threat of the insurrection act and the new police had frightened the disaffected into submission. On 30 September 1814, he wrote, 'I never recollect such a cessation of outrage and disturbance as there has been for the last three months – it would seem presumptuous to say since the passing of the two acts of the last session.'[12] Evidently the Castle decided to use Middlethird as a laboratory to test the effectiveness of the new police, for even in a generally tranquil Ireland, Tipperary could be relied upon to provide plenty of work for the Force. Lord Donoughmore, an influential Irish whig, agreed to co-operate, and the other magistrates followed his lead.[13]

In mid-September 1814 the barony of Middlethird in Tipperary was proclaimed by the lord lieutenant to be in a state of disturbance, and received a force of twenty ex-cavalry sergeants under the direction of their chief magistrate, Richard Willcocks.[14] The new force barely had time to reach Tipperary before a storm of criticism erupted, for which they were in no way responsible. Judge William Fletcher presented to the Wexford grand jury a violent attack on British 'rule' in Ireland and all its trappings. According to Fletcher, rack-rents, tithes, Orange lodges, the magistracy, and corruption, rather than treason and conspiracy, were the causes of crime.[15] The new police did not escape his wrath, for he considered them little more than an addition to Castle patronage. 'There is first an office of £700 a year, a very good office for a loyal man. . . . There are three offices of £150 for second-rate loyalists, and an abundance of offices of £50 a year for inferior loyalists. Oh most excellent peace preservation bills, Oh! Mr Peel, Mr Peel, Oh!' The judge's charges received considerable attention in the opposition press in both England and Ireland, as a condemna-

[12] Peel to Abbot, 30 Sept. 1814, in Peel, *Private papers*, i, 154.

[13] Donoughmore to Willcocks, 13 Sept. 1814 (Peel papers, B.M., Add. MS 40189); Report, Whitworth to Sidmouth, 5 June 1816 (P.R.O., H.O. 100/189).

[14] Whitworth to Peel, 5 Sept. 1814 (Peel papers, B.M., Add. MS 40189); Report, Whitworth to Sidmouth, 5 June 1816 (P.R.O., H.O. 100/189).

[15] For a copy of this speech and the government correspondence concerning it, see P.R.O., H.O. 100/176.

tion of Irish policy in general and of the Peace Preservation Force in particular. Peel was deeply angered, and late in September wrote of the attack, 'I will not say that it is disapproved of by all the friends of good order . . . but I may venture to assert that it has unqualified approbation of . . . every demagogue . . . who survived the periods of 1798 and 1803.'[16] Fletcher's remarks on the new police undoubtedly made the task of gaining public acceptance much harder. As late as 1822, when plans were being made for the reform of the county police, the Dublin *Evening Post* opposed it as a patronage scheme, declaring that the proposed constables were 'second and third order jobbers'.[17]

The bitterness aroused in Peel and his associates by the Fletcher episode was no doubt mollified by the apparent success of the Peace Preservation Force during its first weeks in operation. Willcocks established his headquarters in Cashel, and from there sent out mounted bodies of police to patrol the roads around the town, being careful not to establish a schedule or pattern which could be anticipated by marauders. Whenever the required information was available, detachments of police were sent to sites where trouble was expected, and it appears usually not to have materialized.[18] Peel was able to write on 30 September, 'The practical proof of its efficacy is, that since the day on which Middlethird was proclaimed, I have not had the report of an outrage of any description either in that or in any other part of Tipperary, an extraordinary state of things in that county.'[19] Whitworh was equally enthusiastic: 'Although the police bill has been but a very few weeks in operation, the effect is already such as to justify the most sanguine expectation of its ultimate success.' He pointed out that Tipperary had long been the worst of the counties, and that since this measure had been applied it was 'in a state of perfect tranquillity'. Of equal importance, the 'better class' of people were free from the burden of fear, and now able to react on the worse classes.[20]

[16] Peel to Abbot, 30 Sept. 1814, in Peel, *Private papers*, i, 154.
[17] Dublin *Evening Post*, 2 Feb. 1822.
[18] See Willcocks to Gregory, 1 Oct. 1814 (P.R.O., H.O. 100/181).
[19] Peel to Abbot, 30 Sept. 1814, in Peel, *Private papers*, i, 155.
[20] Report, Whitworth to Sidmouth, 14 Oct. 1814 (P.R.O., H.O. 100/181).

The complacent optimism expressed by Peel and Whitworth in these letters was soon shattered, for they had failed to anticipate the opposition to the peace preservation act which was beginning to appear. The lack of opposition encountered by the act in parliament may have been interpreted by the Irish government as an indication of a general acceptance of its provisions, but events of the near future were to show such an interpretation unwarranted. By November, the 'state of perfect tranquillity' had ended, and the Force in Middlethird found itself caught between the renewed activity of the banditti and the hostility of the magistracy.

As winter approached in 1814, the peaceful conditions characteristic of the troublesome areas in the summer and early autumn were replaced by the dreary and all-too-familiar pattern of crime and violence. Tipperary was no exception, for the district selected for the Peace Preservation Force experiment became the site of a major crime wave. The home of one of the leading country gentlemen of the Cashel area was looted by a gang of thieves in broad daylight, and they added insult to injury by spending an entire afternoon ransacking the house. On another occasion, a gang robbed a mail-coach after forcing it to stop by felling trees across the road. One of the attendants on the coach was shot by the robbers.[21]

It is quite possible that Peel did not know of these incidents for some time after their occurrence in Tipperary. Willcocks was inclined to ignore the portion of his orders calling for weekly reports,[22] and the Castle was often properly suspicious of information from outside sources. If Peel did know of the reappearance of trouble, he chose to overlook it, for the speech he made on 18 November in the house of commons was full of praise for the efforts of the new police. The occasion for the speech was the need for a slight modification in the peace preservation act,[23] and Peel used this opportunity to answer the criticism of the act by 'evil and designing men'. The picture he painted was a rosy one. Not just Middlethird had benefited greatly from the presence of the Force, but the surrounding

[21] State of the country, Nov. 1814 (P.R.O., H.O. 100/182).
[22] Peel to Gregory, 3 Apr. 1815, 13 Apr. 1815 (Peel papers, B.M., Add. MS 40288).
[23] 55 Geo. III, c. 13, 1 Dec. 1814.

districts as well. Freed from the threat of reprisal from the lawless, the lower classes were showing a degree of co-operation with the authorities not known in the past. He cited an instance in which a group of labourers had been responsible for the apprehension of an arms raider, and described this as an example of the hitherto rare 'combination in support of the law of the land'.[24]

The reaction in parliament to Peel's speech may have been quite a surprise to the chief secretary and his associates. Lord Donoughmore, who earlier had lent his support to the use of the Force in Middlethird, now launched a vigorous attack on Peel's picture of an efficient police in a tranquil area. After discussing in detail the recent crime wave in this portion of Tipperary, which he cited as proof that the new police were ineffective, he turned to the provisions of the act, which he characterized as defective and a threat to the constitution. The inefficiency of the Force was due partly to the serious error of picking the personnel from discharged soldiers in Dublin and putting them under the command of a Castle magistrate. Tipperary men and magistrates would have been better acquainted with the area involved and thus better qualified. He also implied that the Castle's desire for additional patronage might have been one of the reasons behind the Peace Preservation Force. Donoughmore strongly supported the insurrection act as a more effective instrument. Strangely enough, he also regarded it as the 'milder' of the new measures, for he saw in the peace preservation act evidences of a danger not present in the other. It gave the Irish government power

to proclaim every barony in every county of Ireland. Thus the lord lieutenant and the chief secretary and . . . the privy council, might if they saw fit, might without any previous application whatever, declare the whole kingdom of Ireland to be in a state of disturbance.

But the financial provisions of the act caused his deepest concern. He saw in them nothing less than 'a bill of taxation'. 'It went to take from those who had property, because that property was attacked, the means of punishing individuals who had no property to lose.' The Irish government could both proclaim and tax all Ireland without consulting the better class of people.

[24] *Hansard 1*, xxix, 335–7.

According to his figures, a chief magistrate in every barony in Ireland would impose a tax of £240,000 on the 'kingdom of Ireland' without the sanction of those taxed. As a final warning, he called attention to the fact that fifty members of the new police in each barony would provide the government with an army of 10,000 men. He offered no explanation of his part in installing the Force in Middlethird, but he did say that when the magistrates had requested the Peace Preservation Force, they had thought that they were requesting the insurrection act![25]

If the Force was less than a success in combating crime, at least the monetary punishment provisions of the act were obviously beginning to make themselves felt. But the Irish government did not withdraw the Force from Middlethird, and the local magistrates showed not the slightest inclination to co-operate.[26] Willcocks and his men continued their operations, apparently with some success, for the 'State of the country' reports during the winter of 1814–15 mention few serious occurrences in his area.[27] In February 1815, some of the magistrates in the proclaimed district evidently tried again to shake off their burden. The Dublin *Evening Post*, a determined foe of the present administration,[28] gleefully printed a full account of the meeting of the Middlethird magistrates. The article began by describing the peace preservation act as a complete failure, and speculated that 'Mr Peele' would probably introduce a bill to repeal his own act. According to the *Post*, it was charged at this meeting that the outrages in the area were now more numerous than at any time since the rebellion of 1798. A resolution was offered stating 'that as the peace preservation bill was insufficient to prevent these outrages and put down an armed banditti, the government would adopt some other mode more efficient'. A magistrate identified only as 'Mr Jacob' seems to have been the leading instigator of

[25] *Hansard 1*, xxix, 501–4.

[26] Whitworth to Sidmouth, 13 May 1815 (Peel papers, B.M., Add. MS 40190).

[27] State of the country, December 1814 (P.R.O., H.O. 100/182); February, March 1815 (P.R.O., H.O. 100/183).

[28] Magee, the editor, had been fined and sentenced to prison for libelling the Dublin police. See Gregory to Peel, 25 June 1813 (Peel papers, B.M., Add. MS 40197).

this resolution, and although he waved a collection of documents purportedly proving his case, their contents were not revealed by the *Post*. The resolution was defeated by a vote of twelve to seven. Yet, while the *Post* was violently opposed to the peace preservation act, it had nothing but praise for Willcocks, 'a meritorious and excellent magistrate', and seemed to blame the Middlethird magistrates for not co-operating with him.[29]

Despite influential opposition, by February 1815 a majority of the magistrates in the proclaimed area were willing to continue with the Peace Preservation Force, and on 3 May the adjoining baronies of Kilnemanaugh and Eliogarty were placed under the provisions of the act. According to Peel, the Force was requested by the magistrates of these baronies because it had proved itself efficient in Middlethird. He suggested to Gregory that this example of the worth of the Force be used to convince other areas to request it.[30] But if the Force was gradually gaining acceptance in Tipperary, it was not yet acceptable elsewhere. On 14 November 1814, Lord Castlemaine (the 'grand alarmist') and fourteen magistrates of Westmeath asked the Irish government to apply the provisions of the insurrection act.[31] There was no evidence whatsoever to justify the panic-stricken claims of 'insurrectionary activities' put forth by this group, evidently victims of fears set going by the 'conspiracy' of the previous June, which continued to plague much of southern Ireland throughout the winter of 1814–15. A 'disorderly spirit' was detected in Killarney, and in Cork 'a great alteration in the behaviour and conduct of the lower orders'. The lower classes in Clare were stated to be 'very riotous and savage'.[32] Yet the Irish government could not completely ignore the rumours, for such rumours had all too often been substantiated. Nor would it have been wise to affront a person of Castlemaine's stature by an unqualified refusal of his request. The insurrection act was not to be considered, for Peel was still determined to use it only in cases of extreme

[29] Dublin *Evening Post*, 11 Feb. 1815.
[30] Peel to Gregory, 17 May 1815 (Peel papers, B.M., Add. MS 40299).
[31] Report, Whitworth to Sidmouth, 5 June 1816 (P.R.O., H.O. 100/189).
[32] State of the country, December 1814 (P.R.O., H.O. 100/182); February 1815 (P.R.O., H.O. 100/183).

emergency. The peace preservation act had been designed for just such a situation, and the government sent an agent to Westmeath to see if there were grounds for its application, and to inform Castlemaine and the magistrates that, were extraordinary measures advisable to maintain law and order, the peace preservation act must suffice.[33] The offer was refused, and no serious trouble in Westmeath appeared during the following months.

Peel was now to find that there were disadvantages in having the insurrection act in reserve for special emergencies. The shock of Napoleon's return from Elba and the possible further diminution of the military establishment increased the apprehensions of some of the magistrates to an alarming degree, and between 15 March and the end of April the Irish government received four requests for the application of the insurrection act. Westmeath's was the first request, followed by Clare, Limerick, and Meath. In no instance was it found that the actual circumstances justified invoking that act. As Peel wrote to Gregory,

We ought to have been impeached if we had enforced the insurrection act upon such grounds as those on which the magistrates of Westmeath and Meath desired it. When we come to consider not their pompous memorials, but the evidence that we have of actual disturbance, is there ground for all the alarm that seems to pervade the country? Are not Waterford, Kilkenny, Tipperary and Queen's County more tranquil than they were last year? Clare appears to be worse, and Limerick no better. I dare say – I have no doubt, indeed – that the disposition of the lower orders in all these counties is very bad, but from proof of actual outrage I cannot discover that it is much worse than usual.[34]

Peel's analysis seems to have been accurate, and Whitworth agreed that the country was more tranquil than the reports would indicate.[35] The Irish government refused each of the four requests in turn, offering always the alternative provisions of the peace preservation act. Gregory tried once more to sell the act to Castlemaine, but was unable to do so. Evidently Castlemaine was continuing his objections to the financial provisions of the

[33] Whitworth to Peel, 23 Nov. 1814 (Peel papers, B.M., Add. MS 40189).
[34] Peel to Gregory, 29 Apr. 1815 (Peel papers, B.M., Add. MS 40288).
[35] Whitworth to Sidmouth, 15 May 1815 (P.R.O., H.O. 100/184).

act, and Gregory was instructed to tell him that the 'tax' in Middlethird was only 10½*d*. per acre. Peel concluded his instructions by reminding the under-secretary that 'the bill is infinitely more likely to work if it is enforced with the concurrence and co-operation of the magistracy'.[36]

The Castle also failed in its proposals to Clare and Limerick. The magistrates refused to request the act, and the Irish government refused to force it on them.[37] By the end of April, Castle tempers had begun to wear a bit thin, and Saurin began to argue for the use of the provisions of the act that allowed the Irish government to enforce it without consent of the magistrates. He wrote to Peel:

The machine of government is at present but ill adapted to the times. We must enforce the peace preservation bill in several places – it should have been done before this time. I am still very confident that it will prove useful and that with a little management it will cease to be unpopular. Fifty good and well armed constables in a barony would in these times be some use against an insurrectionary movement then, as well as a preventive.[38]

Several weeks later, Saurin launched a bitter attack on the magistrates who had requested the insurrection act, stating that 'the niggardly spirit of the gentry and their wishes to get extended powers into their own hands make them blind to any measure but the one for preserving the peace',[39] that is, the insurrection act.

Peel was by now beginning to share Saurin's views on the need to override the wishes of the magistrates. The renewal of the war on the Continent and the demands of Wellington's army were increasing the need for wider use of the new police. In his letter to Gregory of 17 May, Peel said, 'I think . . . that some further attempt should be made to reconcile the magistrates to the peace preservation bill, and then if this attempt is fruitless and after the lapse of a short time the disturbances still continue the bill should be enforced.' The magistrates were to be re-

[36] Peel to Gregory, 3 Apr. 1815 (Peel papers, B.M., Add MS 40288).
[37] Whitworth to Sidmouth, 13 May 1815 (Peel papers, B.M., Add. MS 40190).
[38] Saurin to Peel, 29 Apr. 1815 (Peel papers, B.M., Add. MS 40211).
[39] Saurin to Peel, 16 May 1815 (Peel papers, B.M., Add. MS 40211).

minded and warned that the provisions of the act would apply to all, not just to the disorderly.[40]

But the government's threat to the magistrates did not materialize. Again, with the arrival of warm weather, the disturbances and threats of disturbances disappeared, and by July only Tipperary was in a disturbed state.[41] But there is yet another possible reason for the Irish government's finding it unnecessary to take strong measures at this time. Although the evidence is very incomplete, it is still worth relating. In April, Whitworth wrote to Sidmouth concerning 'the experiment of the peace preservation bill in the part of Meath and Westmeath',[42] and later commented on the effects of the act in Limerick.[43] But Meath, Westmeath, and Limerick were not put under the provisions of the act, not 'proclaimed', until considerably later than this.[44] It is possible that a chief magistrate and a force of constables were sent to these counties on an experimental basis, with the cost defrayed by the government, to see if they could succeed in tranquillizing the parts of these counties alleged to be disturbed. If some such experiment was attempted, it was evidently considered successful in at least two instances. On 3 June, Whitworth wrote to Peel,

There is a magic in the very nature of the peace preservation bill which produces a most salutary effect – It tranquillized Westmeath and has now operated with the same effect on the county of Limerick. It is what you foresaw.[45]

Evidently the magistrates of Westmeath and Limerick did not share Whitworth's enthusiasm, for with the renewal of outrage in the fall of 1815, they turned once more to the insurrection act as a solution to their problems, and vigorously opposed application of the peace preservation act.

Following the final defeat of Napoleon and the 'victory' over the banditti in Limerick and Tipperary in 1815, cabinet atten-

---

[40] Peel to Gregory, 17 May 1815 (Peel papers, B.M., Add. MS 40288).
[41] State of the country, July 1815 (P.R.O., H.O. 100/184).
[42] Whitworth to Sidmouth, 19 Apr. 1815 (Peel papers, B.M., Add. MS 40190).
[43] Whitworth to Peel, June 1815 (Peel papers, B.M., Add. MS 40190).
[44] Proclaimed districts, 1814–22 (Peel papers, B.M., Add. MS 40328).
[45] Whitworth to Peel, 3 June 1815 (Peel papers, B.M., Add. MS 40190).

tion had again been directed to the Irish military establishment. It is difficult to determine the exact strength of the armed forces in Ireland at this or any other time: men deserted, died, or were discharged; regiments and militia units were transferred to and from Ireland; and for various reasons statistics from one source do not tally with those from another. In early April 1815, about a month after Napoleon's escape from Elba, the establishment stood at about 21,000 regulars and 13,500 Irish and English militiamen. Despite cabinet reluctance to diminish the military force in Ireland, on 14 April it was recommended that over 5,000 regulars be withdrawn for continental service.[46] During the spring and summer of 1815, the regulars continued to leave, but various measures were used to maintain the total strength of the establishment. Regiments returning from America were ordered to Ireland, a re-embodiment of the inactive units of the Irish militia was ordered for June, additional British units arrived, and in October the commander of the forces reported 33,000 'effectives' available, a number he considered 'barely adequate'.[47]

In May, realizing that it would take time to return the militia units to strength, Whitworth decided to convert the yeomanry into a sort of substitute militia.[48] The method by which this was accomplished was as follows: Volunteers were requested from the yeomanry corps of certain northern counties (Armagh, Antrim, Fermanagh, Monaghan, and Tyrone). These volunteers served for two- or three-month periods, outside their home counties, performing the same duties as regulars and militia, and subject to military discipline. The government provided their equipment and maintenance, and they were led by their own officers. These units were under the command of the commander of the forces in Ireland, who decided how they could best be used to relieve regular troops and aid the civil power. Each of the counties involved was to provide

---

[46] Cabinet minute, 14 Apr. 1815; Peel to Sidmouth, 23 Apr. 1815; Memorandum, Apr. 1815 (P.R.O., H.O. 100/183).
[47] Whitworth to Peel, 29 June 1815 (Peel papers, B.M., Add. MS 40190); Sidmouth to Whitworth, 24 June, 18 July 1815 (P.R.O., H.O. 100/184); Littlehales to Beckett, 23 May 1815 (P.R.O., H.O. 100/184); Hewett to Peel, 23 Oct. 1815 (P.R.O., H.O. 100/186).
[48] Whitworth to Sidmouth, 15 May 1815 (P.R.O., H.O. 100/184).

140 men.[49] The statutes governing organization and use of the yeomanry made no provision for employment outside their 'districts', and apparently no provision existed under which the government could pay for such an operation. Peel chose to ignore these limitations:

I have no notion of being prevented by the letter of an act of parliament from averting any serious evil to the state, or depriving it of any great benefit. I am sure parliament will always be ready to sanction a liberal construction of its enactments, when the motive is clearly a good one. . . .[50]

There is no indication that this use of the yeomanry under questionable circumstances was ever noted by parliament. In March, General Sir George Hewett, commander of the forces in Ireland, and Sir Edward Littlehales, the Irish military under-secretary, had questioned the wisdom of using the yeomanry in any capacity.[51] Their lack of discipline and general unreliability had recently been demonstrated when a yeomanry detachment sent out to prevent a clash between catholic and Orange factions at Lurgan (Armagh), joined the Orangemen and helped to run the catholics out of town.[52] In April, the activities of one of the Limerick yeomanry units had been singled out by the Dublin *Evening Post* for special attention. The *Post* referred to them as 'the criminal, unpunished, protected disturbers of the peace', and concentrated on the activities of one Captain Fuller, who 'assembles the infatuated people he proposes to attack, and breaks open houses in the night to rob and torture'.[53] In March there had been talk of disbanding the entire force, but Peel had reminded Littlehales that 'the most vehement loyalty in Ireland is apt to take offence', and suggested that they might be gradually diminished instead.[54] Yet by June the past record of the yeomanry was being ignored, and Peel and Whitworth had decided to 'persevere in spite of Sir George's objection'.[55] Thus

[49] Whitworth to Sidmouth, 29 June 1815; Littlehales to the brigade-major, 27 June 1815 (P.R.O., H.O. 100/184).

[50] Peel to Gregory, 17 June 1815 (Peel papers, B.M., Add. MS 40288).

[51] Hewett to Littlehales, 14 Mar. 1815; Littlehales to Peel, 22 Mar. 1815 (P.R.O., H.O. 100/183).

[52] State of the country, Mar. 1815 (P.R.O., H.O. 100/183).

[53] Dublin *Evening Post*, 4 Apr. 1815.

[54] Peel to Littlehales, 27 Mar. 1815, in Peel, *Private papers*, i, 174.

[55] Peel to Littlehales, 4 May 1815, in Peel, *Private papers*, i, 176.

the experiment was launched. By the end of June, Whitworth could write to Sidmouth, 'should the progress of this experiment correspond with the promise of its commencement, a valuable, and perhaps extensive, temporary addition to our military resources may be obtained.'[56] But Whitworth's hopes were to go unfulfilled, for when the next serious agrarian crime wave appeared, the yeomanry once more proved themselves a liability to the government.

The wave of agrarian violence which swept the lower Shannon area during the summer and fall of 1815 provided the first real test of the measures placed at the disposal of the Irish government in 1814. The first indication of serious trouble appeared in late July, with the sudden return of the agrarian secret societies. They first turned up at the fair of Kilfeale, six miles from the Peace Preservation Force's temporary headquarters at Cashel. Two hundred strong, wearing ammunition pouches and white coats, they arrived with the avowed purpose of doing battle with any police who might be present. Since they were not challenged, they left, to appear again several days later at the fair of Roes Green. This time they marched in a crude formation accompanied by fifes, and after firing 'at and about' the fair again withdrew. It appears that this demonstration was staged as an expression of contempt for the judge of the assize sitting in Clonmel, who had just sentenced two men to be whipped and imprisoned for 'being in arms'. The leader of this banditti group was William Crehan, alias Captain Pim, who had recently been released after a similar punishment for the same offence.[57]

It was not long before the banditti made the aims of their agitation known. No one was to pay over two shillings per acre in tithe, and no one was to pay more rent for his holding than had been paid the previous year.[58] The punishment meted out to offenders was, as one might expect, a flogging.[59] As so frequently happened, when one section of the dissatisfied population began active opposition to the authorities, others

[56] Whitworth to Sidmouth, 29 June 1815 (P.R.O., H.O. 100/184).

[57] Representation of the state of the county of Tipperary, Sept. 1815 (P.R.O., H.O. 100/185).

[58] F. Dessrand(?) to Gregory, 4 Sept. 1815; T. Maloney to Gregory, 11 Sept. 1815 (P.R.O., H.O. 100/185).

[59] Davenport to Gregory, 4 Sept. 1815 (P.R.O., H.O. 100/185).

were quick to take advantage of the situation. The two important factions around Cashel, the Ryans and the Dwyers, evidently
decided that this would be a good occasion on which to settle
a few old scores between them, and renewed their noisy feud.[60]
Also, within a period of a few weeks, mail-coaches were robbed
on four occasions and several members of the cavalry escort
were killed.[61] Whether these robberies were committed by
members of the agrarian secret societies or by others was not
reported. As the situation grew worse, the inevitable flood of
rumours reached the Castle. An informant who signed himself
'An Enemy to Bloodshed and Assassination' claimed that he had
overheard a conversation between unspecified individuals who
were discussing a scheduled uprising for Michaelmas night,
directed against all protestants; this was 'substantiated' by a
second report of an uprising scheduled for 29 September.[62] One
of the most influential magistrates in Tipperary solemnly
informed the Castle that he had received information that there
were French officers in Tipperary, and that some of the banditti
now wore Napoleonic uniforms. He had also been informed that
the banditti and their French associates were in contact with St
Helena.[63]

By early September, the secret societies of Limerick had
joined those in Tipperary in opposition to the tithe and higher
rents. But where in Tipperary only the western portion of the
county was disturbed, it was claimed that in Limerick 'the
entire of that county was in a state of disturbance, occasioned
by a very general confederacy among the lower orders'.[64] The
first step taken by the Castle was nearly to triple the military
establishment in these counties. On 24 July, there had been
1,200 troops in Tipperary, and 1,228 in Limerick; towards the
end of September, the establishment in Tipperary was increased

[60] Willcocks to Peel, 15 Oct. 1815 (P.R.O., H.O. 100/186).

[61] Report, Whitworth to Sidmouth, 5 June 1816 (P.R.O., H.O. 100/189).

[62] An enemy of bloodshed and assassination to Major-general Barry,
21 Sept. 1815; Charles Lanley to the attorney-general, 11 Sept. 1815
(P.R.O., H.O. 100/185).

[63] Thomas Westropp to Gregory, 17 Sept. 1815 (P.R.O., H.O. 100/185).

[64] Report, Whitworth to Sidmouth, 5 June 1816 (P.R.O., H.O. 100/189).

to 32 guns, 300 cavalrymen, and 3,603 infantrymen. Lt.-General Meyrick left Dublin to take over the command of the south-east and Shannon districts, and plans were made to move a total of 10,000 men into the two counties.[65] Throughout August, the banditti had concentrated on the tithe proctors and the few farmers who had been unwise enough to pay their tithes. Attacks on members of these groups became daily, and even twice-daily, affairs. On 19 August a proctor named Meagher and his party of eight armed assistants were attacked; Meagher was murdered and his assistants disarmed.[66] By the end of August, the tithe proctors seem to have been driven into the towns, and the banditti now concentrated on arms raids. One of the magistrates commented on this change, '. . . while those disturbers of the peace were only flogging each other, I did not think it necessary to trouble his excellency about them, but now . . . it has taken a more serious aspect'.[67] On 8 September a barracks and a house in Kilnemanaugh, which had been prepared to receive a detachment of troops on the following day, were attacked and destroyed by a large party of marauders; much to the concern of the authorities, the leader of the party proved to be the son of a 'man of considerable property'.[68] The military establishment in Limerick and Tipperary had been increased and was being further strengthened as more troops became available. In September, the government took a further step in the restoration of order by offering the provisions of the peace preservation act to Limerick, which was considered by the government to be in a state of disorder not too advanced to be handled by the Force. The offer was flatly refused, and the spokesman for a group of the Limerick magistrates told the government exactly why. In a letter to Gregory, he said that he was writing because he

perceived it to be determined to grant no other redress than may be obtained by the peace preservation bill which never can be of the

[65] Littlehales to Hewett, 18 Sept. 1815; Whitworth to Sidmouth, 20 Sept. 1815 (P.R.O., H.O. 100/185).

[66] Representation . . . of Tipperary, Sept. 1815 (P.R.O., H.O. 100/185).

[67] Thomas Davenport to Gregory, 4 Sept. 1815 (P.R.O., H.O. 100/185).

[68] Report, Whitworth to Sidmouth, 4 Sept. 1815 (P.R.O., H.O. 100/189).

smallest use in any country in a high state of insurrection. That bill I humbly conceive to be a bill of pains and penalties imposing heavy burthens on the loyal and innocent while the rebels and the guilty . . . are perfectly free from its influence. It is a bill that may be effectual in preserving the peace of a country already quiet, but never can restore that of one agitated . . . by insurrection and rebellion.

Nor was this attack on the act levelled entirely against the 'punishment' provisions. The yeomanry experiment initiated early in the previous summer was now being tried in Limerick, and the Castle's employment of 'voluntary services of the yeomanry corps acting as police' was invoked as a reason for not accepting the Peace Preservation Force. A man and his wife who had given evidence against one of the banditti for flogging them had been brutally murdered by a group of seventy men while the magistrates and their yeomanry detachment were on patrol a short distance away. All the attackers escaped, and this example was cited as an argument against using the Peace Preservation Force:

What could a superintending magistrate, a stranger in the country assisted by a set of constables also strangers, do in opposition to a set of ruffians who have bid defiance to the forces brought against them?

Summing up, the magistrate vigorously pointed out to the Irish government 'that this country does not want a peace preservation bill as they have no peace to preserve – it wants a peace restoration bill'.[69]

Observers could not long overlook the fact that the present troubles had their origins and continued to be strongest in the baronies of Tipperary where the peace preservation act was in effect. As early as 26 August, Military Under-secretary Little-hales had written to the home office, expressing surprise at finding this part of Tipperary greatly disturbed and asking whether Sidmouth knew of the situation.[70] Other letters reached the Castle,[71] complaining of the inefficiency and poor leadership of the Thurles detachment of the Peace Preservation Force under Edward Wilson, and one letter, written by a

[69] Westropp to Gregory. 17 Sept. 1815 (P.R.O., H.O. 100/185).
[70] Littlehales to J. C. Beckett, 26 Aug. 1815 (P.R.O., H.O. 100/184).
[71] See Langley to the attorney-general, 11 Sept. 1815 (P.R.O., H.O. 100/185).

friend of Saurin, was considered important enough to be forwarded to Sidmouth. Its author listed on three folio-sized pages the outrages committed in the Middlethird since the installation of the Force in that barony in 1814.[72] There appeared to be no doubt that the Peace Preservation Force had failed its first major test. None of the objects for which the Force had been organized had been attained, and the magistrates had been neither persuaded nor coerced into supporting the measure.

Whitworth had to meet this mounting crisis alone, for his chief secretary was not in Ireland or England, but in Ostend, awaiting the arrival of Daniel O'Connell. An exchange of insults during the previous summer had resulted in a challenge by Peel, and the duel was to be fought outside Britain, where the practice was illegal. There was no duel after all,[73] but Whitworth was denied Peel's presence at a time when he badly needed it.

Forty of the magistrates of Tipperary assembled at Cashel in late September and once more asked the Irish government to apply the insurrection act. Their petition reached Whitworth on 25 September, and he immediately bowed to their wishes. The provisions of the act were applied to the baronies of Middlethird, Kilnemanaugh, Eliogarty, Sliveardagh, Iffa and Offa East, and Clanwilliam. Several days later, Iffa and Offa West was added, and following a petition from the magistrates of Limerick the entire county was placed under the act on 30 September.[74] Writing to Sidmouth on 25 September, Whitworth listed his reasons for applying the insurrection act to part of Tipperary: the continuing system of terror which made many victims refuse to prosecute and others to testify, the continuing increase in outrages, and the failure of the Peace Preservation Force. Commenting on the last point, he stated that after trying the peace preservation act in Middlethird for a year, and in Eliogarty and Kilnemanaugh for four months, the government had found that it did not work. The system of murder and outrages had not diminished, but rather had increased to an

[72] Samuel Jacobs to the attorney-general, 10 Sept. 1815 (P.R.O., H.O. 100/185).

[73] See Gash, *Peel*, pp 162–7.

[74] Report, Whitworth to Sidmouth, 5 June 1816 (P.R.O., H.O. 100/189).

alarming extent.[75] To drive home this point, Whitworth included a letter from one of the 'active' magistrates of Middle-third, which pointed out that the peace preservation act had completely failed to stimulate the better classes into greater efforts to suppress outrage. As for its effects on the 'lower orders', he wrote, 'I applied to many farmers of approved loyalty and endeavoured to persuade them to enter into associations – the universal answer was, "We dare not, we must take a chance about paying the tax, but we should certainly be put to death if we associated as you advise us".'[76]

Peel returned from the Continent in October, and wasted no time in making his presence felt on the Tipperary magistrates. Their request that the baronies of Upper and Lower Ormond, Ikerrin, and Ourmay be placed under the provisions of the insurrection act he refused as being supported by insufficient evidence, and he let it be known that he had not abandoned the Peace Preservation Force as an effective means of combating crime. For although both Whitworth and Sidmouth seemed ready to discard the Force as an experiment which had failed,[77] Peel refused to withdraw his support. It was fortunate that he took this stand, for at the very time that the Force was bearing the brunt of extensive criticism, it was gradually beginning to prove itself a valuable weapon in the struggle against the agrarian secret societies.

It is impossible to say what portion of the responsibility for the situation in Tipperary should be placed on the Peace Preservation Force. Some sort of an understanding had been reached between the Force and part of the magistrates in Middlethird early in 1815, but in mid-May Whitworth wrote that 'Willcocks received not the slightest support or assistance from any one magistrate of the barony'.[78] In July, Wilson had written from his headquarters in Thurles warning the Castle that a situation was developing in his area of Tipperary which would

---

[75] Whitworth to Sidmouth, 25 Sept. 1815 (P.R.O., H.O. 100/185).

[76] Westropp to Peel, 17 Oct. 1815 (P.R.O., H.O. 100/186).

[77] Sidmouth to Whitworth, 27 Nov. 1815; Minute, 20 Nov. 1815 (P.R.O., H.O. 100/187).

[78] Whitworth to Sidmouth, 13 May 1815 (Peel papers, B.M., Add. MS 40190).

be beyond the power of the Force to control.[79] Whether or not the men of the Force were responsible for allowing such a situation to develop, they certainly proved themselves to be most ineffective when first confronted by serious outrage. There were charges of inefficiency and poor discipline in the Force when in contact with the banditti,[80] and on at least two occasions their bungling had serious results. In the Cashel area, a group of banditti had descended on an isolated farmhouse in search of arms. The attack of the raiders was met by the farmer and his sons, and a battle developed in the farmyard. A Peace Preservation Force patrol heard the firing, rushed to the farm, and in the darkness joined forces with the banditti against the farmer and his sons. As a result of this blunder, one of the sons was killed.[81] Shortly afterward, a group of marauders, apprehended in an arms raid, escaped during the night while the detachment of the Force on guard duty was asleep. Someone had forgotten to handcuff the prisoners, and the Dublin *Evening Post* remarked on learning of the incident, '. . . in no possible way is Mr Peel's peace preservation bill serviceable to the country.'[82] But even at this low point in the fortunes of the Peace Preservation Force, its members showed a certain versatility. In mid-September, Willcocks and a detachment of the Force were called to the scene of a murder. The coroner informed Willcocks that he was unable to get a jury from the area. The chief magistrate and his men conducted the investigation, were then sworn in as jurors, and handed down a verdict of 'wilful murder by persons unknown'.[83]

The turning-point in the fortunes of the Force came late in September 1815. The application of the insurrection act and the strong military reinforcements sent to the disturbed areas relieved the Force of the pressure imposed by a task that had grown to proportions quite beyond their powers to control, and gave them an opportunity to try again to prove their worth. This time they were more successful, but not quite in the

[79] Edward Wilson to Peel, 27 July 1815 (P.R.O., H.O. 100/184).
[80] Charles Langley to the attorney-general, 11 Sept. 1815 (P.R.O., H.O. 100/185).
[81] B. Ormsby to Peel, 22 Sept. 1815 (P.R.O., H.O. 100/185).
[82] Dublin *Evening Post*, 23 Sept. 1815.
[83] Ormsby to Peel, 22 Sept. 1815 (P.R.O., H.O. 100/185).

manner envisaged by Peel and Whitworth. While the army held down the populace by garrisoning the towns and villages and performing most of the routine patrolling of the countryside, the Peace Preservation Force was turned into an 'élite corps' of outrage specialists, free for special assignments. The weekly reports of Willcocks and Wilson show detachments of the Force successfully serving warrants, escorting prisoners to jail, and providing the mounted escort for the collector of excise. Much of their time was spent in investigating information received by the chief magistrate through informers or rumour. Here they seem to have been especially successful – in the week from 15 to 21 October, for example, two murder cases were 'solved', and the six men involved were arrested. Members of the Force appeared as witnesses at trials, and several of the reports mention individual sub-constables directing the activities of military detachments on special assignments.[84]

By the end of October 1815 the Peace Preservation Force had proved itself to be of value in the struggle against agrarian crime. But one part of the Force in particular, the chief or stipendiary magistrate, had proved an outstanding success. The Force was to be supplanted by more efficient police systems in the future, but the stipendiary magistrate was to become a permanent feature of the Irish countryside. One of the reasons for the early success of this office lies in the nature of Peel's first two appointees, Willcocks and Wilson. The chief secretary's insistence that ability rather than patronage or politics should determine the selection of the members of the Force proved sound, for both Willcocks and Wilson served the Irish government long and well. 'Active, intelligent and useful',[85] Willcocks emerges as the key figure in the early history of the Force. Possibly it can be said that Willcocks was Ireland's first truly professional police official. Apparently he avoided serious political involvement, his attitude towards the lower classes seems to have been free of the hatred and fear felt by numbers of the local magistrates, and by the standards of contemporary political morality he was honest. Whatever success the Force had at this time must be attributed to the initiative and leadership of Willcocks and, to a

---

[84] See reports from Middlethird, 25 Sept.–29 Oct. 1815; from Eliogarty and Kilnemanaugh, 24 Sept.–28 Oct. 1815 (P.R.O., H.O. 100/185,/186).
[85] Arthur Moore to Littlehales, 6 Oct. 1815 (P.R.O., H.O. 100/186).

lesser extent, Wilson; for its emergence as a body of 'outrage specialists', and in some respects a primitive detective force, was certainly the work, not of the Castle, but of the stipendiary magistrates.

What may be considered the seal of approval to the Peace Preservation Force was given by the Tipperary magistrates in December 1815. William Baker, an influential magistrate of the barony of Clanwilliam in Tipperary, had been assassinated as he returned from the assize at Cashel. This crime moved seventy-five magistrates to assemble in special session at Cashel on 13 December, under the chairmanship of Lord Donoughmore, the ardent foe of the peace preservation bill in the previous year. Now Donoughmore introduced a motion, which was passed, requesting the application of the peace preservation act to the barony of Clanwilliam. The Force was to discover and apprehend the murderers, and protect the magistrates and their families. If Peel saw the letter conveying this information to the Castle, he must have allowed himself at least a moment of triumph, for as Willcocks reported, 'It is impossible but the proceedings of yesterday must have the best possible effect towards the suppression of outrage and the restoration of tranquillity. Magistrates of the highest respectability, catholic and protestant, are pledged, each to the other, and one and all, to support the laws, and bring to justice those who should offend against them.'[86]

[86] Willcocks to Gregory, 14 Dec. 1815 (P.R.O., H.O. 100/188).

VI

THE FORCE AND THE
MAGISTRATES, 1815-18

~~~~~~

BY MID-NOVEMBER, 1815, only three months after the first
outbreaks of serious outrage in the Tipperary-Limerick area,
a surprising degree of tranquillity had been restored to these
counties. The combination of the insurrection act, strong
military re-enforcement, and the Peace Preservation Force had
suppressed this most recent challenge to authority with little
real difficulty. In Dublin and in Westminster, the men responsible for Ireland saw in the speedy pacification of the disturbed
areas the justification of their new approach to agrarian
outrage, embodied in the insurrection act and the peace
preservation act. Of the measures used by the government to
break the grip of the banditti on Tipperary and Limerick there
can be little question that the insurrection act was most important. It proved to be the one instrument of the state with
which the banditti could not cope, and by providing a protective
cloak under which the military and the Force could operate it
assured their success. In Limerick in November and in Tipperary in February, the courts were busy freeing those caught in
minor infractions of the act and ordering the punishment of
those found guilty of serious crimes. A total of 254 men were
brought to trial in the two counties, but only fifty-nine were
convicted: the most frequent convictions were for administering

illegal oaths, assembling at arms, compelling farmers to quit their lands, assault, and arson.[1]

The success of the insurrection act in 1815 removed from Whitworth's mind the last traces of doubt concerning its efficacy. On 22 November 1815 King's County was placed under the act, followed on 24 November by Westmeath. In proclaiming these counties, Whitworth seems to have acted solely on evidence provided by the local magistrates, without consulting either Sidmouth or Peel.[2] Until his departure from Ireland in 1817, Whitworth remained a staunch advocate of this law as the best medicine for agrarian outrage. Writing in mid-1817 of the peaceful state of Ireland at that time, he said, '. . . it is entirely owing to the existence of that act, this insurrection bill'.[3] But Peel continued to oppose widespread use of this law. He freely admitted that the measure was largely responsible for Ireland's present tranquillity, but stubbornly insisted that the insurrection act solved nothing, that it effected 'no change in the attitude of the lower orders'.[4] In January 1816, he wrote:

I have no hesitation in giving a decided opinion against an application for the insurrection act. We are determined to reserve this strongest and last remedy for occasions of great emergency. . . . Depend on it, however, that nothing will be half so effectual as an active stipendiary magistrate patrolling by night with thirty or forty mounted constables, and occupied by day in detecting and preparing evidence for the trial of offenders.[5]

Throughout 1816 Peel's attitude prevailed, and by April the act was withdrawn from the last of the counties where it had been in operation. The Castle returned to the practice of offering the peace preservation act as a counter-proposal to magistrates who requested the insurrection act, and during the year portions of Louth and Clare received detachments of the Force. But by the end of 1816 the recently-won tranquillity of Ireland was again threatened, this time by events quite beyond the control of the Irish government.

Rain and floods at harvest time apparently had ruined the

[1] Report, Whitworth to Sidmouth, 5 June 1816 (P.R.O., H.O. 100/189).
[2] Ibid.
[3] Whitworth to Peel, 17 May 1817 (Peel papers, B.M., Add. MS 40193).
[4] Peel to Sidmouth, 17 Aug. 1816 (P.R.O., H.O. 100/190).
[5] Peel to James Daly, 18 Jan. 1816, in Peel, *Private papers*, i, 205–6.

potato, grain, and hay crops, and Ireland late in 1816 faced the prospect of famine.[6] The concern of the Irish government was further aroused by the activities of the 'reformers' in Britain. The first Spa Fields meeting was held on 15 November, when Hunt made his way to the platform preceded by a 'cap of liberty' on a pike, and the tricolour flag of the future British Republic. On 2 December, following the second meeting, the Spencean 'uprising' briefly terrorized the City until the rioters were surrounded and captured at the Mansion House.[7] The crop failures in Ireland, unrest in Britain, and the 'wretched depravity and sanguinary disposition of the lower orders'[8] combined to convince the Irish government that it would be unwise to risk a new wave of violence; and – apparently at the first signs of disorders early in 1817 – Louth, Tipperary, and Limerick were placed under the insurrection act.[9] The anticipated trouble did not come; during much of 1817, the lower classes were kept fully occupied by problems of survival. The famine of 1817 (accompanied by a typhus epidemic) was the most devastating in many years, and the government spent considerable sums to ward off starvation in the areas most affected, an effort which, it was claimed, 'made a strong impression in favour of the government with the people.'[10]

The insurrection act was due to expire in July 1817, but Whitworth insisted that it be renewed in fairness to 'our successors', who would 'find it as necessary as we have done'.[11] The act was extended, but for only one year, and in the spring of 1818 Peel announced his opposition to further renewal. Since the chief secretary refused to join those who hoped that the act might be made into a permanent law, similar to the Whiteboy act, it was suggested by Attorney-general Saurin that it should be repealed before it expired, thus making the 'appearance of

[6] See Peel to Sidmouth, 10 Oct. 1816; C. F. Hawthorne to Peel, 9 Oct. 1816 (P.R.O., H.O. 100/191).

[7] See Halevy, *Liberal awakening*, pp 16–21.

[8] Peel to Sidmouth, 1 Nov. 1816 (P.R.O., H.O. 100/191); Peel to Abbot, 25 Dec. 1816, in Peel, *Private papers*, i, 736.

[9] Peel, *Speeches*, i, 88–90.

[10] Peel to Sidmouth, 27 July 1817 (P.R.O., H.O. 100/193); see also Gash, *Peel*, pp 220–5.

[11] Whitworth to Peel, 6 May 1817 (Peel papers, B.M., Add. MS 40193).

giving the people a trial, to see if things work without it'.[12] Two months before the insurrection act was due to expire, it was repealed.

Following the victory of the government over the banditti in Limerick and Tipperary in 1815, cabinet attention had again been directed to the Irish military establishment. Since Britain was no longer at war, it was becoming increasingly difficult to justify the keeping of the militia units on active duty. In January 1816 it was announced that the English units remaining in Ireland were to be gradually removed, and in March orders were issued to begin the process of placing the Irish units on inactive status. By the end of April, the men of the last Irish unit had been sent home. The intention of the civil and military authorities in Dublin had been to replace the disbanded militia units with half of the 50,000 British troops on occupation duty in France as soon as the peace treaty was signed at Vienna.[13] But this plan ran foul of Britain's mounting financial crisis, a crisis which originated in the government's desire to maintain the armed forces at a level necessary to meet its many commitments at home and abroad. The only way to bear the financial burden of a strong army and navy was by retaining the wartime income tax, which the chancellor of the exchequer proposed to reduce from 10 to 5 per cent. But the cabinet had promised that the income tax would be discontinued after the restoration of peace, and the uproar which followed became so intense that the government was forced to keep this promise.[14] The abandonment of the income tax created an annual deficit of about £15,000,000, a figure roughly equal to that previously raised by the tax. Year after year, this deficit haunted the government, which attempted to meet the financial problem by borrowing and by economies in governmental spending.

The armed forces seem to have suffered most from this economy drive: in 1816 the expenditure on the army was £15,416,000, exclusive of ordnance, but in 1817 the military estimates called for an expenditure of only £9,080,000 for the army, a reduction of over one-third.[15] During the Napoleonic

[12] Saurin to Peel, 6 Apr. 1818 (Peel papers, B.M., Add. MS 40211).
[13] Sidmouth to Whitworth, 25 Oct. 1816 (P.R.O., H.O. 100/191).
[14] Halevy, *Liberal awakening*, pp 6–8.
[15] Ibid., pp 36–8.

wars, Britain's overseas commitments had deprived Ireland of the troops necessary to maintain order, forcing the Irish government to take the first steps towards a civil solution for the problem of keeping Ireland tranquil. Now the financial plight of the British government was to have a similar effect.

For years, the civil and military authorities in Dublin had looked forward to the return of peace and, with it, sufficient regular soldiers to garrison Ireland properly. The refusal of the British government to allow a minimum establishment of 40,000 in 1814 seems to have had little effect on the plans of the commander of the forces and the lord lieutenant. When it was learned that the army in Ireland was to be limited to 25,000 men, Whitworth entered a strong protest: the figure was too low, and it would require continued reliance on the Irish militia. The lord lieutenant may also have felt that the reduction in the establishment was not motivated solely by financial problems. He informed Sidmouth that members of the cabinet believed conditions in Ireland to be exaggerated.[16] By late February, Whitworth had apparently abandoned his opposition: he was 'aware of the necessity of reducing . . . the burthens of the country; and it is no less my inclination than my duty to give every possible effort to so desirable an object'.[17] But in April, following the announcement of the end of active service for the Irish militia, the lord lieutenant considered resigning, giving as his reason the reduction of the establishment. He decided to remain in office until the following spring, saying, 'Another year will put it to the proof.'[18]

Peel was equally disturbed to learn of the weakening of the establishment, and it was at least in part due to his efforts that the army in Ireland was not reduced below 25,000 in 1816.[19] In December, however, he suggested that it would be possible to pare an additional 3,000 men from the establishment before 1817, and he asked that the yeomanry be reduced to about one-sixth of their 1814–15 strength.[20] Even these reductions were not

[16] Whitworth to Sidmouth, 19 Jan. 1816 (P.R.O., H.O. 100/189).
[17] Whitworth to Sidmouth, 20 Feb. 1816 (P.R.O., H.O. 100/189).
[18] Whitworth to Sidmouth, 7 Apr. 1816 (P.R.O., H.O. 100/189).
[19] Peel to Whitworth, 28 Feb. 1816; Peel to Hewett, 29 Feb. 1816, in Peel, *Private papers*, i, 210–11.
[20] Peel to Sidmouth, 16 Dec. 1816 (P.R.O., H.O. 100/191).

enough, for Liverpool told Peel that the British army, though not too large in itself, 'was very large when compared with the means which we are likely to have of supporting it',[21] and the reduction continued. By the end of 1818, there were 3,248 cavalrymen and 15,172 foot in Ireland for a total of 18,420 men,[22] less than half the total proposed a few years earlier as the absolute minimum needed for a peaceful Ireland.

Undoubtedly one of the reasons for Peel's support of the extensive reduction in the Irish establishment lay in his belief that the Irish government possessed in the Peace Preservation Force an answer to the problems of agrarian disorders. In February 1816 the magistrates of Louth requested the insurrection act, but were unable 'to make out a sufficient case', and after pressure had been applied by the Castle they agreed to accept the peace preservation act as a substitute. Major D'Arcy was sent to the county with a force of one hundred men.[23] The government considered the efforts of the Force in Louth highly successful and believed that it had gained the general approval of the residents of this area.[24] In May, a detachment of the Force was installed in part of Clare, under the command of Major Warburton.[25] By October, Peel considered Louth and Clare to be 'perfectly tranquil', and ascribed this condition to the presence of the Force. This apparent success convinced him that 'the common law is as well suited for Ireland as England. The truth is it is enforced in one country and not in the other'.[26]

But, as in the past, the attempts of the government to extend use of the Force encountered strong opposition, based ostensibly upon the financial provisions of the act. In July, Peel received an anonymous letter from a magistrate (evidently a resident of Clare) complaining of the 'enormous expenses' of maintaining the Force, and 'the severity and oppression which it has brought on many innocent industrious individuals untainted by the

[21] Liverpool to Peel, 20 Dec. 1816 (P.R.O., H.O., 100/191).
[22] Establishment for the year 1818, n.d. (P.R.O., H.O. 100/191).
[23] Whitworth to Peel, 26 Feb. 1816, 12 Mar. 1816 (Peel papers, B.M., Add. MS 40191).
[24] Saurin to Peel, 13 May 1816 (Peel papers, B.M., Add. MS 40211).
[25] Whitworth to Peel, 2 May, 22 May 1816 (Peel papers, B.M., Add. MS 40192).
[26] Peel to earl of Enniskillen, 10 Oct. 1816 (Peel papers, B.M., Add. MS 40291).

principles and vices which surround us, and totally unable to bear such a burden'.[27] Nor was this criticism an isolated instance, for there was soon evidence of widespread opposition to the peace preservation act, similar to that of Tipperary and Limerick magistrates in 1815. Early in 1817, a series of attacks on grain barges on the canal network in Kildare, occasioned by the widespread crop failure of the previous fall, indicated to the Castle the need for detachments of the Force. The magistrates flatly refused to follow the suggestion of the Castle and openly boasted 'that no grand jury can be found to lay such a burden on the county'.[28]

The outspoken resistance of the Kildare magistrates, added to a series of similar reactions, seems to have convinced Peel of the necessity for making a change in the peace preservation act. By 1817, there could have been little question that the financial punishment provisions of the act made its general acceptance by the Irish magistracy very unlikely. As long as the insurrection act was available and military assistance could be obtained at no expense to a disturbed area, the magistrates were reluctant to incur the costs of the Force. The Irish government was able on occasion either to overawe the magistrates, or, by refusing them the insurrection act, to force them to accept the peace preservation act, but such procedures took time and so defeated one of the most important purposes of the Force, the halting of agrarian crime before it could become dangerous. With the strength of the military decreased, and with the continuation of the insurrection act uncertain, the Force assumed a greater importance. By 1817, Peel was ready to compromise with the magistrates.

In the house of commons on 11 March 1817 he asked permission to introduce a bill enabling the lord lieutenant to determine the proportion of the cost of the Peace Preservation Force to be borne by the district involved, and that to be drawn from public funds. Since financial considerations were of great importance at the moment, the proposed amendment was presented as a method of reducing expenses. The 'employment

[27] A magistrate to Peel, 22 July 1816 (Peel papers, B.M., Add. MS 40291).
[28] Whitworth to Peel, 20 Mar. 1817 (Peel papers, B.M., Add. MS 40193).

of the soldiery, the charge of erecting barracks, and a great variety of other items, formed . . . a considerable aggregate of expense, under the existing system'. The Force could accomplish more at less cost than could the army, but some districts of Ireland were too poor to pay the entire cost of the Force in their areas. As an added incentive, Peel promised to reduce the Irish establishment by 3,000 men should his amendment be accepted.[29] This announcement of the intention of the government to share the cost of the Force seems to have had the desired effect. By the end of March, plans were under way to install the Force in County Kildare,[30] and on 10 June, an additional barony of Clare was placed under the act. On 29 July, part of Donegal was proclaimed,[31] and there is evidence that other counties also received detachments of the Force. The authorities seem to have been somewhat casual about the arrangements involved in installing the Force. A number of letters and reports relate to 'proclaimed districts' that do not appear on official lists of such areas or do not appear until later dates.[32]

By 1818 a sizeable portion of Ireland had been introduced to the 'peelers'. After the passage of Peel's amending bill in 1817, the cost of operating the Force was apportioned between the proclaimed area and the Irish government, with the government allowed to absorb up to two-thirds of the total cost of the Force. By the early 1820s it was established practice to divide the cost evenly.[33] Even this compromise, however, did not satisfy all the magistrates, and in several instances they attempted to have the Force removed before the area had been 'pacified'. Whenever possible, the Castle respected the wishes of the magistrates, for as Peel warned Gregory, 'We must not make the Peelers unpopular by maintaining them against the declared and unequivocal desire of the county in which they act.'[34] But in

[29] See Peel, *Speeches*, i, 73–4.
[30] Whitworth to Sidmouth, 24 Mar. 1817 (P.R.O., H.O. 100/192).
[31] Proclaimed districts, 1814–1822 (Peel papers, B.M., Add. MS 40328).
[32] See Whitworth to Peel, 25 Mar. 1817 (Peel papers, B.M., Add. MS 40193); Proclaimed districts, 1814–1822 (Peel papers, B.M., Add. MS 40328).
[33] See Peel to Gregory, 24 June 1817 (Peel papers, B.M., Add. MS 40293); Proclaimed districts, 1814–1822 (Peel papers, B.M., Add. MS 40328).
[34] Peel to Gregory, 14 Apr. 1818 (Peel papers, B.M., Add. MS 40295).

other areas there appeared no desire to have them removed, especially where there were few resident magistrates and, in areas like Tipperary, where some degree of disorder was always present and the specialized functions of the Force were in constant demand. Early in 1818, detachments of the Force were organized in Tipperary, Louth, Cavan, Clare, and Donegal as a 'separate police establishment',[35] and in 1833, three years before the Force was absorbed into the Irish Constabulary, it was operating in nine counties.[36]

By 1818 it was generally known that Peel intended to resign his position as chief secretary, and he left Ireland in August of that year. Whitworth had left the previous year and had been replaced by Earl Talbot in October 1817. Peel had been largely responsible for the important changes made in Irish law-enforcement practice during his six-year tenure. His most obviously successful contribution was the introduction of the stipendiary magistrate to rural Ireland, but other aspects of his reforms were to have considerable future significance. The provision for a stipendiary was the first step in taking rural law-enforcement from the hands of the amateur and placing it with the professional, a direction that was to characterize future police developments in Britain as well as in Ireland. Peel's Peace Preservation Force had achieved several notable successes since its introduction in 1814, and by 1818 much of the opposition of the country gentlemen had apparently disappeared. But the Force had known failure too, and was to know it again in the future – by 1820 it would find itself under serious attack from both the banditti and the politicians. During the final years of his chief secretaryship, Peel had come to recognize the faults and weaknesses of the Force, but he refused to abandon the basic concepts upon which his police had been created. Thus one of his major accomplishments lay in making Ireland 'police-conscious'. By 1818 the idea of a civil solution to the problems of law and order, although not yet fully implemented, was firmly established in Ireland. The military continued to play an important role in curbing rural lawlessness, but where prior to 1815 the government had encouraged the magistrates to call for military assistance in times of disturbance, in 1818 Sidmouth

[35] Lord Talbot to Sidmouth, 23 Jan. 1818 (P.R.O., H.O. 100/194).
[36] *Return of the Peace Preservation Force . . .* , H.C. 1834 (201), xlvii, 399.

could instruct the new chief secretary to discourage this practice whenever possible, and to teach the magistrates to 'place their chief reliance upon themselves, and upon the civil authorities for their protection'.[37]

At no time did Peel make the mistake of claiming a greater potential for the Peace Preservation Force than was realistically possible. He considered it from the outset to be an adjunct to the existing machinery of rural law-enforcement, a body of trained policemen organized into mobile units to assist the magistrates and the military in dealing with local disorders.

The Force was less successful than Peel had hoped, but his disappointment did not end his interest in police reform. Instead, he seems to have been more determined than ever to solve the problem of the effective policing of Ireland. During his last four years as chief secretary, while he was trying to extend the operations of the Force, Peel considered the possibility of a different, permanent 'general system of police', to replace the baronial constables. He did not press the matter at this time, probably because his belief that it would be impossible to find enough capable, honest men to staff a country-wide general police organization made him doubt the feasibility of too extensive a reform. The plan is none the less of interest, since it was to influence later developments in Ireland.

What Peel envisioned was a system of police based on 'the establishment of a body of gendarmarie to be called by some less startling name' as a permanent institution for all Ireland. Each county would have a separate police establishment, but most of the cost and all of the control would be assumed by the Irish government. The leadership of the police detachments was to be vested, not in stipendiary magistrates, but in police officers who would not possess the judicial powers of the magistracy. One reason for this suggestion may be found in the very success of the stipendiaries, for their widespread use had encouraged the 'imperfect but indispensable' local magistrates to relax their efforts towards keeping the peace even further than before. The Peace Preservation Force had been designed in part to force the magistrates into performance, and the projected new system was intended to encourage them to still greater exertions. The leaders of the police detachments would report

[37] Sidmouth to Charles Grant, 23 Nov. 1818 (P.R.O., H.O. 100/195).

to the government on the activity or lack of activity of the local magistrates; stipendiaries could then be dispatched to areas 'where the ordinary administration of law was unsatisfactory, either by the absence or misconduct of the magistrates'.

At one point in his consideration of a new police plan, Peel did consider extending the use of stipendiary magistrates. He said that there had been frequent suggestions that a stipendiary be appointed for each county, but he noted that these suggestions came 'as frequently perhaps from a desire to fill or recommend the office, as from any disinterested considerations for the public tranquillity'. It would have been difficult to assign stipendiaries on a county basis since the counties differed greatly in size and in 'local circumstances which aided crime'.

Although Peel did not attempt to implement his plan for establishing a permanent general police system for Ireland while he was chief secretary, in 1822 he sent the outline of his proposal to the then lord lieutenant, the marquess of Wellesley,[38] and this outline seems to have provided the basic design for the County Constabulary established in that year.

When Peel left Ireland in 1818, it was undoubtedly with a feeling of relief at being free from the eternal Irish problem and from a people whom he had neither liked nor truly understood. But the relief was to be short-lived, for in 1822, when he returned to office as home secretary, he found himself once more associated with the perplexities and problems of Ireland.

[38] Peel to Wellesley, 12 Apr. 1822 (Wellesley papers, B.M., Add. MS 37299).

VII

TALBOT AND GRANT, 1818–21

WHITWORTH'S SUCCESSOR, EARL TALBOT, arrived in Ireland in October 1817. The new lord lieutenant had Irish family connections, was opposed to catholic emancipation, and is remembered chiefly for his interest in the problems of Irish agriculture and for his determined efforts to win the good will of the country.[1] Although his intentions were of the best, he remains one of the lords lieutenant of Ireland often relegated to a footnote.[2]

Peel's successor, Charles Grant,[3] took office in August 1818, fated to become the most controversial chief secretary in many years. Grant was a man of some ability, considered by an 1827 observer to be one of the three ablest men in the government and, with Huskisson, the best informed.[4] But his selection as chief secretary at this time was unfortunate. Somewhat liberal in his political views, he was placed in close association with men like Sidmouth, who were still busy rooting out Jacobinism. And at this stage of his career, Grant was a rather poor administrator, inclined to be careless and forgetful.[5] At the time of his appointment, however, it was the new chief secretary's advocacy

---

[1] O'Mahoney, *Viceroys of Ireland*, pp 218–22.
[2] See Lady Gregory's description of Talbot in *Letter-box*, p. 108.
[3] Created Baron Glenelg, 1831.
[4] *The Greville memoirs, 1814–1860*, ed. L. Strachey and R. Fulford (London, 1938), i, 304.
[5] Ibid., i, 356.

of catholic emancipation that made him suspect in the eyes of such staunch 'protestants' as Talbot, Sidmouth, and Gregory. Apparently Grant's appointment was not made as a concession to the 'catholics', but rather as a matter of political necessity. Liverpool had found it impossible to discover a qualified candidate, willing to accept the position, who held the right views on emancipation; when one possible appointee was rejected because of his 'opinions on the catholic question', Peel observed that 'this is an objection which equally applies to nearly all if not to all those who may be considered competitors for the office . . .'.[6] Grant's appointment was not to prove very successful; religious questions may have furthered the alienation that developed between him and other members of the Irish executive, but the errors and indiscretions of the chief secretary himself seem to have been a more potent factor.

Late in 1818, Lord Liverpool decided to try for a further reduction in the Irish military establishment. The estimate for 1819 provided for a force of 18,000 men, and in the interest of economy the prime minister hoped to reduce the figure by another 1,000. Initially, Sidmouth was opposed to the reduction, and it was Grant who set about convincing the home secretary of the proposal's merits. The correspondence between them shows the nature of Grant's views on the problem of keeping Ireland at peace. Giving his 'considered views on Ireland', Grant wrote,

. . . if we could once make the magistrates urgently rely upon their own exertions under the sanction of law, instead of flying for resource on every occasion to military aid, a more rapid improvement might be expected. I cannot help adding that the sure method, or one sure method, would be a further reduction of our army here.[7]

This 'sure method' of decreasing the demand for military assistance, by reducing the number of troops available, made little impression on Sidmouth, who patiently instructed the new chief secretary that 'it too often happens . . . that the danger is of such magnitude and character, that the magistrates and civil officers cannot be . . . expected to act without . . . support and assistance from the military'.[8]

[6] Peel to Talbot, 18 May 1818 (Peel papers, B.M. Add. MS 40295).
[7] Grant to Sidmouth, 3 Nov. 1818 (P.R.O., H.O. 100/195).
[8] Sidmouth to Grant, 28 Nov. 1818 (P.R.O., H.O. 100/195).

Grant continued to present his case, writing that there was widespread optimism over the peaceful state of Ireland and that there might be serious opposition in parliament to the size and expense of the Irish establishment. 'I cannot forget that the ordeal of parliament awaits me,' he wrote, and he asked permission to attempt reducing the establishment by one thousand men. He then proceeded to a more fully developed discussion of his views: 'If I am asked whether I think the state of the country is such as to require 18,000 men to keep it in order, I cannot . . . give that as my honest conviction . . . the occurrence of lawless attacks, which would justify the maintenance of 18,000 would warrant also the maintenance of 20,000 or 30,000 or a larger number.' Grant again insisted that so long as military assistance was available, local authorities would rely on it instead of on their own efforts, and he added that while an army was necessary against an insurrection, in Ireland 'the great want is a good police'. This want, he said, was 'universally acknowledged', and 'the peace preservation bill which [Peel] introduced is a much more efficient guardian of public tranquillity than a numerous army. . . . That bill even in its present state would, I think, enable us to secure the peace of the country considerably below the proposed estimate'.[9]

Grant's attempt to economize at the expense of the army was a complete failure. After securing Sidmouth's approval of the figure of 17,000 men for 1819, Grant turned to the military officials in London. The commander-in-chief, the duke of York, immediately informed the chief secretary of his opposition to any reduction in the Irish establishment, and wrote directly to Liverpool, stating that such a suggestion would 'not be listened to' until a careful investigation showed the reduction to be feasible.[10] Investigations into any aspect of Irish affairs were avoided by Liverpool whenever possible, and the matter was allowed to drop.

Throughout the late summer and fall of 1819, police informers stationed on the quays at Dublin and Belfast kept a close watch on the incoming passengers from Great Britain, searching for people who might be 'Hunt's agitators'. The 'Peterloo massacre',

[9] Grant to Sidmouth, 9 Dec. 1818 (P.R.O., H.O. 100/195).
[10] Memorandum, 16 Feb. 1819; Commander in chief to Liverpool, 15 Feb. 1819 (P.R.O., H.O. 100/196).

which had occurred in Manchester on 16 August, seems to have caused more alarm in Ireland than any other event since the escape of Napoleon from Elba in 1815. To the lord lieutenant and a number of lesser officials, it appeared that 'Peterloo' might be the opening engagement in a vast lower-class revolution. Reports of nightly meetings held by great numbers of armed men 'in correspondence with the disaffected in England', and rumours of strangers who were busy administering oaths began reaching the Castle.[11] Talbot ordered the bayonets and locks to be taken from the guns of the Irish militia only to learn that all militia weapons had been sent to ordnance depots when the militia was disbanded in 1816.[12] One nervous magistrate took the unprecedented step of suggesting that his barony be placed under the insurrection act (then non-existent) before a single outrage had been committed.[13] After the failure of the Cato Street conspiracy in London in 1820, Talbot informed the home secretary that he had evidence that Thistlewood had recently been in Ireland.[14] Grant and Gregory, however, seem to have been unaffected by the wave of fear that had caught up so many of their associates. Wrote Gregory,

It matters not how many of Hunt's addresses are disseminated through Ireland. The lower orders here have no feelings in common with the same class in England; the national hatred is much too strong to make them rejoice . . . whether the people or the government are successful.

It was Gregory's opinion that the great mass of Irish catholics knew nothing of parliamentary reform and Grant agreed with him, adding that the only place where 'reformers' might find allies would be among the Ulster protestants.[15]

But the fears of Talbot were not entirely without substance; during the winter of 1819–20, and again from 1821 to 1823, a considerable portion of rural Ireland was swept by terrorism. After 1816, the activities of the banditti had declined to such an extent that they had been negligible annoyances; but now,

[11] Précis, Dec. 1819 (P.R.O., H.O. 100/197).
[12] Talbot to Sidmouth, 20 Nov. 1819 (P.R.O., H.O. 100/197).
[13] Précis, Dec. 1819 (P.R.O., H.O. 100/197).
[14] Talbot to Sidmouth, 7 Mar. 1820 (P.R.O., H.O. 100/198).
[15] Gregory to H. Hobhouse, 22 Aug. 1819; Grant to Sidmouth, 6 Sept. 1819 (P.R.O., H.O. 100/197).

beginning in 1819, secret organizations appeared throughout Ireland, seemingly stronger and better organized than the agrarian secret societies of 1812–16. Letters written by 'reformers' to individuals and groups in various parts of the British Isles were intercepted by the authorities.[16] In 1821, Dublin police claimed to have uncovered a 'revolutionary committee' – with connections in England, the north of Ireland, and the United States – whose purpose was to co-ordinate activities among the disaffected and to await England's next war.[17] Grant wrote of the revival of the secret organizations and the disturbances that followed:

It does not appear that the disturbances . . . differed in any essential respect from the local commotions which have been so frequent in Ireland during the last 80 years; and there is no proof that they deserve the name of a radical, or a popish insurrection. . . . There are indeed many reports that secret emissaries have been dispatched from England to various parts of the country; but . . . no such persons have been discovered nor has any proof been obtained of a connection between the radicals and the Ribbonmen . . . although it is probable that the accounts of the English troubles . . . have increased the irritation excited in the people by other causes.[18]

Grant was correct. Despite reports of widespread 'reformer' activity, and the claim of the Dublin police to have uncovered a 'revolutionary committee', reliable evidence of close ties between the disaffected in Ireland and 'radicals' in other countries did not exist. But it is quite likely that the Ribbonmen mentioned by Grant – members of a Dublin-based secret organization – were instrumental in the spread of a variety of Ribbonism to the countryside during the autumn and winter of 1819–20. Efforts to explain to what purpose Dublin Ribbonism became involved with agrarian protest remain highly speculative. The Dublin conspirators seem to have shared a name, a hatred of protestants, and a fraternal bond with the Ribbonmen of the north – but little else. Despite Grant's denial of the

[16] For example, one Richard Kearny appeared to be a 'very disaffected man desirous of promoting a connection between the Irish malcontents and the English radicals', but his letters failed to convey 'precise information'. Hobhouse to Grant, 28 Feb. 1820 (S.P.O., C.S.O., Private and official correspondence books, vol. 3).

[17] Talbot to Sidmouth, 9 Jan. 1821 (P.R.O., H.O. 100/200).

[18] Grant to Sidmouth, n.d. (1820), (P.R.O., H.O. 100/198).

connection, the primitive and ill-defined radicalism of the Dublin Ribbonmen had more in common with British lower-class radicalism than with the programmes of disaffected Irish peasants. Prior to this time, the major activities of the organization seem to have been clashes with local Orange groups and participation in the more elementary forms of trade unionism. But, crude as it seems to have been, Dublin Ribbonism at this time represented the most sophisticated body of lower-class protest in all Ireland.[19]

As autumn approached in 1819, the Castle was informed of a sudden upsurge of 'bad spirit' among the peasants of a considerable portion of central and western Ireland. In November, Clare, Limerick, and Tipperary were added to the growing list of disturbed counties. By winter, reports and letters from police officials, military commanders, and local magistrates were emphasizing the unique character of this most recent manifestation of peasant discontent. The harvest had been good; thus the peasants were not threatened by that frequent cause of disorder, hunger. 'Outside agitators' from distant places were reported active in the countryside. Ribbon societies were appearing in areas where organized Ribbonism had been generally unknown. And in contrast to the local and economic interests of the agrarian secret societies, it was suspected that the new Ribbon societies were formed to further broadly based religious and political interests – by implication, to prepare for a catholic revolution.[20]

It is impossible to determine the extent of 'new' Ribbon influence at this time: by the final third of 1821, its influence had largely evaporated, leaving behind little more than a residue of increased hostility between catholics and protestants. Nor is it possible to determine the relationship between the new movement and the agrarian secret societies. It seems most unlikely that banditti groups such as those in Tipperary and Limerick would agree to submerge their identities in an 'alien' organization; logically, the most the Ribbonmen could count on from a long-established agrarian secret society was co-operation. If the leaders of the Ribbon movement hoped to

[19] See pp 12–13 above; McDowell, *Public opinion & govt policy*, pp 63–5.
[20] Précis, Dec. 1819; Talbot to Sidmouth, 17 Nov. 1819 (P.R.O., H.O. 100/197).

organize lower-class catholic Ireland in preparation for a future rebellion, and this is a reasonable assumption, the failure of their plan was apparent with the outbreak of widespread violence in the winter of 1819–20. If such a plan existed, it would seem that only the 'traditional' Ribbonmen of Ulster obeyed orders, and even in the north Antrim and Donegal were disturbed. Elsewhere the new Ribbonism provided a 'cause' for the agrarian secret societies to rally upon and added new members to the ranks of organized disaffection. Once under attack by the forces of authority, and with centralized leadership uncertain or non-existent, the new Ribbon societies became old-style agrarian secret societies. And outside Ulster, regardless of their chosen name, Ribbonmen became banditti.

By December 1819 'Ribbonmen' were active to some extent in fourteen counties, and in Galway, Westmeath, King's County, Tipperary and Limerick, their activities had reached serious proportions.[21] The outbreak of disturbances in the autumn had found the Irish government poorly prepared to cope with extensive agrarian disorder. During the preceding three years, comparative peace in Ireland and the pressing need for economy had combined to reduce the strength of the army, while the militia for all practical purposes no longer existed. The yeomanry was still around, but the military authorities considered it of little value, and more far-sighted men at the Castle saw in it a factor for increasing disturbance wherever it might be used. In November, the Castle began belated preparations against widespread disturbances of an 'insurrectionary' nature, caused by a 'very bad spirit among the lower classes in five counties'.[22] By early 1820, Galway had become the most seriously disturbed county, and the military garrisons in the west were increased as much as was possible without dangerously depleting the strength of the establishment elsewhere. The number of troops in the Connaught district was raised from 2,542 men in January to 5,886 in March, with 3,696 men concentrated in Galway alone.[23] To release more troops for duty in the disturbed area, 1,200 members of the

---

[21] Précis, Dec. 1819 (P.R.O., H.O. 100/197).
[22] Talbot to Sidmouth, 17 Nov. 1819 (P.R.O., H.O. 100/197).
[23] Galway summary, 25 Apr. 1820 (P.R.O., H.O. 100/198).

yeomanry in the north were activated,[24] and a new source of potential reserve strength was tapped. The Royal Hospital of Kilmainham was an organization for the residence and support of invalid and aged regular soldiers of long service, similar to the Royal Chelsea Hospital near London. The rolls of the Hospital were combed for pensioners fit for limited duty, and by March, 3,145 of them (mostly out-pensioners) had been formed into military units.[25] In February it had been announced that a veterans' unit was 'on the way to Galway'.[26] There is no record of the success or failure of this particular experiment, though it was to be repeated in future years.

As the disturbances in the west reached serious proportions, Grant was faced with the first real test of his ability to meet the demands of his job. The Castle was informed that an infantry regiment was to be sent to Ireland, and the chief secretary announced his firm opposition to such a move. He informed Sidmouth that military reinforcements might 'excite alarms' and he suggested that instead the regiment be held in readiness to come at a moment's notice. A very confusing exchange of letters followed. On 10 January, Grant told Sidmouth that 'accounts are improving' and that 'alarms will subside', and he repeated his request to withhold reinforcements. A month later, on 16 February, he wrote to the lord lieutenant about the 'alarming state' of Galway and Roscommon, where the 'gentlemen' had either fled to the towns or were living in a state of siege. But two days later, he assured the home secretary that the situation in Galway was improving.[27] Signs of disunity were appearing within the small group most closely involved with the conduct of Irish affairs.

The chief secretary was convinced that the best way to restore order in the disturbed areas was by use of an expanded Peace Preservation Force, supported by the existing military establishment. Talbot believed the situation was serious enough to warrant an increase in the establishment, and was supported

[24] Talbot to Sidmouth, 7 Mar. 1820 (P.R.O., H.O. 100/198).

[25] Talbot to Sidmouth, 20 Nov. 1819 (P.R.O., H.O. 100/197); Galway summary, 25 Apr. 1820 (P.R.O., H.O. 100/198).

[26] Grant to Sidmouth, 21 Feb. 1820 (P.R.O., H.O. 100/198).

[27] Grant to Sidmouth, 4 Jan., 10 Jan., 16 Feb., 22 Mar. 1820; Grant to Talbot, 14 Feb. 1820 (P.R.O., H.O. 100/198).

by Sidmouth. The home secretary was clearly annoyed. In a letter of 27 March, he called Grant's attention to the fact that the chief secretary had neglected to keep the home office informed of events in Ireland and, as a challenge to Grant, Sidmouth wrote, 'It would be a great satisfaction to me to be convinced that further augmentation of the army, and consequently the staff in Ireland would not . . . be absolutely necessary'.[28] As for Gregory, the under-secretary, by February he seems to have reached the conclusion that the Force was incapable of dealing with serious disorder without the backing of the insurrection act.[29]

Despite high-level bickering, Grant's wishes seem generally to have prevailed during the troubles of 1819–20. On 5 November, the entire county of Roscommon was placed under the peace preservation act on the representation of twenty-nine magistrates of that county. The Force was under the command of Major Wills and consisted of three chief constables, twelve mounted police, and 118 foot police.[30] Meetings were held by the magistrates in Limerick, King's and Galway to determine whether or not to ask the government to install units of the Force in these counties, but the familiar problem arose once more. Even the modified financial provisions of the act did not make its operation inexpensive enough for the magistrates of Limerick and King's County, who refused to ask the government for it.[31] Among the Galway magistrates, the supporters of the act had to override extensive opposition before they were able to gain a majority, but on 15 December, the government was asked to 'proclaim' four baronies. Two additional baronies were proclaimed on 26 January 1820, and seven more on 18 February, placing all but four western baronies of Galway under the act.

The decision to proclaim the initial four baronies in Galway had immediately revealed a serious flaw in the organization of the Force, one hitherto overlooked or ignored by the authorities – the lack of reserves. According to the provisions of the act, units not assigned to an area were paid off. The existing units

[28] Sidmouth to Grant, 27 Mar. 1820 (P.R.O., H.O. 100/198).
[29] Gregory to Talbot, 20 Feb. 1820 (P.R.O., H.O. 100/198).
[30] Proclaimed districts, 1814–22 (Peel papers, B.M., Add. MS 40328).
[31] Talbot to Sidmouth, 14 Nov. 1819 (P.R.O., H.O. 100/197).

seem to have been fully occupied where they were, and by 1819 the supply of qualified available men with military experience was dwindling. The lack of reserves was particularly damaging to a police designed at least in part to stop disturbances before they reached dangerous proportions. The request from Galway in December caught the Castle completely unprepared, and more than three weeks were spent forming a detachment consisting of a chief magistrate and sixty men.[32] To complicate matters further, the most disturbed areas in Galway had few local magistrates, and some of these had fled when banditti activities became more than they could handle. The Castle adopted an unusual expedient to meet the problem: all field officers and all captains commanding military posts in the proclaimed districts were given commissions of the peace and thus made into magistrates.[33]

In February 1820 the Galway magistrates 'rebelled'. The government had attempted to extend the provisions of the peace preservation act to the four remaining baronies of that county, but the forty-seven magistrates who had been assembled for the purpose of giving their consent refused to do so.[34] On 17 February, the magistrates assembled again, and this time 'censured the government severely'.[35] The solution they request-ed was the usual one: they wanted the insurrection act.[36] Several months later, the Galway grand jury repeated the magistrates' charges, criticizing the Castle for its slowness in attending to applications for assistance.[37] Talbot countered by accusing the Galway magistrates of failure to perform their duties, suggesting that if they had acted earlier and with more vigour, strong government measures might have been un-necessary.[38] Grant used the complaints of the magistrates to justify his opposition to using the military for maintaining order, asserting that aid had not been rushed in at once because of doubts created by the 'perpetual demands made on the

[32] Grant to Sidmouth, 24 Jan. 1820 (P.R.O., H.O. 100/198). Eventu-ally the Force in Galway numbered about 300 men and 9 chief constables under the command of Major D'Arcy. Proclaimed districts, 1814–22 (Peel papers, B.M. Add. MS 40328).

[33] Galway summary, 25 Apr. 1820 (P.R.O., H.O. 100/198).
[34] Ibid.   [35] Ibid.   [36] Ibid.
[37] J. W. Blakeney to Talbot, 8 Apr. 1820 (P.R.O., H.O. 100/198).
[38] Talbot to Sidmouth, 8 Apr. 1820 (P.R.O., H.O. 100/198).

government for military protection. . . . If all the demands were answered at once, 100,000 men would not be enough'. He also pointed out that the step taken by the magistrates at the first appearance of trouble was always a request for strong military assistance, followed shortly afterwards by a cry for the insurrection act. With the experience of the recent disturbances to draw upon, Grant was certain that the government should furnish only enough military assistance to give the magistrates confidence. This step should be followed by installation of the Peace Preservation Force, and if both steps failed to restore tranquillity, the government would have to assume full responsibility for restoring order even if it meant acting independently of the country gentlemen.[39]

With the success of the insurrection act in 1815–16 still widely remembered, it is not surprising that the request of the Galway magistrates for such legislation should have found some support in Dublin Castle. Gregory was among the first to advocate revival of the act as the 'only solution' for the disturbances in the west. Grant's insistence on the Force as the best method of suppressing outrage was brushed aside by the undersecretary, who pointed out that 'the Peelers were no doubt successful in restoring tranquillity to Tipperary and Louth, but in both of those counties the insurrection act was in force'. But Gregory doubted that there was sufficient time remaining during the present session of parliament to push such a bill through both houses in the face of inevitable opposition.[40] Nothing more was heard of this proposal until late in March 1820 after the first phase of the current cycle of disturbances had ended. Surveying the situation in the west, Talbot decided that the lower orders were 'at present intimidated by the large military force and the police establishment now stationed in the proclaimed districts', but he could detect 'no change in the attitude of the people'. He therefore suggested to Sidmouth that it might be wise to revive the insurrection act.[41] His support of such extreme action was somewhat qualified: 'While I advocate strong measures for repressing disturbances, it is my duty no less broadly to state, that the peasantry of Ireland have great

[39] Report, Ireland, 1820 (P.R.O., H.O. 100/198).
[40] Gregory to Talbot, 20 Feb. 1820 (P.R.O., H.O. 100/198).
[41] Talbot to Sidmouth, 23 Mar. 1820 (P.R.O., H.O. 100/198).

cause for complaint.'[42] Once more, Grant found himself in opposition to the policy of his associates. He reminded Sidmouth that an 'extensive disturbance' had just been put down without the aid of the insurrection act.[43] In Galway the reluctance of the magistrates to incur the expense of the Peace Preservation Force and their willingness to 'delay and temporize' could be traced to their belief that the government would come to their rescue with the insurrection act.[44]

But with the arrival of spring in 1820 the disturbances faded away, and with them went the debate over the act. By May, Chief Magistrate D'Arcy was able to report that the county was 'perfectly tranquil'.[45] No clearly discernible programme had emerged from the activities of the banditti; arrests were made, but the societies appear to have remained unbroken. During the months that followed, little was done to prepare for the renewal of trouble in the future. It was suggested that the militia should be restored to some degree of efficiency, but the enlistment periods of most of the men had expired, and when it was determined that it would cost the government almost £35,000 to call up the militia for a twenty-eight-day training period, interest declined.[46] Even the correspondence between the Castle and Westminster during the summer of 1820 was sparse; the fears of the previous fall and winter had given way to lethargy.

Late in September 1820, near the beginning of the traditional outrage season, the chief secretary turned his attention to the areas which had been the scenes of disturbance during the previous winter. The total number of troops in the Connaught district was now 4,760, with 2,100 in Galway alone. Parts of Galway, Tipperary, Meath, Westmeath, and Donegal, and all of Limerick, Clare, and Roscommon were under the peace preservation act. The total strength of the combined units of the Force was 805 foot and 250 mounted.[47] Between 5 November 1819 and 15 April 1820 the Force had been expanded to cover all of Roscommon, all but two baronies of Galway, the remain-

[42] Talbot to Sidmouth, 8 Apr. 1820 (P.R.O., H.O. 100/198).
[43] Grant to Sidmouth, 1 Apr. 1820 (P.R.O., H.O. 100/198).
[44] Report, Ireland, 1820 (P.R.O., H.O. 100/198).
[45] D'Arcy to Gregory, 10 May 1820 (P.R.O., H.O. 100/198).
[46] Gregory to Hobhouse, 12 Apr. 1820 (P.R.O., H.O. 100/198).
[47] Grant to Sidmouth, 28 Sept. 1820 (P.R.O., H.O. 100/199).

ing 'unproclaimed' areas of Clare, and all of Limerick. This rapid expansion of the Force logically should have given considerable satisfaction to the chief secretary, but by September 1820 Grant's attitude towards the Force had changed. He saw in its expanded size 'a frightful number; especially in addition to the soldiery; and they cost no small sum to the public. The expense galls the resident gentry, as part of it is borne by the district; but in general the police establishment gives satisfaction. . . . As a permanent and universal system it might on principle be objectionable.'[48] Grant did not offer an explanation for this change of attitude, but like other men in his time, the chief secretary might have feared the growth of a powerful police, which could become a weapon of oppression in the hands of the unscrupulous. By late 1820, the strength of the Force had risen to 1,050 men, at a time when the memory of Fouché and his Napoleonic 'political' police still disturbed many Britons. An indication of the nature of Grant's concern appears in one of his statements on the possibility of establishing a new system of rural police for all of Ireland: '. . . it is easy to foresee that no measure founded on true principles will satisfy the parties more clamorous for a vigorous system of police by which they mean a *gendarmerie*.'[49] Perhaps the chief secretary felt that even an inefficient magistracy, free from the domination of the government, could act as a check to a too-powerful police.

Grant's doubts about certain aspects of the Force did not mean that he had abandoned police as a means of combating crime, but he was less enthusiastic than he had been in the past. His consideration of a new system of rural police never progressed beyond the planning stage. In November he wrote that he was 'trying to frame a bill regarding the police, "ordinary police" or rather the constabulary of the country', but was disturbed that the poor quality of the magistracy was making his task much more difficult.[50] Perhaps because the winter of 1820–1 was relatively tranquil, or because Grant's proposals were not acceptable to his superiors, the plan was not mentioned again.

In 1821 the bickering with his associates and the sporadic outbursts of violence in the rural areas had combined to end the

[48] Ibid. [49] Ibid.
[50] Grant to Sidmouth, 4 Nov. 1820 (P.R.O., H.O. 100/199).

earlier optimism of the chief secretary. Writing in January, Grant described the condition of the Irish countryside:

In the first place with regard to outward tranquillity it is in its usual state. There are local outrages, and robberies sometimes accompanied with brutal murders; there are vindictive excesses – and burglaries in search of arms – there are fightings at fairs, and many symptoms of the disorders incident to a country without an adequate system of civil authority.[51]

There was ample evidence throughout the winter of widespread activity by secret organizations in the familiar trouble spots. The Dublin Ribbonmen seem to have been making a final attempt at extending the influence of their organization into the rural areas. 'Swearing' was detected in Kildare; King's County was reportedly in a 'dangerous state', but the 'proprietors would risk their lives rather than incur the expense' of the Force; and Limerick was considered the worst of all.[52] In January, the meeting of the 'revolutionary committee' was raided in Dublin, and the information thus gained indicated a possible connection between the disaffected in Dublin and those in the rural areas.[53] Some violence appeared, usually in the form of arms raids, but the main effort of the banditti was towards extending their influence by use of the oath. It was suggested that larger numbers of the peasantry were now associated with the societies than at 'any time in the last sixty years'.[54]

The reaction of the Irish government to these disclosures was, to say the least, uncharacteristic. Talbot's attitude was that there was no reason for alarm; the government should be vigilant and 'not let these beginnings grow into an organized rebellion',[55] but there the matter rested. Perhaps the Castle believed that in breaking up the 'revolutionary committee' in Dublin they had destroyed the possibility of independent action by peasant organizations in the rural areas. Such an idea might have been reinforced by the fact that the remainder of the winter found Ireland relatively quiet. But even these apparently

[51] Grant to Sidmouth, 2 Jan. 1821 (P.R.O., H.O. 100/200).
[52] Grant to Sidmouth, 4 Nov. 1820 (P.R.O., H.O. 100/199); Grant to Sidmouth, 2 Jan. 1821 (P.R.O., H.O. 100/200).
[53] See p. 109 above; Talbot to Sidmouth, 9 Jan. 1821 (P.R.O., H.O. 100/200).
[54] Ibid.
[55] Ibid.

reassuring circumstances cannot adequately excuse the blunders made at this time.

Still guided by considerations of economy, in July Liverpool proposed a further major reduction in the size of Britain's army,[56] and Sir David Baird, commander of the forces, was given the task of convincing the duke of York that the strength of the Irish establishment could be safely reduced. The duke agreed, Talbot apparently raised no objection, and Grant was willing to support a cut in military strength if there was 'any possibility at all to do so'.[57] There was some opposition at a lower level. A member of Baird's staff wrote that he could not understand why money could be spent on policemen and not on soldiers: '. . . it is difficult to understand the economy of a measure which gives 1s. 6d. a day to a private policeman, instead of 1s. to a soldier, and seven or eight hundred a year to a police magistrate for the direction of a force not exceeding generally one hundred men'.[58]

The summer of 1821 witnessed the arrival of the king, making George IV the first monarch to visit Ireland since William III. His subjects greeted him with enthusiasm, but the brief period of goodwill was ended in October by a series of events that led to a period of almost uninterrupted agrarian outrage, lasting with brief intermission for the next two years. This time the trouble began in Limerick and spread into Cork, Tipperary, Mayo, and Cavan; by the end of the year, the entire province of Munster was in a state of disturbance perhaps deeper than any Ireland had witnessed since the end of the last century. A later writer has seen the basic cause of this turmoil as economic, lying in the landlords' determination to continue collecting the high rents that the tenants could no longer pay.[59] The investigation by the Irish government in 1821 seems to support this explanation.[60] One of the immediate reasons for the outbreak

[56] Liverpool to George IV, 27 July 1821 (Liverpool papers, B.M., Add. MS 38289).

[57] Thomas Sorell to Sir Herbert Taylor, 27 Oct. 1821 (P.R.O., H.O. 100/201); Grant to Sidmouth, n.d. (P.R.O., H.O. 100/200).

[58] Sorell to Taylor, 27 Oct. 1821 (P.R.O., H.O. 100/201).

[59] G. Locker Lampson, *A consideration of the state of Ireland in the nineteenth century* (London, 1907), p. 232.

[60] See Report of Willcocks and Warburton, 25 Oct. 1821 (P.R.O., H.O. 100/201).

of violence lay in the activities of the agents of the infamous Courteney estates in Limerick, who had been conducting a programme of wholesale eviction against the tenants who were behind in their rents. Contrary to orders, and to the annoyance of Grant, soldiers had been used to assist the agents, the tenants had begun to collect arms for the purpose of redress against 'oppressive acts', and the authorities had again let the situation develop until it was beyond their control.[61]

In October 1821 Sidmouth took the initiative in preparing to meet the spreading disorder in Munster. Writing that 'delay, compromise or concession, will be fatal', he insisted that the power of the banditti could be broken only by an overwhelming military force.[62] But it was difficult to create such a force, for government economy measures had reduced the army in England as well as in Ireland. It is doubtful that even the combined strength of the two could have made up the force envisioned by the home secretary.[63] Once again the military authorities began to exert pressure to have the small detachments in the disturbed areas withdrawn and combined into larger units,[64] and the military situation was further complicated by political considerations. Earlier in the year the duke of York had allowed himself to be convinced that it was possible to reduce the size of the Irish establishment. To save the duke from parliamentary criticism, the military authorities now insisted that the Irish government take responsibility for the weakened state of the establishment, and that the civil authorities make the request for reinforcements.[65] Talbot, possibly disturbed by rumours of his possible replacement and also anxious to avoid being the target of parliamentary censures, sought reasons to believe that the situation in Munster was not serious and that additional troops were not needed. The situation clearly permitted no such optimism, however, and on 30 October Talbot reluctantly admitted that reinforcements were

[61] A. McCarthy to Gregory, 29 Oct. 1821; Talbot to Sidmouth, 13 Oct. 1821 (P.R.O., H.O. 100/201); Grant to Henry Bateman, 19 Jan. 1820 (S.P.O., C.S.O., Government correspondence books, private, 1820–2).
[62] Sidmouth to Talbot, 23 Oct. 1821 (P.R.O., H.O. 100/201).
[63] See Sidmouth to Grant, 21 Nov. 1821 (P.R.O., H.O. 100/202).
[64] Baird to Talbot, 21 Oct. 1821 (P.R.O., H.O. 100/201).
[65] Sorell to Taylor, 27 Oct. 1821 (P.R.O., H.O. 100/201).

needed. 'If Ireland is to be kept in a state of general tranquillity,' he wrote, 'the means which government possesses of effecting this desirable object, must be increased.'[66]

By the end of 1821, the Irish establishment had received a number of the regiments stationed in Britain, but even this reinforcement failed to repair the damage done during the previous spring. Rebuilding proved difficult; regiments and battalions from other portions of the world were drawn in, but by mid-1822 the number of troops in Ireland was only about 16,000 men.[67] As in the past, the Castle was forced to turn to the yeomanry, and in late October, Talbot called to 'permanent duty' units of the Tarbert (Kerry) and Palatine (Tipperary) corps.[68] Sidmouth gave his full approval and suggested that other units be called out, for 'we will not be deterred by considerations of expense, however important under other circumstances, from resorting to it'.[69] Early in November, orders went from the Castle to call out 3,000 members of Ulster yeomanry corps to replace line regiments from the north that were to be sent to Munster.[70]

But Talbot had not consulted Grant, and the chief secretary, acting on his own initiative, promptly cancelled the lord lieutenant's orders to the Ulster units. As soon as this action was reported to Sidmouth, the home secretary dispatched a fiery letter to Grant, asking for an explanation.[71] Grant's letter was already on its way to London, and in it the chief secretary pointed out that the Ulster yeomanry corps were protestant in composition and strongly tainted with Orangeism. To call them out would create added tension in the disturbed areas, and would almost certainly result in new incidents. Grant reminded Sidmouth that the mobilization of the yeomanry in Ulster might plunge that area into the kind of trouble now rapidly spreading throughout Munster.[72] In taking this stand Grant found a temporary ally in the lord lieutenant. On 22 November, Sidmouth wrote to Talbot, asking him why the rest of the

[66] Talbot to Sidmouth, 30 Oct. 1821 (P.R.O., H.O. 100/201).
[67] Military in Ireland, 7 Aug. 1822 (P.R.O., H.O. 100/206).
[68] Talbot to Sidmouth, 22 Oct. 1821 (P.R.O., H.O. 100/201).
[69] Sidmouth to Talbot, 27 Oct. 1821 (P.R.O., H.O. 100/201).
[70] Talbot to Sidmouth, Nov. 1821 (P.R.O., H.O. 100/202).
[71] Sidmouth to Grant, 21 Nov. 1821 (P.R.O., H.O. 100/202).
[72] Grant to Sidmouth, 19 Nov. 1821 (P.R.O., H.O. 100/202).

yeomanry in the south had not been called out,[73] and in reply Talbot wrote that additional units would be used only after an investigation had proved them reliable. As for the Ulster corps, Talbot opposed their use, adding to Grant's arguments the observation that they were 'too far away'.[74] But the lord lieutenant's opposition weakened under pressure from Sidmouth, and on 28 November Talbot yielded to the extent of calling out two Ulster units and all of the Dublin yeomanry.[75] Grant continued to oppose using the yeomanry; in December he indicated his belief that a substitute for them had been found in the now-reactivated veterans corps. The pensioners were to be used to free regular troops stationed in the north, and the danger inherent in the use of the yeomanry would thus be avoided. The yeomanry, Grant insisted, were 'perfectly useless, as they are very reluctant to march from their own places – so that they are of little use except to excite . . . irritation'.[76] There is no indication that Grant's arguments convinced Sidmouth, but his opposition had stopped their widespread use until December, when a new lord lieutenant, the marquess of Wellesley, came to Ireland. Wellesley flatly refused to sanction the use of the yeomanry corps,[77] and from 1822 to 1831, a most critical period in Irish history, the yeomanry were generally absent from the scene. Not until 1831, when the whigs returned to office, did they appear in sizeable numbers – to resume once more their traditional role of Orange-tinged troublemakers.

In mid-October 1821 a chief constable of the Peace Preservation Force in Limerick, Major Going, was riding from Limerick City to Rathkeale, when he was attacked by a group of armed men. In a matter of seconds, his body 'was made a riddle of'. It was necessary for a military escort to recover the body, to keep the villagers from tearing it to pieces. Within an hour after the attack, Going's death 'was announced to the country by bonfires on all the hills, and echoed by a savage yell of exultation

[73] Sidmouth to Talbot, 22 Nov. 1821 (P.R.O., H.O. 100/202).
[74] Talbot to Sidmouth, 24 Nov. 1821 (P.R.O., H.O. 100/202).
[75] Talbot to Sidmouth, 28 Nov. 1821 (P.R.O., H.O. 100/202).
[76] Grant to Sidmouth, 24 Dec. 1821 (P.R.O., H.O. 100/202).
[77] See Wellesley to Peel, 22 June 1823 (Peel papers, B.M., Add. MS 40324).

from the villages'.[78] The news of the outrage itself undoubtedly caused enough alarm in Dublin Castle, but the government was to receive another shock upon completing its investigation into the attack. In the report submitted by Willcocks and Warburton, the Force in Limerick was described as 'unpopular' and made more so by 'character assassination'. The local magistrates had failed to co-operate, and the chief magistrate was 'completely inexperienced' and without military training. The men were 'better than expected', but lacking in discipline. But the shocking part of the report was the revelation that an Orange lodge existed within the Limerick Force, a situation made even more damaging by the presence of catholics in the detachment; the resulting division within the ranks must have weakened the effectiveness of the Force. To say that rumours of Orange leadership and personnel 'made the police very unpopular in the area' was an understatement. Going, reputed to be an Orangeman, was singled out as the target of the most violent hatred by the Limerick peasantry, and when a rumour reached the countryside that a wounded member of the banditti had been buried alive by the police, Major Going paid with his life.[79] By early November, it was claimed that the Limerick agrarian secret societies were offering rewards for the assassination of members of the Force,[80] an honour frequently accorded to particularly obnoxious Orangemen. The Going incident and the investigation following it lent substance to the complaints that accumulated after the rapid expansion of the Force in 1819–20. The police were accused of showing 'bad spirit in dealing with the inhabitants', of taking arms from 'honest and respectable farmers' in an unproclaimed area,[81] and of acting in a manner 'likely to irritate and exasperate'. At Tyragh the police were suspected of having provoked an 'affair', and the chief magistrate of Roscommon was accused of having been absent without leave for three weeks, during which an 'upsurge' of

[78] *Annual Reg., 1821*, p. 129.

[79] Report of Willcocks and Warburton, 25 Oct. 1821 (P.R.O., H.O. 100/201); *Second report . . . disturbed districts in Ireland*, H.C. 1825 (35), xiii, 82–3.

[80] Gregory to Sidmouth, 9 Nov. 1821, in Gregory, *Letter-box*, p. 159.

[81] Grant to Col. Brown, 6 Mar. 1820; Gregory to Jam. O'Donoghue, 7 Mar. 1820 (S.P.O., C.S.O., Government correspondence books, private, 1820–2).

Ribbonism had taken place.[82] The death of the unfortunate chief constable merely underlined a fact long recognized by numerous country gentlemen and by certain elements in Dublin Castle: the Peace Preservation Force, as it had evolved by 1821, was not a satisfactory instrument to combat agrarian disorder. It had succeeded neither in preventing major outbreaks nor in effectively coping with them once they had occurred. The task assigned to the Force was too big for it to handle, and as long as the local magistrates continued to oppose it, even its limited value to the government was perforce restricted.

Government attempts further to extend the use of the Force in the autumn of 1821 met with a wave of criticism, some of it from rather unexpected sources. Willcocks, the senior chief magistrate of the Force, reported to his superiors in October: '. . . it would be highly beneficial to have such establishments completely formed, before they go into the district for which they are intended – as their awkward and undisciplined conduct is at first observed, and once held cheap, it is almost impossible to obtain any ascendancy over the people.' Like several other critics of the Force at this time, Willcocks had a plan to enable the government to cope with the banditti. Even a modified Force and a strong military establishment were not enough; Willcocks suggested that the situation demanded an arms act to limit the number of people eligible to possess guns, an act to limit the sale of gunpowder, and a permanent 'modified' insurrection act, always at the disposal of the government.[83]

Willcocks was by no means alone among members of the police and military in expressing doubts about the Force. Colonel Thomas Sorell, a member of the staff of the commander of the forces, evidently favoured disbanding the Force altogether. As Sorell saw the matter,

The inefficiency of this Force for keeping the country quiet has been . . . clearly demonstrated in Limerick. . . . Whilst tranquil, they

[82] Grant to Lord Clonbrooke, 8 Mar. 1820; Gregory to C. L. P. French, 3 May 1820; Grant to Wills, 31 Jan. 1820 (S.P.O., C.S.O., Government correspondence books, private, 1820–2).

[83] Report, R. Willcocks, 25 Oct. 1821 (P.R.O., H.O. 100/201).

were all that was required – but the moment the disturbances began, a general outcry for troops took place. . . . I fear however, that this government is strongly prepossessed in their favour but I am persuaded they will disappoint its expectation.[84]

On 12 November, Lord Aylmer, the adjutant-general in Ireland, joined the attack, suggesting that there was so much objection to the peace preservation act in the disturbed areas that its suspension might be the wisest course for the present. Many of those who had formerly supported the Force were now against it. There was a need for magistrates 'with no local interests', but military officers could perform that function without 'the expense of the peace preservation act'.[85] Three days later, Aylmer informed Sorell that the 'better class' of farmers had a deep dislike of the act, which could 'drive them into the insurgent camp'.[86]

When steps were taken by the Castle to install the Force in several baronies of Cork in early November, a meeting of the 'nobility, magistrates, and gentry' of the baronies of Fermoy, Condon, and Clongibbon protested loudly to the Castle. The peace preservation act they characterized as a failure, and added that the present disorder could be controlled only by reviving the insurrection act and administering a 'loyalty oath' to the residents of the disturbed areas.[87] In spite of objections, however, three baronies of Cork were placed under the act on 13 November 1821.[88] Even Talbot was now justifying the lack of exertion by the magistracy in the disturbed areas, explaining that their hesitancy to act was 'not without reason' where a bolder stand would make them 'marked men for the rest of their lives'. The lord lieutenant now believed that the insurrection act was vitally necessary, and should be revived at once.[89]

The mounting criticism of the Peace Preservation Force did not go unanswered by men who still placed the blame for agrarian outrage on the magistrates. The bishop of Raphoe

---

[84] Sorell to Taylor, 27 Oct. 1821 (P.R.O., H.O. 100/201).
[85] Lord Aylmer to ——, 12 Nov. 1821 (P.R.O., H.O. 100/202).
[86] Aylmer to Sorell, 15 Nov. 1821 (P.R.O., H.O. 100/202).
[87] 'Meeting', 7 Nov. 1821 (P.R.O., H.O. 100/201).
[88] Proclaimed districts, 1814–22 (Peel papers, B.M., Add. MS 40328).
[89] Talbot to Sidmouth, 7 Nov. 1821 (P.R.O., H.O. 100/201).

claimed that opposition to the Force by the magistrates in Donegal was based on resentment caused by attempts of the chief magistrate to stop the collusion between the local gentry and certain dissident elements. A magistrate might associate himself with a local 'faction', which in turn would protect his property from the depredations of factions associated with other magistrates and gentry. What Ireland needed most, the bishop wrote, was a 'uniform police system' for the entire country.[90] Criticism of the magistrates for corruption and self-interest also came from a member of the magistracy itself. Opposition to the Force, he wrote, was based on the fact that it checked the 'shameful trading of . . . corrupt justices of the peace, who are a disgrace to the commission and make considerable profit of it, by means most cruel, oppressive, and illegal. . . . The justices and the baronial police [are] the encouragers and protectors of every species of villainy, fraud and outrage.' And again the solution suggested to the Castle was a system of police for all Ireland.[91]

By the end of 1821, there could no longer be any reasonable objection to proposals for a radical overhaul of the entire system of maintaining law and order in rural Ireland. Peel's ambitious plan for forcing the magistracy to perform its duties had failed, and the army had dwindled in size until it could no longer perform the functions traditionally assigned to it. The militia had virtually ceased to exist, and there was still strong opposition from the chief secretary and other 'enlightened' persons to the use of the yeomanry. The Castle was forced to make extensive use of the Peace Preservation Force, but evidently no one in government circles now viewed it as the answer to the problem. Yet if extensive changes were to be made in the existing system, they had now to be undertaken at a time when the situation in Ireland appeared to be growing more critical than at any time in recent decades. The obvious solution seemed to lie in the revival of the insurrection act and in a new police system. Perhaps this solution was being considered at Westminster in December 1821, when the first step was taken towards remedying the situation in Ireland: Talbot and Grant were both recalled, and replaced by the marquess

[90] Bishop of Raphoe to Grant, 24 Nov. 1821 (P.R.O., H.O. 100/202)·
[91] John Minton to Gregory, 8 Nov. 1821 (P.R.O., H.O. 100/201).

of Wellesley and Henry Goulburn. As the *Annual Register* put it, 'Among the measures taken by the government to restore tranquillity in Ireland was the recall of Lord Talbot and Mr Grant.'[92] And in January, Peel replaced Sidmouth as home secretary.

[92] *Annual Reg., 1821*, p. 129.

VIII

THE COUNTY CONSTABULARY,
1822–5

~~~~~~

THE WELCOME ACCORDED the new lord lieutenant, the marquess of Wellesley, upon his arrival in Dublin on 29 December 1821 was anything but reassuring. The city was in a state of great alarm. The entrances had been reinforced with barricades and cannon; the Castle guard had been doubled; the gates were closed. Stones had been carried to the roofs of public buildings, to be dropped on assailants. Dublin gave every appearance of a city preparing to withstand a siege.[1]

The arrival of the lord lieutenant and the military precautions were not unconnected. For the appointment of a political 'catholic' had horrified the Orangemen and other ultra-ascendancy protestants, who saw in the coming of Wellesley, coupled with certain vaguely alarming statements made by the king during his recent Irish tour, a sure sign of approaching catholic emancipation. Throughout Ireland, the Orange lodges began to muster their forces and enrol recruits to meet this 'threat to the constitution'. Inevitably this activity by the Orangemen alarmed the Ribbon societies, in particular those around Dublin. Rumour had it that Lord O'Neill, the grand

---

[1] See Col. Meyrick Shaw to Sir William Knighton, 18 Sept. 1827, in *The letters of King George IV, 1812–1830*, ed. A. Aspinall (Cambridge, 1938), iii, 301.

master of the Orange lodges in Ireland, was marching south with a hundred thousand Orangemen 'to put down the catholics', and the nightly meetings and oath-swearings by Ribbonmen in the Dublin area increased to such proportions that the Castle believed an attack on the city to be imminent.[2]

The reactions and counter-reactions created by the appointment of a 'catholic' lord lieutenant were symptoms of the growth of a problem that was to plague the Irish government for many years. The Irish ultra-protestants saw themselves being deserted by *their* government. As a result, the traditional alignment of a 'loyal' ascendancy against a 'disloyal' catholic Ireland was disrupted. The Irish government soon found itself in the middle, subject to attacks from both the protestant 'right' and the catholic 'left'. The new alignment emerged gradually, and in many respects the victory of the emancipationists in 1829 merely intensified already existing bitterness. The government was to discover that protestant 'treason' was as subversive of law and order as the catholic variety.

Wellesley had been sent to Ireland, not to prepare the way for catholic emancipation, but 'to administer the existing laws in a spirit of mildness and impartiality'.[3] To retain the allegiance of the pro-emancipation Grenville faction, which had broken with the whigs at the time of the queen's trial, the government gave Ireland a 'catholic' lord lieutenant. Wellesley's appointment was also symptomatic of the cautious liberalization of the tory leadership during the remaining years of Liverpool's tenure as prime minister.[4] Wellesley was given a policy for Ireland best described as one of official neutrality. The lord lieutenant was

to administer the existing laws in a spirit of mildness and impartiality, which might give to the different religious sects and political parties of that country a confidence in the equal and unbiased dispensation of justice: to correct the notion which has long unhappily prevailed in Ireland, that there was one law for the rich and another for the poor – one law for the protestant and another for the catholic.

He was also instructed to determine 'the causes of the continual

2 *Letters of George IV*, iii, 301–2.
3 *Letters of George IV*, iii, 297.
4 McDowell, *Public opinion & govt policy*, p. 102.

appearances of discontent . . . and disturbance in Ireland and to suggest the proper remedies'.[5] This policy, perhaps a tacit admission that government solely in the interests of the ascendancy was no longer feasible, was more than a pious pronouncement. It was to be implemented by a programme of reform. Within the next year and a half, Ireland received a new police system, a reform of the magistracy was instituted, an attempt was made to alleviate the burden of the tithe, and the practice of holding petty sessions of the magistracy was introduced. The reforms were all designed to make it easier for the Irish peasant to look to the government instead of to the secret societies for protection and justice.

The new Irish policy was to be administered by a man who seemed eminently qualified for the task. The marquess of Wellesley, elder brother of the duke of Wellington, had served as viceroy of India from 1797 to 1805, and in that capacity had 'transformed "a little patchwork of crimson spots on the map of the Indian continent" into an Indian empire'.[6] A twentieth-century writer has referred to him as 'the great governor-general',[7] but officials of the East India Company had taken a different view of his rapid acquisitions of territory and political responsibility. Following Wellesley's return to England in 1805, unsuccessful attempts had been made in parliament to accuse him of high crimes and misdemeanours, and the court of proprietors of the Company had passed a vote of censure on him by a large majority, a verdict reversed by the directors of the Company thirty years later. A vain and autocratic man, Wellesley deeply resented the series of rebuffs, and he had waited impatiently for an opportunity to restore his tarnished reputation. Now in 1821 it seemed that the opportunity had arrived. The appointment of Wellesley, committed as he was to catholic emancipation (and soon to marry a catholic), seemed to many a portent of significant changes in Ireland. He was to remain in Ireland as lord lieutenant until 1827, and during this period a number of important reforms were to be instituted, but Wellesley would actually have little to do with them. The

[5] Shaw to Knighton, 18 Sept. 1827, in *Letters of George IV*, iii, 297.

[6] P. Guedalla, *Wellington* (New York, 1931), p. 105.

[7] G. M. Trevelyan, *British history in the nineteenth century and after, 1782–1919* (London, 1948), p. 107.

great viceroy of India was fated to be a mediocre lord lieutenant of Ireland, a noble figurehead, while the actual administration passed even more than in the past into the hands of the chief secretary and the home secretary.

One of Wellesley's first official actions was the dismissal of Saurin, the attorney-general who had been Peel's close associate during his years as chief secretary. Wrote Wellesley, 'When I went to Ireland in 1821, I found . . . an old Orangeman named Saurin, then attorney-general by title, who had really been lord lieutenant for fifteen years.'[8] Saurin was replaced by the Irish solicitor-general, William Conyngham Plunket, who was also the member for Dublin University and was gradually emerging as the spokesman for emancipation in the house of commons. Thus the lord lieutenant and the attorney-general represented the 'catholic' viewpoint in the reconstituted Irish government.

But the upper level of the Irish government was to be balanced as well as neutral, and the protestant point of view was ably represented by the new chief secretary, Henry Goulburn, who normally reflected the ideas and attitudes of his friend Peel. The persisting insinuation that Goulburn was an Orangeman[9] is completely without foundation, although the strength of his opposition to emancipation was equal to Peel's. Thomas Moore called Goulburn 'a secretary, worthy of the good old anti-popery times, and to whose spirit I would ensure a safe passage over Mahomet's bridge into Paradise'.[10] But in spite of his identification with a losing cause, Goulburn was intelligent and conscientious, and was to become one of Ireland's better chief secretaries.

Peel's appointment as home secretary followed the resignation of Sidmouth early in 1822. As home secretary, Peel was to exercise more influence on the Castle hierarchy than Sidmouth had. By this time, Peel's ability was widely recognized, owing to a considerable extent to his success as chief secretary. The tendency in Dublin and London was to look to him for leadership on Irish matters. Fortunately Wellesley and Peel worked

[8] Wellesley to Lady Blessington, n.d., in Peel, *Private papers*, i, 302.
[9] See J. A. Reynolds, *The catholic emancipation crisis in Ireland, 1823–1829* (New Haven, 1954), p. 109.
[10] T. Moore, *Memoirs of Captain Rock* (Paris, 1824), p. 309.

with a minimum of friction. In January 1822, Peel wrote to the lord lieutenant,

I lament that on one great question materially affecting Ireland I have the misfortune to differ with your excellency, but I will not allow myself to believe that that difference can countervail the force of other impressions arising from the strongest attachment to Ireland, and the sincerest desire to co-operate with you in the promotion of her welfare.[11]

The sentiments expressed in Peel's letter may be said to typify the outward relationship between the two factions. In the Castle as in the cabinet, catholic emancipation had become an 'open question'. The dislike and suspicion that seemed almost inevitable between men of opposing views on such an incendiary subject were successfully hidden from the public, but such emotions did exist.

Peel, Goulburn, and Gregory were suspicious of Wellesley on grounds other than emancipation alone: the lord lieutenant was not just vain and autocratic, he was also lazy and inept. Thus Peel treated him with icy courtesy; Goulburn, outwardly proper in his relations with his superior, seems on occasion to have been hard pressed to control his irritation; Gregory, who believed himself to have been personally affronted by the lord lieutenant, was surprisingly open in expressing his hostility.[12]

It is fortunate that open dissension did not appear within the Irish government at this time, for by 1822 the Castle was no longer referring to the chaos in Munster as but another series of 'disturbances' or 'outrages'; it was frankly admitted that the situation bordered on rebellion in parts of the province.[13] The 'deluded wretches' in this area had conceived a wild plan to force the landowners to flee from banditti violence, allowing the tenants to occupy the land without paying rent.[14] By January 1822 the banditti had succeeded in at least the first part of their plan: most of the 'better classes' had fled for their lives, for 'those who dared to be obedient to the law, were punished by the control of a predominant power, exercising lawless, cruel,

[11] Peel to Wellesley, 17 Jan. 1822, in Peel, *Private papers*, i, 305.
[12] See Gregory to Goulburn, 1 July 1823 (Surrey Record Office, Goulburn papers, box C, pt 1).
[13] Wellesley to Peel, 31 Jan. 1822 (P.R.O., H.O. 100/203).
[14] Shaw to Knighton, 18 Sept. 1827, in *Letters of George IV*, iii, 300.

and savage tyranny'.[15] In north Cork, the greater part of the male population left home and established camps in the mountains. From these camps, bodies of men descended upon the neighbouring towns to seize food, bedding, and arms. The Castle believed, with apparent justification, that attempts were being made to form a banditti army beyond reach of the authorities.[16]

At no time in many years had the banditti appeared in such large numbers and shown such willingness to attack military and police detachments. On 21 January 1822 Lord Bantry and a body of fifty-five men, consisting of soldiers and police, left Bantry in Cork to march to Macroom, a distance of roughly thirty miles. About twelve miles from Bantry, on the other side of a mountain pass, they were attacked by a group of possibly four hundred men acting under crude military discipline. Bantry's party were able to regain the pass by sending out flankers to keep themselves from being surrounded, but for three miles the retreating soldiers and police waged a running battle with the banditti.[17] Near Buttevant, in Cork, a barracks occupied by the Peace Preservation Force was destroyed, and of the seventeen men stationed there eight were killed or wounded. Shortly after this, a body of 'one thousand Whiteboys', well-armed and commanded by a stranger, fought an engagement with an unspecified number of soldiers and police. This affray ended when the 'Whiteboys' ran out of ammunition and negotiated surrender terms. A short distance away, another detachment of soldiers listened anxiously to the sound of firing without marching to the aid of their comrades. Information had been received by their commander that a false attack would be staged to lure them out of camp and into a trap, and they had been ordered to remain where they were.[18] With exceptions, the discipline of the banditti during the attacks left much to be desired, and in most cases after a few shots had been exchanged the attackers would break and run. But there was no assurance

[15] Wellesley to Peel, 1 May 1822 (P.R.O., H.O. 100/204).

[16] Wellesley to Peel, 29 Jan. 1822 (P.R.O., H.O. 100/203); Gregory to Goulburn, 6 Mar. 1822 (Surrey Record Office, Goulburn papers, box C, pt 1).

[17] Wellesley to Peel, 29 Jan. 1822 (P.R.O., H.O. 100/203).

[18] Major Carter to the chief secretary, 1 Feb. 1822 (P.R.O., H.O. 100/203).

that they would continue doing so, and by February 1822 the Castle had unconsciously increased the stature of the banditti by discussing the possibility of 'war' in Ireland.[19]

Before the country could enjoy the benefits of the new Irish policy, order obviously had to be restored in Munster, and to this end Wellesley and Goulburn concentrated their first efforts. The revival of the insurrection act was requested, and further to strengthen the efforts of the government the lord lieutenant also asked for a bill to suspend habeas corpus for a limited period.[20] Peel, as home secretary, gave his reluctant support to both measures,[21] but while he could see the need for the insurrection act, he was uneasy about suspending habeas corpus. To reassure his friend, Goulburn explained its purpose as a means of combating the secret societies.[22] Since the members of these groups would give no information when apprehended, and since it was difficult to get victims or witnesses of their crimes to testify against them, only by suspension of habeas corpus could suspected members of the societies be arrested and held until the disturbed area was tranquillized. The two bills, for the insurrection act and suspension of habeas corpus, were introduced in the house of commons by Lord Londonderry on 7 February 1822. The purpose of these measures, he said, was 'to furnish the executive authorities in Ireland with additional powers for the restoration of the public peace', these powers to be in effect only until 1 August 1822. The need for such 'painful' legislation was justified by

. . . nothing short of absolute rebellion, prevailing in a considerable portion of the south and southwest of Ireland. Rebellion was in the field: it was characterized by every mark belonging to insurrection; resistance to the law, defiance of the constituted authorities, and every component principle of rebellion.

The house was warned that to hesitate in passing these bills was to 'encourage the spirit of disaffection, and to appal and dismay the loyal subject . . .'. The rebellion at the moment was neither

[19] Wellesley to Peel, 15 Feb. 1822 (P.R.O., H.O. 100/203).
[20] Wellesley to Peel, 31 Jan. 1822 (P.R.O., H.O. 100/203).
[21] Peel to Goulburn, 2 Feb. 1822 (Surrey record office, Goulburn papers, II/14).
[22] Goulburn to Peel, 30 Jan. 1822 (Peel papers, B.M., Add. MS 40328).

political nor religious, but if the house 'delayed to act with vigour', it might become both.[23]

Londonderry did not present the measures convincingly. Evidently disturbed from the outset by the knowledge that both bills would be challenged sharply from the floor, he was on the defensive from the moment he began to speak. The attack was led by Sir John Newport, supported by C. H. Hutchinson, Thomas Spring Rice, Sir Francis Burdett, and Henry Brougham. The line of argument followed by those in opposition to the bills was stated by Newport:

The noble lord might say that the safety of the state required the executive government to be armed with those extraordinary powers. He, on the other hand, who conceived those powers to be too extensive, would say, 'let the government have what is necessary, and no more'. If more troops were required, let them have more.

The members opposing the proposed legislation were lavish in their praises of Wellesley, and Brougham went so far as to suggest that instead of these measures the lord lieutenant should be given unrestricted powers for a limited time. Wellesley could be trusted not to abuse extraordinary powers; the magistrates could not. But in spite of Spring Rice's warning that 'if the English members . . . allowed ministers to contract the habit of suspending the constitution, . . . their fate could easily be predicted', and Burdett's question, 'Was it to be tolerated, that Ireland should know nothing of this country, but through bloodshed and gibbet?' the government was able to command a safe majority at every stage of the progress of the bills. On 11 February 1822 both bills received the royal assent.[24]

The new Irish government had inherited, along with a near-insurrection, the usual resultant problems of punishment for the offenders. By 1 February 1822, three hundred persons were awaiting trial for crimes associated with the 'war' in Munster, and the government was arranging in advance for transporting two hundred convicts.[25] Since most of those committed and waiting for the special assize had been arrested for crimes of an 'insurrectionary nature', the number of capital convictions was

[23] *Hansard 2*, vi, 104–12.
[24] *Hansard 2*, vi, 112–50, 163–219.
[25] Goulburn to Hobhouse, 1 Feb. 1822 (P.R.O., H.O. 100/203).

certain to be high, and it appeared to the lord lieutenant that here would be the logical starting-point for the 'new policy'. Wellesley feared that the death sentences would reach a number 'neither humanity nor policy could sanction', and suggested that transportation be substituted for the gallows whenever possible.[26] Here was an opportunity to try a 'spirit of mildness', to attempt to win respect for the government by invoking mercy instead of retribution. The lord lieutenant's fears were realized, for at the special assize held in mid-February, thirty-six capital convictions were handed down, or more than one in ten of the total number committed for trial.[27] But Wellesley's suggestion that leniency be used wherever possible was apparently given a somewhat diabolical twist by the man responsible for applying it. Plunket, the attorney-general, selected fourteen men to be hanged in the future – 'unless the state of the country shall be such as to warrant the extension of mercy, they must abide their sentence'.[28]

Transportation as a substitute for the death sentence, when feasible, was a common practice. Gregory, commenting on recent convictions in Cork, expressed established policy when he wrote, 'It is not, of course, intended to execute them all. I conclude these convictions will have the effect of inducing many of the untried to plead guilty on the terms of transportation.'[29] But Peel and Goulburn were obviously disturbed by Wellesley's policy, possibly because the lord lieutenant seemed to be moving beyond the commutation of the death sentence whenever possible and towards some broad amnesty for the banditti. The suggestion that those who voluntarily surrendered their arms should be pardoned evoked a strong protest from the chief secretary. To Goulburn, 'before any amnesty is granted or any general remission of punishment takes place, sufficient examples ought to have been made to prove to the deluded people that punishment will always follow crime . . .'.[30] Peel

[26] Wellesley to Peel, 21 Jan. 1822 (P.R.O., H.O. 100/203).
[27] Attorney-general to lord lieutenant, 26 Feb. 1823 (P.R.O., H.O. 100/203).
[28] Ibid.
[29] Gregory to Goulburn, 21 Feb. 1822 (Surrey record office, Goulburn papers, box C, pt 1).
[30] Goulburn to Wellesley, 22 Mar. 1822 (Wellesley papers, B.M., Add. MS 37298).

supported the chief secretary, and by May 1822 Wellesley was forced to conclude that his offer of pardons for arms had not resulted in a 'general surrender'.[31] The well-meaning gestures made by the lord lieutenant to win the support of the disaffected evidently went unnoticed by the lower orders, but practical considerations caused the authorities to continue the commutation of death sentences – 'I do not know what can be done with so many persons under sentence of death, it will not be possible to execute them all,' wrote Gregory.[32] Wellesley's policy reached a kind of sordid climax in September, one somewhat symbolic of the lord lieutenant's efforts to do what he believed best for Ireland. It was suggested that certain prisoners awaiting execution in Cork should be reprieved, and Wellesley wrote on 20 September, 'I am always happy to find any reasons for respite of capital sentences'. But three days later Goulburn informed him, 'It is most painful to me to have to announce to you that the messenger did not reach Cork in time. . . '.[33] In 1822, Wellesley had intended 'to administer the existing laws in a spirit of mildness and impartiality', but by 1823 he would be forced to turn instead to the 'effectual and impartial administration of the law'.[34]

Unlike the insurrection act of 1814, the similar measure of 1822 failed to insure a speedy victory over the banditti armies. To be sure, banditti activities at this time were much more widespread and more intense than they had been in 1815, but the government's real handicap lay in the weakness of the military establishment, which numbered around 16,000 men in mid-1822. As soon as some degree of peace had been restored to one area, troops had to be withdrawn for service in another, leaving the first to revert to its original state of disturbance. By 1 May 1822, Limerick, Kerry, parts of Tipperary, Westmeath and Kilkenny, and all of Cork, including the city of Cork, had been placed under the act, and there were disturbing signs of growing unrest in almost every county in Ireland. Even though

[31] Wellesley to Peel, 1 May 1822 (P.R.O., H.O. 100/204).

[32] Gregory to Goulburn, 26 Apr. 1822 (Surrey record office, Goulburn papers, box C, pt 1).

[33] Wellesley to Goulburn, 20 Sept. 1822; Goulburn to Wellesley, 23 Sept. 1822 (Surrey record office, Goulburn papers, II/21).

[34] Wellesley to Peel, 27 Apr. 1823 (P.R.O., H.O. 100/208).

signs of disturbance were appearing in the north, that region was stripped of soldiers, who began 'slowly and imperfectly' to re-establish the authority of the government in the areas abandoned to the banditti.[35]

But by the end of May the activities of the banditti had ceased – not, however, because the government had succeeded in bringing order. The ominous stillness of the Irish countryside resulted rather from the grim prospect of starvation. The autumn of 1821 had been unusually wet, and much of the potato crop had rotted in the ground; by the following May, Clare, Cork, Mayo, Limerick, Kerry, Roscommon, and Sligo were faced with famine. It is related that in Clare the population of one barony was willing to be sent to jail for the sake of obtaining food. 'Outrage and insurrection disappeared, and the miserable peasantry sank into the peace which is the result of utter exhaustion.'[36] Within a relatively short time, the government acted to provide relief for the victims of the famine, and rather considerable sums of money were allocated, to be used primarily to provide employment for those unable to buy food.[37] With autumn and the new potato crop, the famine faded away and 'the people, relieved from their fear, lapsed again into their normal condition of alternate ferocity and good humour, gaiety and despair'.[38] The Irish government received official notice that the worst of the famine had passed in September 1822, when the Castle was informed of a fresh wave of outrages in Tipperary.[39]

While the Castle was devoting its efforts to keeping a sizeable portion of the peasantry from starvation, steps had been taken at Westminster in anticipation of the almost certain return of disorder to Ireland in the autumn. The insurrection act was due to expire in August; the early expiration date had been offered in return for quick, certain passage of the act. As early as February 1822, deliberations had begun on whether it should be extended. During the February debates on the act, it was

[35] Wellesley to Peel, 1 May 1822 (P.R.O., H.O. 100/204).
[36] S. Walpole, *A history of England from the conclusion of the great war in 1815* (London, 1902), ii, 276.
[37] Gregory, *Letter-box*, p. 212.
[38] Walpole, *England from 1815*, ii, 277.
[39] Willcocks to Gregory, 23 Sept. 1822 (P.R.O., H.O. 100/206).

frequently suggested that a strong military establishment would make the measure unnecessary, and Peel sought advice from the logical authority on military matters, the duke of Wellington. The duke declared himself in favour of the act, stating that he had long believed that the military alone, without the help of the insurrection act, would never 'get the better of the disturbances in the south of Ireland'.[40] The pronouncement of the great duke was enough to remove any lingering doubts. The home secretary suggested that the act should be renewed for an additional year, and Wellesley agreed.[41] The decision as to whether or not the habeas corpus suspension act should also be renewed was left to the lord lieutenant,[42] and since this measure had not been used it was allowed to expire. The bill to extend the duration of the insurrection act was introduced at Westminster early in July, and was presented and guided through the various stages by Goulburn, with the aid of Plunket. The only serious opposition to the measure was offered by Spring Rice, who asked why trial by jury had been suspended in proclaimed areas where it had been possible to empanel a jury. But the government was relieved of the necessity for answering this embarrassing question; as the *Annual Register* stated, 'There was, undoubtedly, considerable weight in this objection; but it was forgotten amid the mass of heterogeneous matter which the other speakers introduced into the debate.' On the first division the opponents of the bill mustered only seventeen votes, and the measure passed through the subsequent stages with little opposition.[43]

But by the end of 1823, when there seemed reason to doubt that the continuation of the act was necessary, once again the Castle showed extreme reluctance to let it lapse. Wellesley and, to a lesser extent, Goulburn were anxious to keep the act as an emergency measure for possible future use 'only held, not enforced'.[44] The chief secretary denied that he wished to make

[40] Wellington to Peel, 27 Feb. 1822 (Peel papers, B.M., Add. MS 40306).

[41] Peel to Wellesley, 12 Apr. 1822 (Peel papers, B.M., Add. MS 40324).

[42] Ibid.

[43] *Annual Reg., 1822*, p. 43; Hansard 2, vii, 1498–1500, 1522–47, 1653–7.

[44] See Blacker to Goulburn, 30 July 1823 (P.R.O., H.O. 100/204).

the act permanent, but his arguments are somewhat unconvincing: 'I have always thought also that the extent of the
power which the law confers is in itself advantageous to liberty
as it effectively prevents the adoption of the law as a permanent
measure of government in Ireland.'[45] Wellesley viewed the time
when the insurrection act could be safely removed as still far in
the future:

To induce the habit of abstaining from excess is some advance
towards the introduction of habits of good order, and lawful
obedience; and if general tranquillity can be maintained for a
considerable period of time, the natural course of moral causes may
be expected to open and facilitate the channels of industry and
honest labour; and the common sense of the people may gradually
prefer the advantages of peace and security to the perils of illegal
adventure.[46]

Evidently in the areas still under proclamation the provisions
of the act were not generally enforced. But this tendency to regard
the act as a semi-permanent emergency measure ran counter to
the continuing doubts of Peel concerning the wisdom of such a
course.[47] The wishes of the Irish government prevailed over the
doubts of the home secretary, and in June 1824 the life of the
act was again extended, but in his speech in support of the
extension Peel implied that it would be the last such request by
the government.[48] By July 1824 the Castle was informed of
growing opposition by the magistrates of King's County and
Limerick to the continuation of the act in these areas,[49] and by
September the chief secretary had abandoned his advocacy of
the measure and declared with Peel in opposition to any
further extension.[50] Wellesley remained strongly in favour of
the act,[51] but evidently his advocacy was not enough to override

[45] Goulburn to Peel, 16 Apr. 1824 (Peel papers, B.M., Add. MS 40330).
[46] Wellesley to Peel, 28 Jan. 1825 (Wellesley papers, B.M., Add. MS
37303).
[47] Peel to Wellesley, 5 Feb. 1824 (Wellesley papers, B.M., Add. MS
37302).
[48] Peel, *Speeches*, i, 318.
[49] George Bennett to Goulburn, 14 July 1824; Blackbourne to Goulburn, 20 July 1824 (P.R.O., H.O. 100/210).
[50] Goulburn to Peel, 16 Sept. 1824 (P.R.O., H.O. 100/210).
[51] Wellesley to Peel, 28 Jan. 1825, 30 Jan. 1825 (Wellesley papers,
B.M., Add. MS 37307).

the combined opposition of Peel and Goulburn. In 1825, the insurrection act was finally repealed.

One of the reasons for Goulburn's willingness to allow the act to expire was his belief that the success of the new County Constabulary established in 1822 made the act less necessary.[52] On 30 January 1822, while re-enactment of the insurrection act and the proposal to suspend habeas corpus were still being discussed, Goulburn had written to Peel of 'another measure on the anvil . . . which is a general police for the country . . . to be grafted to [Peel's] bill'.[53] The need for a new rural police had been repeatedly demonstrated and became all the more pressing in the light of official dissatisfaction with the record of the Peace Preservation Force.[54]

During the first half of 1822, in spite of the increasing seriousness of the situation in Munster, the Force had been installed in only one additional barony.[55] The bitterness between the local magistrates and the Force continued to hamper the operations of this organization. In February, Major Carter, chief magistrate of Cork, wrote to Goulburn that because the Force was so unpopular with the 'gentlemen' of the area he was completely unable to obtain information 'on anything' and was forced to act without their co-operation.[56] But in 1822, as in 1815, when the insurrection act lightened the burden of maintaining order and allowed the Force to concentrate on its duties as 'outrage specialists' it was able to prove its worth. Especially was this true in Tipperary, where the success of the Force in 'patrolling, detection and preparing evidence' moved Wellesley to state in May 1822, '. . . it is impossible to bestow too much commendation on the exertions of the police under Major Willcocks . . .'.[57] But by this time, plans for a new system of police were being readied for presentation to parliament, and there is no indication that the Castle even considered abandoning the new in favour of the old. Possibly the success of the

[52] See Goulburn to Peel, 16 Sept. 1823 (Peel papers, B.M., Add. MS 40329).

[53] Goulburn to Peel, 30 Jan. 1822 (Peel papers, B.M., Add. MS 40328).

[54] Wellesley to Peel, 2 Feb. 1822 (P.R.O., H.O. 100/203).

[55] Fermoy, in Cork.

[56] Carter to the chief secretary, 1 Feb. 1822 (P.R.O., H.O. 100/203).

[57] Wellesley to Peel, 1 May 1822 (P.R.O., H.O. 100/204).

Force at this time may have influenced the government to keep it as a group of specialists when the new County Constabulary was formed in the autumn of 1822.

The Irish constables bill was an indispensable part of the new policy of Wellesley and his associates. On 7 June 1822 the home secretary informed the house that '. . . before they could give up the operation of such extraordinary measures as the peace preservation bill, or the insurrection bill, they must have an improved police, and habituate the people of Ireland to that which was the greatest of all national blessings – an equal, unvarying, and impartial administration of justice'.[58]

Although the evidence is incomplete, it would appear that initially Goulburn had contemplated a modified Peace Preservation Force, established on a permanent basis, and expanded to include all Ireland.[59] By the end of March 1822 a police bill had been drafted by Plunket, and only after it had been completed did the chief secretary realize that the proposal contained the features that had made the application of the peace preservation act so difficult. The problem of paying the costs of the proposed police was not solved, nor was that of the relationship between police and magistracy. For although under the earlier measure only the magistrates of a proclaimed area were superseded by the stipendiaries, application of the same principle to a system of police for all Ireland would place the entire magistracy under the authority of Castle magistrates. Goulburn believed that opposition to the proposals might be reduced by giving the local magistrates the right to appoint the constables, subject to certain qualifications established by the government, including the right of the Castle to dismiss them. Wrote Goulburn, 'We should not be subject to the injust imputation of desiring to grasp at the constable patronage.'[60]

It was logical that the chief secretary should turn to Peel for advice in formulating plans for the new police. From scattered bits of information[61] it would appear that Goulburn yielded to

[58] Peel, *Speeches*, i, 203.

[59] Goulburn to Peel, 30 Jan. 1822 (Peel papers, B.M., Add. MS 40328).

[60] Goulburn to Wellesley, 29 Mar. 1822 (Wellesley papers, B.M., Add. MS 37298).

[61] See Peel to Wellesley, 12 Apr. 1822; Goulburn to Wellesley, 13 Apr. 1822 (Wellesley papers, B.M., Add. MS 37299); *Hansard 2*, vii, 852 ff.

the home secretary's greater experience in Ireland and accepted a proposal based on the county police plan worked out, but never used, by Peel between 1815 and 1818. The police were to be established by counties; the detachments were to be commanded by chief constables (without the powers of magistrates) who would have a force of constables and sub-constables. The local magistrates would direct operations of the police, but the Irish government, not the magistrates, would select the chief constable and the members of his force and have the power to discharge them. Apparently stipendiaries could be installed by the government wherever the magistracy was inefficient or numerically weak: 'Thus we would not immediately supersede all local magistrates without reference to abilities and actions, but would have the power to do so if necessary.' To complete the new police, an 'inspecting magistrate' was to 'overlook' the chief constables and their men.

The news that the government was planning to establish a 'general system of police' had two immediate, and hardly surprising, results. Once more letters from job-seekers began to reach the home office and Dublin Castle, and the Dublin *Evening Post* launched a violent attack on the proposed police reorganization. As early as 2 February 1822, the *Post* denounced the resident nobility and gentry of Ireland for failure to perform their duties, a failure which '. . . we are afraid will lead to A NEW PRINCIPLE INTO OUR CONSTITUTIONAL CODE. Having either abandoned their station or perverted their authority, they must be virtually superseded by a GENERAL POLICE.' On 16 March, in a statement in many ways typical of this newspaper, the editor decided that the proposed system of police was unnecessary, for 'Deduct the disturbances of four southern Counties, Limerick, Tipperary, Kerry and Cork from those which are stated to have occurred in other parts of the Kingdom, and the remainder will amount to little more than nothing'. In other editions, the new police were criticized as 'counter to the constitutional justices of the peace'. or were characterized as no more than a colossal patronage scheme.[62] But by August, following the passage of the amended Irish constables bill, the *Post* surrendered and admitted that the County Constabulary was better than a permanent insurrection

[62] Dublin *Evening Post*, 28 May, 11 June 1822.

act: 'Something is needed, but we are still not certain this is it.'[63]

The *Post* was not alone in its opposition to the police proposals. After the intentions of the government had been revealed by the introduction of the Irish constables bill, a number of the Irish members announced their reluctance to support the measure as it stood. Commenting on this opposition, Goulburn wrote,

I have had much difficulty in persuading Irish members to support the constabulary bill and am not sure that I shall secure any very effectual support from them at all. It is not a little disheatening to find that while they admit the evils of the existing system even to a greater degree than I presume to state them they nevertheless will not lend their aid to applying the only effectual remedy.[64]

Clearly the government was faced with a dilemma: the need for a force similar to the proposed Constabulary was widely recognized, but if the measure were pushed through against the wishes of the Irish members, quite probably the Constabulary would encounter the kind of opposition from the country gentlemen that had so limited the effectiveness of the peace preservation act. Compromise was obviously indicated, and compromise could only mean giving a greater degree of control over the new forces to the corrupt, inefficient magistracy.

The most common criticism levelled against the new police system was that it was 'unconstitutional', a term which covered a wide range of opposition. Some of the Irish members felt that it was unconstitutional for the Castle to appoint the personnel for the new police. The Irish magistracy appointed the baronial police; now the Castle proposed to increase its patronage by depriving them of that right. At the other extreme were the opponents of the measure who saw a threat to the constitution in the existence of a large, government-controlled police, 'a species of *gens d'armerie*, hitherto unknown to the laws or practice of a British parliament'.[65] At all levels, there was concern for the financing of such a system. But only on the second reading of the bill on 7 June 1822 did opponents of the measure make the extent of their opposition fully known.

[63] Dublin *Evening Post*, 24 Aug. 1822.
[64] Goulburn to Wellesley, 15 June 1822 (Wellesley papers, B.M., Add. MS 37299).
[65] *Annual Reg.*, 1822, p. 45.

Goulburn opened the debate, justifying the need for police legislation on grounds of the notorious inefficiency of the existing rural police in Ireland. He realized that the bill

might be met with the objection that it was against the principles of the constitution to vest such a power in the hands of the government as the appointment of these constables, but he thought the first constitutional duty of every man was to enforce the observance of the laws.

Plunket was somewhat more effective, presenting the proposed measure as an economy move. The new police would be more expensive than the existing force by only about £40,000 a year, and the efficiency of the new system would result in economies that would outweigh the additional expenditure. 'If the house took into its consideration the saving of public morals, and the probable restoration of peace, obedience, and sober habits to the country, the advantage in favour of the new system would be prodigious.'

The bill was opposed by Spring Rice, Sir John Newport, Sir Henry Parnell, and James Abercromby. In general their arguments concerned the expense of the proposed system, the threat to the constitution, and the increase in patronage for the Castle. It would greatly augment the power of the executive while failing to attain its avowed objectives. But the most surprising, and the strongest, attack made against the constables bill came from Charles Grant, late chief secretary for Ireland and usually a supporter of the present government. By June 1822, the nature of his opposition was clear. To Grant, it was the duty of any government to see justice administered and property protected. But there was another duty of equal importance, to see that in fulfilling these obligations the government did not sacrifice constitutional freedom. The present bill 'went to place the whole of Ireland under an armed police, to subject it to a species of *gendarmerie*, and to render the whole magistracy of the country liable to the control of the lord lieutenant'. Grant was willing to admit that one of the great evils in Ireland was a corrupt, inefficient magistracy and police, but he insisted that the solution to the problem lay, not in changing the system, but in removing the flaws in the old one. He asked the government to tell the members what steps had been taken to purge the magistracy of undesirable elements, and what measures had been applied to obtain a better type of baronial constable. The reply of the government was a simple question: Why hadn't he taken the steps he now advocated, when he was chief secretary?[66]

On the second reading of the bill, the government was able to obtain a majority of fifty-five votes,[67] but evidently Goulburn felt that further and perhaps more serious opposition awaited the bill in its future stages. On 19 June 1822, he complained to Wellesley about the difficulties he was encountering in getting the measure accepted:

I have during the last week worked hard with some of the leading Irish members and have made some impression on them as to the necessity of having such a police as that for which the bill provided. I have made some modifications which do not appear to me to weaken the force of the bill, but if they should be found in practice to do so it will be easier to amend the bill next year than to carry it without modification now.[68]

The modifications mentioned by the chief secretary were more important than his letter implied, and represented a considerable victory for the opponents of the bill. As modified, the bill gave the Irish magistrates the right to appoint the constables and sub-constables for the detachments established in each county. The nature of these appointments could well have a strong influence upon the future success or failure of the Constabulary. But evidently the majority of the Irish members flatly refused to deprive the magistrates of the patronage they possessed in the right to appoint the baronial constables under the existing rural police system. Some time between April and mid-July the portion of the original proposal reserving to the government the right to install stipendiaries at its discretion disappeared from the bill. In the final draft, such a step could be taken by the government only after seven magistrates of the county involved asked the Castle to do so. Furthermore, the stipendiaries used in conjunction with the County Constabulary were to be the equals, not the superiors, of the local magistrates, a major concession to the country gentlemen.

[66] *Hansard 2*, vii, 852–73.

[67] *Hansard 2*, vii, 873.

[68] Goulburn to Wellesley, 19 June 1822 (Wellesley papers, B.M., Add. MS 37299).

Once the necessary concessions had been made to the Irish members, the modified bill passed through the remaining stages without difficulty. The Act[69] which was to regulate the Irish County Constabulary for the next fourteen years was a truly radical departure from the old baronial system. The Constabulary was to be established by counties, and the units, when required to do so, were to obey the 'orders and commands of the magistrates of the county'. The senior Constabulary officers were the inspectors, one for each of the four provinces of Ireland. They were appointed by the lord lieutenant at a salary of £500 per year, and their duties included formulating the rules and regulations for the separate county units. These rules and regulations were to be submitted to the magistracy of the county for confirmation or correction, and sent to the lord lieutenant for his approval. Each county was to be divided into police districts; separate detachments of the Constabulary were to be installed in each barony, half barony, or other division or combination in the same county. The detachments were under the command of a chief constable, also appointed by the lord lieutenant. The chief constable would receive not more than £100 a year, and a house would be provided for him. He was to live in his appointed area, conduct monthly inspections of his force, and report to the chief secretary every three months; he could be dismissed by the lord lieutenant. Constables and sub-constables[70] numbering not more than sixteen for each barony or half barony were to be appointed by the magistrates of the county, at a salary of not more than £30 a year. They were to be under forty years of age, of good character, and able to read and write; no constable or sub-constable could be a 'game-keeper, wood ranger, tithe proctor, viewer of tithes, bailiff, parish clerk, hired servant or tavern keeper'. While the constables and sub-constables were appointed by the magistrates of the county, the lord lieutenant reserved the right to discharge them, and if the magistrates wanted a larger force in a given area than the sixteen men allowed by the act, permission could be given by the lord lieutenant.

[69] 3 Geo. IV, c. 103, 5 Aug. 1822.
[70] The constables acted as non-commissioned officers. Apparently care was taken to avoid military titles; as the *Evening Post* pointed out, 'constable was a good English word' (2 Feb. 1822).

The Constabulary was to be established in the several counties by proclamation of the lord lieutenant. If within fourteen days after this proclamation, the magistrates of the county failed to meet and appoint the necessary constables and sub-constables, the lord lieutenant would make the appointments for them. Arms, equipment, and horses were to be provided by the Irish government, and the lord lieutenant could order the Constabulary of one area to be used in another if the number transferred was not more than two-thirds of the total strength in the home area and if the men were returned when they were no longer needed. When transferred, the constables and sub-constables were under the direction of the magistrates of the new area. Stipendiary magistrates were to be sent into an area where the absence or non-residence of a magistrate made them necessary. Seven magistrates of a county meeting at general sessions were to request the lord lieutenant to take such action, and he was empowered to appoint one or more 'resident magistrates' at a salary of £500 per year plus suitable living quarters. These resident magistrates were not to be the superiors of the local magistrates, but were to work in co-operation with them.

The establishment of the County Constabulary did not end the existence of the Peace Preservation Force. It remained intact, with its powers unchanged, until it was disbanded in 1836. The reasons for continuing the Peace Preservation Force as a separate organization were not stated. It was to be used often in future years where its services as a group of outrage specialists were needed, and evidently the Castle considered it a reserve force over which the government retained complete control, to be used as occasion demanded.

The costs of operating the County Constabulary were to be paid initially by the Irish government; one-half the costs, less certain fines and recognizances collected by the county, were to be repaid by the county to the Irish government by presentment. The method of paying the costs of the Constabulary was evidently satisfactory to the gentry, although some complaints of its expense were to be heard in the future. Under the new system, the maximum payment from any police district was to be approximately one-half of the salaries of the chief constable and a force of sixteen men, plus a percentage of the salary of the inspector. A larger Constabulary establishment could not be forced upon a district, but could be created only with the permission of the magistrates. The difference between the cost of the Peace Preservation Force and that of the County Constabulary to a barony was thus very significant.[71]

Even a summary of the Irish constables act indicates the extent of the retreat of the Irish government from its previously established position concerning the magistracy. From 1812 to 1822, successive members of the Irish government had castigated the magistrates for timidity, inefficiency, and corruption, and the peace preservation act had been designed as an instrument for use against the magistracy as well as against the banditti. Practical considerations had forced the Castle to modify the punitive provisions of the act, but the dissatisfaction with the magistracy remained. In March 1822, noting the plans of one magistrate for bringing about the 'subjugation of his rebellious subjects', Gregory wrote that he had 'no doubt he will succeed, if they do not fire at him too soon; if they do he will be off as fast as his jaunting car will convey him, in which he proposes to head the troops'.[72] In November, Peel, commenting on the problems of a Mr Franks, observed, 'I have heard of more instances of shots through the hat in Ireland without the head being affected, than in any other country.'[73] Yet by the provisions of the constables act, the local magistrates were given control over the operations of the Constabulary and a share in its administration.

One probable reason for the government's concessions has already been given: evidently it was determined not to repeat the mistake made with the peace preservation act by making the Constabulary so unpopular with the 'better classes' that its utility would be impaired. But there is another, less obvious, reason. Apparently no one in government circles questioned the worth of the venerable institution of the magistracy; rather the criticism was directed at its unworthy members. If the institution could be purged of the timid, the inefficient, and the

[71] A sixteen-man detachment cost a barony roughly 75 per cent less than the cost of a complete fifty-man detachment of the Force.

[72] Gregory to Goulburn, 1 Mar. 1822 (Surrey record office, Goulburn papers, box C, pt 1).

[73] Peel to Goulburn, 6 Nov. 1822 (Surrey record office, Goulburn papers, II/14).

corrupt, there was no reason that the Constabulary should not be placed in the hands of a 'reformed' magistracy. Possibly when the Irish members announcd their opposition to a police system which failed to provide a prominent role for the magistracy, it was decided that the solution to the problem lay in purging this institution. The idea of such a reform was not new; a number of lord lieutenants and chief secretaries had considered the possibility of improving the magistracy, only to abandon their plans for various reasons. As early as April 1822, Peel suggested to Wellesley that some plan might be devised for improving the quality of the Irish magistrate, and two possible solutions occurred to the home secretary. It might be possible to comb the rolls and remove the 'bad' magistrates, but it would be even more desirable to issue 'an entire new commission of the peace, superseding all, and reappointing the good ones'.[74] Early in September, Goulburn informed Peel that 'All agree that a reform of the magistracy is necessary'.[75] Here was the solution to the problems created by the necessity of placing the County Constabulary partly under the control of the magistrates. Whether the decision to reform the magistracy came before or after the Irish members forced Goulburn to modify the bill, it is impossible to say. But either way the decision explains the readiness of the government to defer to the wishes of the country gentlemen: a reformed magistracy would not be a serious threat to the success of the new police.

But agreement that reform was necessary was not enough. For all its corruption and inefficiency, the magistracy included men of political significance, and any attempt at wholesale revision was bound to have repercussions in England and Ireland. A majority of Castle and law-court officialdom seem to have favoured the issuing of an entire new commission of the peace, and after a period of responsibility-shifting the matter was forwarded to the king. In October, Peel wrote Wellesley, 'His Majesty has commanded me to signify to your excellency his entire approbation of the proposed revision of the magistracy of Ireland.' A new commission of the peace was to be issued, retaining the names of magistrates with the proper qualifications

[74] Peel to Wellesley, 12 Apr. 1822 (Wellesley papers, B.M., Add. MS 37299).
[75] Goulburn to Peel, 5 Sept. 1822 (Peel papers, B.M., Add. MS 40328).

and adding the names of other 'gentlemen of respectability whose appointments would be desirable'.[76] Liverpool was anxious for the revision to proceed as rapidly as possible, and expressed the hope that 'the Irish government will not sleep on it.'[77] By mid-October 1822 the reform was well under way. The entire matter of issuing the new commission was placed in the hands of the Irish lord chancellor, Lord Manners – with rather confusing results.[78] No attempt was made by the Castle to supervise the selection of those considered qualified for the magistracy. According to Gregory, the 'chancellor's regulations', establishing that attorneys and bankrupts could not be magistrates, were set forth by Manners without consulting the government.[79] On 22 November 1822, Goulburn noted that the new commission for Antrim would be ready the following Monday and that the commissions for the other counties would be compiled in alphabetical order, but the following day he informed Peel that new commissions had been issued for ten counties without any communication with the government.[80]

Just how many magistrates were removed from the rolls in 1822–3 is uncertain, but there are indications that the lord chancellor's efforts were not so far-reaching as the originators of the plan had intended. Possibly attorneys, bankrupts, and some of the more obviously unfit were dropped; but, according to one rural magistrate, out of fifty magistrates in Meath, only four were removed.[81] Even as early as January 1823 the lord lieutenant realized that the revision was 'not perfect' and would need 'frequent and careful reconsideration'.[82] But it was important; as the lord lieutenant noted, 'the mere knowledge . . . of a plan of revision had produced salutary consequences by increasing the diligence, accuracy and careful conduct of the

[76] Peel to Wellesley, 4 Oct. 1822 (P.R.O., H.O. 100/206).

[77] Liverpool to Peel, 9 Oct. 1822 (Peel papers, B.M., Add. MS 40304).

[78] See Greville, *Memoirs*, i, 178.

[79] Gregory to Goulburn, 3 Mar. 1823 (Surrey record office, Goulburn papers, box C, pt 1).

[80] Goulburn to Peel, 22 Nov., 23 Nov. 1822 (Peel papers, B.M., Add. MS 40328).

[81] Testimony of Lord Killeen, *Second report . . . disturbed districts in Ireland*, H.C. 1825 (35), xiii, 164.

[82] Wellesley to Peel, 29 Jan. 1823 (P.R.O., H.O. 100/208).

magistrates'.[83] And following the revision, an effort of sorts was made to achieve 'frequent and careful reconsideration' of the institution – even Gregory's friend Osbourne was told he could not become a magistrate because he was a bankrupt.[84] Willcocks, an eminently qualified observer, believed that following the revision corruption was ended among the magistrates.[85] Even Daniel O'Connell thought that the revision had accomplished good; it did remove some 'bad' men, although it also left some untouched.[86]

The majority of those testifying before the select committee on Irish disturbances in 1825 declared themselves pleased with the new magistracy.[87] But, as the drive for catholic emancipation increased in tempo, the incompleteness of the lord chancellor's revision was to be revealed when the 'new' magistracy met its first real test.

Two additional reforms instituted in Ireland in 1822–3 represent a cautious attempt to lessen discontent by attacking its causes. At the instigation of the lord lieutenant and in the name of 'the equal and unbiased dispensation of justice', strong government pressure was exerted on the magistrates to hold petty sessions in which two or more magistrates would sit publicly, and thus eliminate the possibility of arbitrary action by a single magistrate.[88] This practice was given legal sanction by the petty sessions act of 1827, which also provided for a clerk, fixed fees, records, and established times.[89] The second reform seems to have been suggested by Liverpool and is of some interest, not for what it accomplished, but as the first step in the long struggle to free the Irish peasant from the burden of the tithe. The prime minister was convinced that 'the disturbed state of

[83] Ibid.

[84] Gregory to Goulburn, 1 Mar. 1826 (Surrey record office, Goulburn papers, box C, pt 1).

[85] Testimony of Richard Willcocks, *Second report . . . disturbed districts in Ireland*, H.C. 1825 (35), xiii, 128.

[86] Testimony of Daniel O'Connell, *Second report . . . disturbed districts in Ireland*, H.C. 1825 (35), xiii, 61.

[87] But see Testimony of Michael Collins, *Second report . . . disturbed districts in Ireland*, H.C. 1825 (35), xiii, 345.

[88] See Peel to Wellesley, 22 Mar. 1822 (Wellesley papers, B.M., Add. MS 37328).

[89] McDowell, *Public opinion & govt policy*, p. 81.

the south of Ireland does not originate in . . . political or religious grievances, but . . . with the complicated relation of society and property'. The solution seemed to lie in measures for leasing or commutation of tithes.[90] The result was the Irish tithe composition act of 1823, which allowed the clergyman and the parishioners to appoint arbitrators to determine a fixed money payment due from the parish, as a substitute for the tithe. The act was slow in taking effect, but by 1832 over half the parishes in Ireland had adopted composition, and, as McDowell states, 'if the burden of the tithe was not lessened, the element of uncertainty and other causes of parochial friction were removed'.[91]

The 'peace' that had returned to Ireland in the spring of 1822 was the direct result of the ravages of the famine; it reflected no change in the attitude of the peasantry, and no victory for the government over the banditti. By September, outrages were occurring once more, and since the tithe question was receiving widespread attention in the Irish press, the tithe received equal attention in the programme of the disaffected. Arms raids by gangs continued, and incendiarism became a major problem. A large portion of the burnings were obviously punishments meted out to those who had offended the banditti, but apparently the rest could be explained only as wanton destruction. Bafflement of the local authorities may have turned to suspicion after an investigation revealed that in several instances piles of straw had been set on fire by their owners, who planned to file claims at the assizes for grain destroyed by the banditti.[92]

Throughout the winter of 1822–3, the same dreary situation occupied the Irish authorities. In January, the Castle hopefully reported that the outrages were no longer 'of the former insurrectionary character'.[93] But by spring, disturbing signs of increased activity by the disaffected began to appear throughout Munster. Incendiarism was still widely used by the banditti, causing Wellesley to complain bitterly that few of the perpetra-

---

[90] Liverpool to Wellesley, 22 Mar. 1822 (Wellesley papers, B.M., Add. MS 37328).

[91] McDowell, *Public opinion & govt policy*, p. 74.

[92] See A. Cookley (?) to Carter, 22 Oct. 1822 (P.R.O., H.O. 100/206).

[93] Wellesley to Peel, 29 Jan. 1823 (P.R.O., H.O. 100/208).

tors were arrested, since it was easy to set a fire and disappear.[94] Early in April, over one hundred petitions were filed in Cork requesting compensation for crops destroyed and cattle killed by the terrorists,[95] and there was 'seldom a night without a fire'.[96] By mid-May, however, much to the surprise of the Castle, which was evidently beginning to consider insurrection a normal state of affairs, the banditti armies began to melt away.[97] The combined weight of the insurrection act, the military establishment, and the new Constabulary finally proved too much for the disaffected, and the four-year period of intermittent conflict came to an end.

A logical explanation for the coming of 'peace' in 1823 would be found in the sheer exhaustion of the banditti,[98] and their inevitable realization of the hopelessness of their cause. But Wellesley saw a victory for his reforms,[99] and others gave particular praise to the County Constabulary, which 'by the firm and at the same time temperate conduct of those employed commanded the respect and confidence of the people everywhere'.[100]

The task of forming the detachments of the Constabulary had begun in October 1822, but over two years later the organization was still incomplete, with Antrim, Down, Dublin County, and Louth not yet under the act.[101] The government was determined not to force the Constabulary upon an unwilling magistracy, and the Castle wanted time to gain control, wherever possible, over the appointments of constables and subconstables. To allow patronage to fill the ranks of the Constabulary with incompetents while members of soon-to-be-disbanded units of the Peace Preservation Force were available was

[94] Wellesley to Peel, 8 Apr. 1823 (P.R.O., H.O. 100/208).

[95] Petition of the grand jury of Cork, 5 Apr. 1823 (P.R.O., H.O. 100/208).

[96] Wellesley to Peel, 9 Apr. 1823 (P.R.O., H.O. 100/208).

[97] Wellesley to Peel, 18 May 1823 (P.R.O., H.O. 100/209).

[98] Wellesley comments briefly upon the 'general distrust of each other among the banditti', Wellesley to Peel, 29 Jan. 1823 (P.R.O., H.O. 100/208).

[99] Wellesley to Peel, 27 Apr. 1823 (P.R.O., H.O. 100/208).

[100] See Mahoney to ——, 3 July 1823 (P.R.O., H.O. 100/209).

[101] Police establishment, 24 Nov. 1824 (Peel papers, B.M., Add. MS 40330).

patently ridiculous. The Castle decided that the 'reformed' magistrate could be persuaded to surrender to the Constabulary inspectors his right to appoint the constables and sub-constables.

In King's County and Limerick, the Castle gained the right of appointment without recorded opposition, and in Limerick the ranks of the Constabulary were filled from the Peace Preservation Force detachments in the county.[102] But in other counties the government's task was less easy. The Tipperary magistrates met in November 1822 to decide whether they should appoint the constables and sub-constables of the Constabulary, or give this right to the inspector of the province of Munster. The vote divided at 63–63, and it was necessary for Willcocks (the acting inspector) to reach an agreement with the chairman. It was agreed that Willcocks should appoint several of the baronial constables recommended by the chairman to the Constabulary in return for the chairman's tie-breaking vote.[103] In Cork, the magistrates retained the right to choose four of the sixteen men selected for each barony; the remaining twelve were to be selected by the inspector.[104] The initial success of the Castle in undermining the magistrates' right of appointment caused Goulburn to comment that the magistrates were 'thereby admitting in the fact the propriety of the provisions of the original bill which they all opposed and which they all now professed to wish for'.[105]

It is impossible to say how many of the counties gave the power to appoint constables and sub-constables to the inspector of police or how many took back the power of appointment at a later date. In one instance, Kerry, the Castle met with a flat refusal, due to the influence of the knight of Kerry (Maurice Fitzgerald), who was 'always promoting some little job of his own'.[106] Evidently the magistrates in most of the counties resisted the blandishments of the Castle and retained the right

[102] Testimony of Richard Willcocks, *Second report . . . disturbed districts in Ireland*, H.C. 1825 (35), xiii, 77.

[103] Willcocks to Goulburn, 25 Nov. 1822 (Peel papers, B.M., Add. MS 40328).

[104] Willcocks to Gregory, 8 Apr. 1823 (P.R.O., H.O. 100/208).

[105] Goulburn to Peel, 22 Nov. 1822 (Peel papers, B.M., Add. MS 40328).

[106] Goulburn to Peel, 23 Nov. 1822 (Peel papers, B.M., Add. MS 40328).

of appointment. Initially the Castle had viewed the constables act of 1822 with considerable suspicion, and early in 1823 officials were considering 'alterations and amendments' in the act of the previous session.[107] But by September 1823 Goulburn was able to write, 'The constable bill works remarkably well ... even those originally opposed to it are now loud in its praise, and [it] has been called for in places where we expected strong opposition.'[108]

But the Castle remained fully aware of the faults of the Constabulary, faults that were either unknown or overlooked by many of the country gentlemen who continued to view the 'exemplary police' with high favour.[109] During the early years of the Constabulary, the Castle frequently expressed concern about the character of the men hired as constables and sub-constables. Inspector Powell described his early experiences with the 'ignorant countrymen' of the Constabulary in Leinster:

Unaccustomed as they were to control ... I was obliged to enforce obedience and discipline in a most rigid manner, as the sub-constables disputed the authority of the constable, which brought on repeated altercations and very frequent blows.[110]

Evidently many of the disciplinary problems encountered by the Constabulary officers were caused by excessive drinking within the ranks, and the majority of those dismissed during the first years of the Constabulary were charged with drunkenness. But considering the size of the undertaking – the establishment of an entirely new police system for all Ireland – the men employed were in general satisfactory. During the period from 1822 to 1824, dismissals in no county exceeded 10 per cent.[111]

Nor is there any evidence that religious differences caused serious dissension in the ranks of the Constabulary. In 1824

---

[107] See Willcocks's plan for 'preservation of the tranquillity of the country by private information', 20 Feb. 1823 (Surrey record office, Goulburn papers, box C, pt 1).

[108] Goulburn to Peel, 16 Sept. 1823 (Peel papers, B.M., Add. MS 40329).

[109] W. Blackburn to Gregory, 1 July 1823; W. Newenham to Gregory, 24 July 1823 (P.R.O., H.O. 100/209).

[110] *Minutes of evidence taken before the commissioners appointed to enquire into charges of malversation in the police establishment of the Leinster district*, H.C. 1828 (486), xxii, 198.

[111] *Return of the Constabulary in Ireland*, H.L. 1824 (4), xiii, 111–12.

there were 1,825 protestants and 845 catholics in the organiza-
tion.[112] The ardent supporters of catholic emancipation saw the
Constabulary as a dangerous stronghold of protestantism:
Richard Sheil, O'Connell's close associate, said,

When I find a decided minority of Roman catholics in the police
where there is a decided majority in the population, and where I find
the police are selected from the lower orders, I must consider
religion as the principle on which the selection is made.[113]

In contrast to Sheil, Willcocks maintained that in his area, half
of the police and eight of the chief constables were catholic, and
that he paid no attention to the numbers of catholics and
protestants in the police and 'knew of no distinction between
them'.[114] One of the judges, relying on information gained while
on circuit, agreed that protestants did predominate in the
Constabulary, but insisted that this situation was largely
traceable to the requirements that all applicants for the jobs
with the police must be able to read and write. It is possible that
not even the chief constables knew for certain just how many
catholics served in their units. According to one police official,
when the Meath Constabulary was formed, twenty-eight men
were chosen from the militia, and the charge was made that not
one of the group was catholic. An investigation was conducted,
and Powell claimed that twenty of the twenty-eight were found
to be of that religion; they had hidden the fact out of fear of
dismissal.[115] But there was no directive from Dublin Castle
establishing a catholic–protestant ratio within the units of the
Constabulary.

With the restoration of a 'normal' degree of tranquillity to
the countryside in 1823, the question of the Irish military
establishment again presented itself. It had taken over two years
to repair the damage caused by the economy drive of the
Talbot–Grant period, and by mid-1823 the strength of the

[112] Number of police by religion and offences, Apr. 1824 (Peel papers,
B.M., Add. MS 40611).
[113] Testimony of Richard Sheil, *Third report . . . disturbed districts in
Ireland*, H.C. 1825 (36), xi, 98.
[114] Testimony of Richard Willcocks, *Second report . . . disturbed districts in
Ireland*, H.C. 1825 (35), xiii, 86.
[115] Gregory to Goulburn, 7 Mar. 1824 (Surrey record office, Goulburn
papers, box C, pt 1).

establishment had risen only to about 21,000 men.[116] Now it appeared that another reduction was imminent, for troops were needed for the West Indies, and it was proposed to take them from Ireland. As home secretary, Peel had to break the news to Goulburn, and he presented the case for reduction by pointing to 'the probabilities . . . that the gradual extension and improvement of the police system will enable you to execute the law with a smaller military force than you at the present have'.[117] In his reply to Peel, Goulburn used arguments that Peel himself had used under similar circumstances when he had been chief secretary:

I do not consider that the police force is likely to relieve you for some time to come from the necessity of keeping up a considerable military force. At the present it is rather a substitute for the old civil force of constables than for troops and . . . we should risk the efficacy of the new system if we left it too soon to struggle unsupported. . . .[118]

The chief secretary was apparently able to convince Peel that a sharp reduction of the military force was unwise, and the figure of approximately 20,000 men became the accepted one for the establishment during the next seven years.

In January 1825 the four inspector-generals of police, Thomas D'Arcy for Ulster, Thomas Powell for Leinster, George Warburton for Connaught, and Willcocks for Munster, were officially installed in their positions.[119] Under their command was a force now totalling 4,500 men, 'greatly improved in efficiency, conduct, appearance and discipline', and viewed with satisfaction by the local authorities.[120] As for the condition of the Irish countryside, Willcocks stated that in eighteen years of service he had never seen Munster in 'better shape'.[121] In describing Connaught, Warburton wrote of 'peace

---

[116] Goulburn to Peel, 15 Nov. 1823 (Peel papers, B.M., Add. MS 40329).

[117] Peel to Goulburn, 23 Oct. (?) 1823 (Peel papers, B.M., Add. MS 40329).

[118] Goulburn to Peel, 15 Nov. 1823 (Wellesley papers, B.M., Add. MS 37301).

[119] Wellesley to Peel, 26 Jan. 1825 (P.R.O., H.O. 100/210).

[120] Willcocks to Goulburn, 20 Sept. 1825 (P.R.O., H.O. 100/210).

[121] Ibid.

and prosperity as I have never before witnessed',[122] and D'Arcy found 'perfect tranquillity' in Ulster.[123] With one reservation, the lord lieutenant shared the optimism of the inspectors. Writing to Liverpool, Wellesley said,

Every measure, insurrection act, police, tithe bill, revisions of magistracy, petty sessions, better administration of law, has succeeded beyond my most sanguine hopes. The general prosperity of the empire begins to reach Ireland. Prices have improved, rents and even tithes are better paid, and in the districts which had been most disturbed the people are turning their attention to pursuits of industry and honest labour, instead of plotting or executing schemes of outrage and violence. . . . In short, I should have been able . . . to present the gratifying tribute of *Ireland tranquillized* to his majesty were not the general prosperity and happiness disturbed by the noisy fury of the Catholic Association. . . .[124]

The exception to the 'general prosperity and happiness' was a notable one, for from 1825 to 1829 the history of Ireland was in many ways to be the history of the Catholic Association.

[122] Warburton to Goulburn, 12 Aug. 1825 (P.R.O., H.O. 100/210).
[123] D'Arcy to Goulburn, 16 Sept. 1825 (P.R.O., H.O. 100/210).
[124] Wellesley to Liverpool, 22 Nov. 1824, in C. D. Yonge, *The life and administration of Robert Bankes Jenkinson, second earl of Liverpool* (London, 1868), iii, 312–13.

IX

CATHOLIC EMANCIPATION,
1823–9

EVENTS IN IRELAND between 1823 and 1829, when Daniel
O'Connell and his associates led the final drive for catholic
emancipation, are among the most dramatic in the history of
modern Britain. For years, the Castle had been examining
reports of banditti activities, fearful of finding evidence of
leadership of 'a higher order' that might convert the dis-
organized, faction-ridden Irish peasantry into a revolutionary
army. With O'Connell and the Catholic Association, the
peasantry found such leadership, and with it a common purpose.
For catholic emancipation was the one goal on which all catholic Ireland could agree, the one cause which could unite the
small landowner, the townsman, the peasant, and – of great
importance – the priest in a common effort. Although the
removal of the catholic disabilities was a goal but imperfectly
understood by the Irish peasant, emancipation was accepted as
a kind of embodiment of victory over an ascendancy responsible
in some way for all the grievances of the Irish countryside. Thus
the catholic peasantry, organized and disciplined as never
before, were willing to place themselves at the disposal of the
eloquent O'Connell. Undoubtedly had O'Connell called upon
this group to take arms at any time between 1826 and 1829 the
majority would have done so, but armed revolt was not his
intention. Instead, he considered the massive organization that

he and his associates had created to be a political pressure group with which to conduct a propaganda campaign, calling the attention of Great Britain to the plight of the Irish catholics, challenging and harassing the politicians and making the task of governing Ireland as difficult as possible, and exploiting to the utmost the threat of revolution. But in the need for an effective threat O'Connell had created a problem for the Association as well as for the government, for the emotions of the Irish peasantry had to be kept at fever pitch, without allowing them to erupt into serious violence. The major question for the government and for the Association became one of O'Connell's continuing ability to control a peasantry poised on the edge of revolt.

During the early years of the Association, the Irish government appeared confident that the military establishment and the Constabulary could handle any uprising, even one on the massive scale that appeared to threaten at this time. But by 1828 there were serious doubts of the reliability of the army and the police. Under the strains of the emancipation crisis, the system of law enforcement revealed flaws that demanded mending; and at the same time the army once more proved itself an imperfect instrument for maintaining order. These weaknesses in the forces at the disposal of the government were to contribute to the victory of the emancipationists in 1829.

The Catholic Association was founded by O'Connell and a group of fellow-barristers in 1823. During its first year, despite the talents of its leader – described at a later date as 'such a master of the law that he can do ten times more mischief than Lord Edward Fitzgerald and Mr Emmet without incurring any legal penalty'[1] – the Association proved no more effective than similar organizations of the past. In November, Goulburn explained to Peel that he had not sent a report on recent proceedings of the Association because 'the newspapers have given as full an account as that furnished by our short-hand writer'; unless the situation changed, he proposed to follow the same procedure in the future.[2] To the chief secretary, the 'popish parliament' appeared dull rather than dangerous, and

---

[1] Lord John Russell to Sir Herbert Taylor, 21 Oct. 1835 (P.R.O., Russell papers, series 30/22, box 1).

[2] Goulburn to Peel, 10 Nov. 1823 (Peel papers, B.M., Add. MS 40329).

he thought that probably it would soon fade from existence.[3] Peel was less willing to dismiss the new organization as unimportant; he wanted more information about its membership and activities, and suggested steps the government might take to limit its influence.[4] But at this time the tendency in the upper reaches of government was to view the Association as a nuisance, an organization to be watched, but no real threat to the established order. In the spring of 1824, the attention of the Castle was diverted to the Irish countryside, where more familiar signs of trouble were beginning to appear in a sudden revival of the agrarian secret societies, which seemed bent on 'the subversion of order and the war against property'. Although Kilkenny was the centre of their efforts, indications of their presence were felt in the surrounding counties also.[5]

In the midst of the growing concern occasioned by these outrages, the government was confronted for the first time with the agents of the Catholic Association and the collection of the 'catholic rent' in rural areas. After the initial period of inefficiency, the Association had made a momentous decision. At the instigation of O'Connell, it had decided to raise a 'fighting fund' by collecting small regular subscriptions from catholic Ireland. O'Connell realized that he was suggesting something more than a method of raising funds, for the payment of a small subscription would commit the contributors to the aims of the Association, and thus give the movement a powerful unity and sense of direction absent from previous efforts to remove the catholic disabilities.[6] But even O'Connell, for all his vanity and imagination, could hardly have foreseen the result of the catholic rent. As the Association grew in numbers and influence, the catholic clergy abandoned their traditional reluctance to become directly involved in politics and openly worked for the movement – on occasion even collecting the rent in their parishes. Within a few months of the inception of the catholic rent, the Association experienced an outstanding growth; from

[3] Goulburn to Peel, 16 Nov. 1823 (Peel papers, B.M., Add. MS 40329).
[4] Peel to Goulburn, 13 Nov., 14 Nov. 1823 (Peel papers, B.M., Add. MS 40329).
[5] Goulburn to Peel, 16 Apr. 1824 (Peel papers, B.M., Add. MS 40330).
[6] 'The beginning of the rent marks the transition of the Catholic Association from a small club into a mass movement.' Reynolds, *Catholic emancipation*, p. 17.

a small group of Dublin barristers meeting above Coyne's Book Shop, it expanded to include all Ireland in a network of committees, so that by the beginning of 1825 it was claimed that every parish had an Association agent.[7]

The simultaneous appearance of disturbances and Association agents in 1824 spread uneasiness and alarm from the police barracks and magistrates' homes of the Irish countryside to the home office in London. Peel expressed 'anxiety and apprehension' over the activities of the Association and deplored its 'imitating the forms of parliament' and 'levying a rent or tax or whatever it may be called . . . for very indefinite public objects'.[8] Legal action was considered, but Plunket, the attorney-general, advised that the organization could not be prosecuted under existing law, and the lord lieutenant seemed reluctant to support the necessary new legislation.[9] Thus about all that was done at this time was to examine the numerical strength of the police, army, militia, and yeomanry in Ireland,[10] possibly in anticipation of the need to act against the banditti, the Association, or both working together. Meanwhile tension continued to rise. A chief constable in Kilkenny placed the blame for the disturbances in that region directly at the feet of one Mr Ford, an agent for the Catholic Association: '. . . this man's machinations have of late not only created a dislike on the part of the peasantry towards the Constabulary, but even great opposition to law – for previous to this committee being formed all was tranquillity'.[11] Goulburn considered the spread of Ribbonism (to the chief secretary, all banditti were Ribbonmen), new outbreaks of violence, and the catholic rent as certainly connected,[12] an understandable attitude in the light of reports from the Constabulary. The uneasy tranquillity of such traditional trouble-spots as Limerick had become an unnatural silence connected with the 'machinations' of the priests and the

[7] Fitzgerald to Peel, 24 Jan. 1825 (Peel papers, B.M., Add. MS 40332).

[8] Peel to Goulburn, 14 Apr. 1824 (Peel papers, B.M., Add. MS 40330).

[9] Peel to Goulburn, 14 Apr. 1824; Goulburn to Peel, 20 Apr. 1824 (Peel papers, B.M., Add. MS 40330).

[10] Goulburn to Peel, 5 June 1824 (Peel papers, B.M., Add. MS 40330).

[11] John Henderson to Powell, 20 Oct. 1824 (P.R.O., H.O. 100/210).

[12] Goulburn to Peel, 10 Nov. 1824 (Peel papers, B.M., Add. MS 40330).

expectations of some great event, undoubtedly a general uprising of the Irish catholics.[13]

As the association grew, the 'popish parliament' accelerated its flow of criticism against the government. Considerable attention went to the activities of the police, and there followed a series of Association-conducted prosecutions against policemen involved in affrays with the peasantry. A sub-constable named Talbot was convicted of murder after he had accidentally killed a suspect during a struggle. An angry Gregory wrote to his superior, 'Talbot, according to popish impartiality, deserved death being not only a policeman, but a protestant.'[14]

By November 1824 those responsible for Irish affairs were bracing themselves for the shock of revolution. Peel informed Goulburn of 'the apprehensions entertained by many persons of some immediate danger', and warned the chief secretary that he could not express 'too strongly' his opinion 'that every precaution should be taken'.[15] The warning was hardly necessary, for Goulburn was expecting 1825 to be a 'year of war'. For the moment, he rejected an offer of additional troops; the present establishment of 20,232 men was in excellent shape, and more soldiers would only stir up discontent. As for other instruments at the disposal of the Castle, the chief secretary had 'a tolerable assurance in the fidelity and intelligence of the police', who covered Ireland so completely that no meeting could take place without their knowledge. The Constabulary now numbered 4,300 men, 'trained in the use of arms and to a certain degree as soldiers'. The chief secretary appeared quite optimistic concerning the ability of the Irish government to cope with an uprising, but was bothered by the lack of accurate information, especially about 'what goes on in the chapels'.[16]

It was Wellesley who was finally able to separate the activities of the agrarian secret societies from those of the Association, thus enabling the Irish government and the cabinet to drop their

[13] G. Draught to Goulburn, 1 Nov. 1824; Goulburn to Peel, with enclosures, 16 Nov. 1824; H. Wray to Powell, 29 Nov. 1824 (P.R.O., H.O. 100/211).

[14] Apparently the sentence was commuted. Gregory to Goulburn, 16 Aug., 22 Aug. 1824 (Surrey record office, Goulburn papers, box C, pt 2).

[15] Peel to Goulburn, 19 Nov. 1824 (Peel papers, B.M., Add. MS 40330).

[16] Goulburn to Peel, 26 Nov. 1824 (Peel papers, B.M., Add. MS 40330).

military preparations and concentrate on less spectacular methods of breaking the power of O'Connell and his organization. Writing for the lord lieutenant, his secretary said, 'He has looked most narrowly into the rumours and representations of danger from all quarters and he feels no alarm. This is not the result of ignorance or prejudice, but of knowledge.' The Irish people in general were well disposed, and looking to the Catholic Association 'for some indefinite good of which they have no clear idea. I do not think [they] look to obtain it by force of arms . . . I do not think that violence is the present game of the Association . . .'.[17] Liverpool accepted Wellesley's analysis without reservation,[18] and by mid-December Goulburn had come around to the belief that an uprising was not imminent.[19] But Peel was more difficult to convince: '. . . even if you are perfectly satisfied that there are no preparations for insurrection and massacre, that fact – though it may expose the absurdity of some and the exaggeration of others – must not by any means be considered decisive. . . .'[20]

By the end of 1824, there was a growing realization in Dublin Castle and at Westminster that O'Connell and the Association hoped to achieve their goal by peaceful methods, but no one dared assume that this situation would continue. The connection linking the secret societies, outrage, and the Association had been weakened in the minds of Castle officialdom, but it had not been broken. The emotions of the Irish peasantry were dangerously near the boiling point, but under the discipline imposed by the Association outrages and other crimes declined rapidly, and faction fights decreased in number. The question remained of the ability of O'Connell and his associates to control the force they had helped to create. As Goulburn saw the situation in December 1824,

The immediate danger that I contemplate is a sudden ebullition of fanatical fury in particular places, originating not in any settled or premeditated plan, but in some casual circumstance operating upon

[17] Col. Shaw to Liverpool, 6 Dec. 1824 (Peel papers, B.M., Add. MS 40304).
[18] Liverpool to Peel, 10 Dec. 1824 (Peel papers, B.M., Add. MS 40304).
[19] Goulburn to Peel, 14 Dec. 1824 (Peel papers, B.M., Add. MS 40304).
[20] Peel to Goulburn, 24 Dec. 1824 (Surrey record office, Goulburn papers, II/13).

the mind of a people easily excited at all times and now in a state of unusual and extreme excitation.[21]

Here was a situation that no government could endure: the Association was becoming a substitute government to which much of Ireland gave allegiance. The policy-makers of the Irish government shared O'Connell's determination to avoid revolution if possible, but were equally determined to break the power of the Association – even the Castle 'catholics' seemed frightened by the magnitude and success of the movement. One effort to break the Association resulted in the passage in March 1825 of an act, to remain in force until 1828, making societies similar to the Association illegal.[22] The association was promptly dissolved, only to reappear as the New Catholic Association, with its programme tailored to avoid violating the law. While the activities of the Association were slowed down somewhat, the government had found no answer to the power of the movement.

The act of 1825 indirectly aided the Association in imposing discipline on the peasantry by curbing the activities of the Orange lodges. The arrival of Wellesley in 1822 had caused an upsurge of Orange activity. The anger felt by the Dublin Orange lodges over the appointment of a 'catholic' lord lieutenant had led to the Dublin playhouse 'riot' of December 1822. Wellesley had been hissed as he entered the theatre, and during the performance a bottle had been thrown at him as he sat in his box. 'Wellesley's attention was thus forcibly directed to the proceedings of the Orange societies.'[23] In 1823, an ineffective act had been passed prohibiting the administering of 'unlawful oaths' – an example of 'neutral' legislation, applying as it did to both the agrarian secret societies and the Orange lodges. As events progressed, it became apparent that any attempt to suppress the Association by legislation would have to apply to the Orange lodges.[24] The Orangemen, with their drums, flags, and anti-catholic songs, threatened the fragile peace of the countryside. As Peel had said several years earlier, it was

[21] Goulburn to Peel, 14 Dec. 1824 (Peel papers, B.M., Add. MS 40304).
[22] 6 Geo. IV, c. 4, 9 Mar. 1825.
[23] Walpole, *England from 1815*, ii, 294.
[24] Peel to Wellesley, 24 Sept. 1824 (Peel papers, B.M., Add. MS 40330); Peel to Goulburn, 24 Sept. 1824 (Surrey record office, Goulburn papers, II/13).

necessary 'to keep the laws which exclude catholics from a place in the direction of public affairs, but the . . . mortification arising from such exclusion should not be increased by irritating ceremonies'.[25] The act of 1825 forbade 'political confederacies', and the Orange lodges were considered to be organizations of this description.

From 1825 to 1828 the Orange organization was illegal, and the leadership – the 'lawyers, placemen, and political Orangemen' – chose not to act in defiance of authority.[26] But the rank and file of the northern lodges were quite capable of ignoring both leadership and the law. In 1826, riots followed processions staged by Ulster Orangemen, but serious religious disorders did not develop at this time. One reason for this is obvious: as Goulburn pointed out, 'The protestant proceedings are of a nature to render them accessible to the law. They hoist flags, they carry swords, they go in procession to church decorated with ribbons.'[27] And it has been suggested that during 1825–8 the activities of O'Connell and his associates were not of the sort to pose the serious and immediate threat to Ulster protestantism that was necessary for a revival of militant, lower-class Orangeism.[28] It was fortunate for the public peace that the Orange lodges did not choose to challenge the rising power of the Association at this time. By 1826, Goulburn believed that the biggest threat to the peace in Ireland lay in the bitterness existing between the two religions: 'Never were Roman catholic and protestant so decidely distinguished and opposed – never did the former act with so general a concert.'[29] There must have been many in Ireland at this time who viewed the restraint imposed upon the lodges with surprise and wondered how long the truce could last. The duke of Wellington undoubtedly expressed the feelings of many of those associated with Irish affairs when he wrote, 'We are in a curious state in all our relations, and it appears to me scarcely possible that we should get out of all our difficulties without a crisis.'[30]

[25] Peel to Wellesley, 11 Nov. 1822 (Peel papers, B.M., Add. MS 40324).
[26] Senior, *Orangeism, 1795–1836*, p. 280.
[27] Goulburn to Peel, 25 July 1826 (Peel papers, B.M., Add. MS 40332).
[28] Senior, *Orangeism, 1795–1836*, pp 217–19.
[29] Goulburn to Peel, 25 July 1826 (Peel papers, B.M., Add. MS 40332).
[30] Wellington to Peel, 1 Aug. 1826 (Peel papers, B.M., Add. MS 40307).

The 'curious state' was to continue, for the initiative had passed completely from the government to the Association. The Castle could do nothing but wait anxiously for a mistake that would allow the Irish government to break O'Connell's hold on Ireland. In the general election of 1826, the Irish forty-shilling freeholders 'revolted' and, against the wishes of most of the landlords, elected pro-emancipation candidates in Waterford, Lough, Westmeath, and Monaghan. Prior to 1829, the forty-shilling freehold franchise in Ireland included those who rented as well as those who owned the requisite amount of land; thus the landlord was in a position to control the votes of his tenantry by threats of eviction. But the 1826 revolt was not unexpected, since for several years the Castle hierarchy had assumed that the next general election would be a lively one. In March, plans were made to protect pro-'protestant' freeholders, for as Gregory noted, '. . . if they have not protection, they will be murdered on the road'.[31] Considerable disorder occurred during the elections, but there was no widespread violence of a serious nature. Waterford, considered a likely trouble-spot, was flooded with soldiers and policemen and remained relatively calm. Some violence appeared in Galway. But the most serious outbreak came in Kerry, where according to the military authorities the magistrates had failed to take the necessary precautions; several were killed and fourteen wounded in a clash between the rifle brigade and the crowd at Tralee, and it was necessary to postpone the poll until military reinforcements arrived.[32] Weeks later the commander of the forces was still concerned with the 'legacy' of the election, which caused 'exultation on one side, and a good deal of indignation upon the other', and with the possibility of a serious clash caused by 'accident'.[33]

Although the 'year of war' that Goulburn had expected in 1825 had not materialized, and no serious trouble had arrived by the beginning of 1826, the peace was still an uneasy one. Some officials viewed the situation optimistically. In January

[31] Gregory to Goulburn, 15 Mar. 1826 (Surrey record office, Goulburn papers, box C, pt 2).

[32] 30 June, 5 July 1826 (P.R.O., W.O. 80/6).

[33] Gen. Murray to Sir Herbert Taylor, 23 Aug. 1826 (P.R.O., W.O. 80/6).

1826, Willcocks reported on the 'exceptional peace' in Munster, and added that 'what renders it still more gratifying is that the relinquishment of outrage has not been effected by coercive measures but gradually attained by legitimate causes'.[34] But it had been almost three years since the last period of protracted rural violence had ended, and in October it seemed that even the influence of the Association and the priests could not stop the working of the agrarian crime cycle. The summer of 1826 was both hot and dry, and was complicated by an outbreak of 'fever'. A poor harvest was followed by an increase in rents; trouble appeared in Athlone in early October and quickly spread into Westmeath, Longford, Roscommon, and Sligo, and by December into Mayo and Galway. The pattern of these disturbances was the familiar one: arms raids, incendiarism, and brutal punishments for those who offended the banditti. The Castle immediately took advantage of the provisions of the constables act to appoint resident magistrates for the thinly-populated areas in Westmeath and Longford, and moved detachments of the Constabulary from the quiet areas of these counties into the disturbed portions. It is interesting to note that the police officials in these areas did not blame this most recent outbreak of disorder on the Association, but placed the blame on economic causes.[35] Even Goulburn, arch-opponent of O'Connell and the Association, suggested that the reasons for the disturbances were to be found in the 'timidity and ineffici-ency of the magistrates' and in the 'misery' of the lower classes.[36]

The disturbances of the winter of 1826–7 offered the first real test of the capacities of the reformed magistracy, on which Wellesley and his associates had looked so benignly a few years earlier. But in the face of outbreaks of violence, the confidence of the government in its 'reformed' magistracy proved sadly unjustified. Late in December 1826, Goulburn lashed out at the magistrates of Westmeath and Roscommon, who were acting surprisingly like the old magistracy. The recent general election had left considerable bitterness between the magistrates of these counties, and they refused to meet to 'make a declaration of their determination to stop outrage'. Portions of Roscommon were

[34] Willcocks to Wellesley, 12 Jan. 1826 (P.R.O., H.O. 100/216).
[35] Inspectors of police, 2 Jan. 1827 (P.R.O., H.O. 100/217).
[36] Goulburn to Peel, 29 Dec. 1826 (P.R.O., H.O. 100/216).

without the services of a magistrate, but there was no application for a resident magistrate; instead there came the familiar request for the insurrection act.[37] Peel and Goulburn made no effort to hide their feelings of disgust over this reversion to type. The request for the insurrection act was brushed aside, and it was suggested that steps be taken to install the Peace Preservation Force in the disturbed areas.[38]

The failures of the 'reformed' magistrates in Roscommon and Westmeath were not isolated instances. By January 1827, Tipperary was considered threatened with disturbance, and the current Tipperary magistracy also proved strikingly like its predecessors. Willcocks complained angrily about the lack of assistance given to the Constabulary by the Tipperary magistrates. Frequently '. . . it could not be had, or . . . would not be afforded, arising out of some cause or other, . . . frivolous excuses have frequently been made to the chief constable when he made such requisitions to individuals.'[39] On 27 January 1827, Wellesley received a petition from Tipperary asking for the insurrection act,[40] and there followed the familiar deadlock between the government and the magistrates. In October 1827 a resolution from the magistrates assembled at Cashel re-stated the case for the act, describing Tipperary as 'a vast depot of hidden arms',[41] but again the Castle refused to consider their wishes. A resident magistrate in Munster reported in late November that he was trying to 'help' the magistrates of Tipperary to work with the police, but with disappointing results; at the most recent 'riotous' fair, not a single magistrate had appeared.[42] By the end of 1827, it was obvious that the reform of the magistracy, considered reasonably successful two years earlier, had been at best incomplete. This fact offered little reassurance to a government faced with the possibility of full-scale revolution.

[37] Ibid.

[38] Goulburn to Peel, 29 Dec. 1826 (P.R.O., H.O. 100/216); Peel to Goulburn, 2 Jan. 1827 (P.R.O., H.O. 100/217).

[39] Willcocks to Gregory, 16 Mar. 1827 (P.R.O., H.O. 100/220).

[40] The grand jury of the county of Tipperary to Wellesley, 27 Jan. 1827 (P.R.O., H.O. 100/217).

[41] Resolution of the magistrates at Cashel, 20 Oct. 1827 (P.R.O., H.O. 100/218).

[42] Carter to Thomas Spring Rice, 24 Nov. 1827 (P.R.O., H.O. 100/219).

The precarious truce achieved for the Catholic camp by the Association and the priests, and for the Orange lodges by the restrictions imposed by the government, continued to hold with occasional exceptions well into 1827. But by July the Castle was growing increasingly apprehensive. Information received by the government indicated that 12 July, the Orangemen's 'independence day', was to be the date of a show of strength by the lodges throughout Ireland, and the Castle was determined to stop them. Throughout the country, wherever Orangemen lived in sufficient numbers to cause trouble, the Constabulary was alerted and detachments of soldiers were moved in to assist if needed.[43] The 12th of July passed in Dublin without incident,[44] and the first reports received at the Castle from the rest of Ireland seemed to indicate that the precautions taken by the government had been successful. The situation had been in doubt for a while in the Granard area of Longford, where an armed procession of Orangemen had marched through the countryside firing guns and singing anti-catholic songs. The constables and troops were not strong enough to disperse them, but fortunately members of the 'opposite party' refrained from giving battle.[45] On the 14th, Wellesley added a personal note to the sheaf of reports, crediting the success of the government's efforts to the police and the 'display of public force', and commenting that there had been no trouble in the entire country.[46]

But Wellesley had written before the last of the reports reached the Castle; the exception to the otherwise tranquil state of Ireland proved to be, of course, Tipperary. Much to the astonishment of the Constabulary officers in Tipperary town, the soldiers sent to help them had marched into the town wearing orange-coloured lilies. The reaction of the townspeople was instantaneous, and order was restored only after the troops had been withdrawn and a reinforcement of sixty-six constables had been rushed from another area.[47] Fortunately this disturbance remained localized, and the inhabitants of Tipperary town

[43] Wellesley to inspector of police, 2 July 1827 (P.R.O., H.O. 100/220).

[44] Richard Butt to military secretary, 13 July 1827 (P.R.O., H.O. 100/217).

[45] Lt. Home to Lt. Charles Cotter, 13 July 1827 (P.R.O., H.O. 100/217).

[46] Note by Wellesley, 14 July 1827 (P.R.O., H.O. 100/217).

[47] Willcocks to Gregory, 14 July 1827 (P.R.O., H.O. 100/217).

showed no inclination to continue the argument after the troops had left. With 12 July behind, the government had weathered another crisis, and evidently the majority of both catholic and Orange camps were still anxious to avoid trouble. But the Tipperary incident had underlined for the Castle the ease with which similar events could destroy the precarious truce between the two parties, and plunge all Ireland into chaos.[48]

The remainder of 1827 passed without serious incident. Late in July, at Edenderry in King's County, the yeomanry made their first appearance in years, twenty strong, marching in an Orange procession.[49] In Tipperary in November, the local factions resumed their feuds, and for several weeks the Magpies and the Black Hens tested their strength against each other and the police.[50] But as the year ended, Ireland was exceptionally quiet; only Tipperary remained disturbed.[51]

The autumn harvest had been excellent, and there was 'no cause to apprehend a scarcity of provisions during the winter'; but as one observer noted, 'the tranquillity or otherwise will depend much on the description and temper of the speeches made at the Catholic Association'.[52] By January 1828, however, the Castle had something more serious to contend with than inflammatory speeches. After the general election of 1826, the Association had avoided direct action, but on 13 January 1828 the first of the simultaneous parish meetings organized by the Association were held in about 1,600 of the 2,500 parishes of Ireland, attended by those who supported O'Connell and emancipation. Obviously these meetings were intended as a show of strength and perhaps as a gesture of defiance to the newly formed Wellington government. If so, they had the desired effect, for to Peel they seemed to provide the 'fatal precedent of a people gathered into a solid and perilous confederacy'.[53] The parish meetings marked the opening round of the final campaign for catholic emancipation.

[48] See Carter to Gregory, 18 July 1827 (P.R.O., H.O. 100/220).
[49] Lord Lansdowne to lord lieutenant, 30 July 1827 (P.R.O., H.O. 100/217).
[50] O'Donoghue to William Lamb, 6 Nov. 1827 (P.R.O., H.O. 100/219).
[51] Maj. Miller to Spring Rice, 6 Dec. 1827 (P.R.O., H.O. 100/219).
[52] Powell to Lamb, 14 Oct. 1827 (P.R.O., H.O. 100/219).
[53] *Memoirs by the Right Honourable Sir Robert Peel*, ed. Earl Stanhope and E. Cardwell (London, 1856), i, 50.

One of the major reasons for the Association's limiting its activities in 1827 primarily to verbal barrages lay in political events in Great Britain. In January 1827, Liverpool had been followed as prime minister by Canning, a supporter of emancipation. Peel resigned the home office to be replaced by Canning's friend Sturges Bourne, and Goulburn was replaced by another supporter of emancipation, William Lamb (the future Lord Melbourne). Emancipation was still an 'open question' in the reconstituted cabinet, but the 'catholics' had strengthened their position, and it seemed possible that under the leadership of Canning emancipation might finally be achieved. But in August Canning died, and was succeeded by the bumbling, incompetent Lord Goderich. In January 1828 a new government was formed under Wellington, with Peel as home secretary and leader in the house of commons. Thus by the beginning of 1828 the government was under the leadership of two opponents of emancipation, and the possibility that the cabinet might take the lead in removing the catholic disabilities appeared most unlikely.

In December 1827, Wellesley resigned as lord lieutenant and left Ireland, 'where he had perhaps neither friend nor foe but wished him away'.[54] Wellington's former commander of cavalry, the marquess of Anglesey, was selected to succeed Wellesley, and when the duke formed his cabinet in January 1828, Anglesey's appointment was continued. The new lord lieutenant, who has been characterized as knowing 'nothing whatever about anything except women and war',[55] may have appeared eminently qualified to the ultra-protestants in Ireland. In 1825 he had told the Lords that 'if the battle must be fought, I would fight it in the best position I could find; and I can look to none so good as that in which we at present stand'.[56] Actually, Anglesey's public pronouncements on the catholic question tended to be somewhat misleading; prior to his appointment, he seems to have been inclined to favour emancipation itself, but was militantly opposed to the Association and its activities.

Anglesey's relations with Wellington deteriorated rapidly. Anglesey was arrogant and outspoken, and Wellington was

[54] Gregory, *Letter-box*, p. 235.
[55] O'Mahoney, *Viceroys of Ireland*, p. 229.
[56] Marquess of Anglesey, *One-leg* (London, 1961), p. 180.

made even more uneasy by the lord lieutenant's whig-Canningite connections and possibly also by his rather emotional attachment to the Irish people. The rift was further widened by Anglesey's changing attitude towards the catholic question: the former cavalryman knew when a battle was lost, and in July he wrote to the chief secretary, 'There may be rebellion, you may put to death thousands, you may suppress it, but it will only put off the day of compromise, and in the meantime the country is still more impoverished and the minds of the people are if possible still more alienated. . . .'[57] The remainder of his tenure as lord lieutenant was punctuated by a series of quarrels with Wellington. Following O'Connell's victory in the Clare election, the prime minister and the home secretary were forced to accept emancipation as the only sensible way out of an impossible situation. Convinced that their decision must remain completely secret until the king's opposition to emancipation was overcome, they did not inform Anglesey that concession was in the offing. Thus in an atmosphere of mounting anger the lord lieutenant bombarded Wellington with demands for action, while the prime minister refused to inform him that O'Connell had in effect already won. In December 1828 the cabinet agreed to Anglesey's recall.

The new lord lieutenant, the duke of Northumberland, held office until the resignation of the tory cabinet in 1830. Reputedly the wealthiest peer in Britain, Northumberland was described by Greville as 'a very good sort of man, with a very narrow understanding, an eternal talker, and a prodigious bore'.[58] This opinion of the lord lieutenant was echoed by others – Lady Gregory relates a standing joke concerning Northumberland's giving a deputation of distressed weavers an order for a waistcoat.[59]

Lamb remained as chief secretary until his resignation in late May 1828. He was succeeded by Lord Francis Leveson Gower, who brought to Ireland a slight reputation as a poet, excellent family connections, and limited talents for the demanding job he had assumed. But he enjoyed good relations with Peel and Northumberland, and survived as chief secretary until 1830.

The news of the parish meetings scheduled by the Association

---

[57] Ibid., p, 201.   [58] Greville, *Memoirs*, i, 241–2.
[59] Gregory, *Letter-box*, p. 262.

for January 1828 seemed to Lamb to herald the arrival of Armageddon. The county authorities were instructed to have the Constabulary in a state of readiness, but 'out of sight' to avoid creating apprehension and alarm.[60] An impressive number of people attended these meetings, but there was surprisingly little violence, and of course no revolution.[61] It is impossible to determine how greatly the excitement caused by the parish meetings in January was responsible for the outbreak of agrarian crime in central Ireland during the following month. By early February, Leitrim was showing signs of restlessness, and the spread of 'Ribbonism' in Roscommon caused the Castle some alarm, for it was 'occurring at the wrong time of year'.[62] Tipperary, which had never been entirely peaceful since 1826, now became seriously disturbed, and during May the baronies of Eliogarty, Middlethird, and Clanwilliam witnessed an average of at least one outrage every other day.[63] The recurrence of widespread violence in these baronies was obviously the work of the agrarian secret societies; their efforts were directed against rent increases and evictions, and in some instances their goal seems simply to have been robbery for profit.[64] No attempt was made by the Castle to blame this state of affairs on the Association, and the authorities proceeded to move against the secret societies as they had so often in the past. An informer was placed in the 'headquarters' of the secret society of Louth, and by the time he had completed his task two hundred banditti were reported to have fled to Scotland and America.[65]

By mid-May the disturbances began to diminish and soon ceased entirely, but this relatively unimportant outburst of rural crime aided, if indirectly, the victory of the emancipationists. The parish meetings of January, and the disorders that followed, had caused the Castle to conduct an investigation into the efficiency of the Irish military establishment,[66] and here

[60] Lamb to lord lieutenant, 6 Jan. 1828 (P.R.O., H.O. 100/221).

[61] Reports, inspectors of police, n.d. (P.R.O., H.O. 100/221).

[62] Gregory to Lamb, 19 Feb. 1828; Case and opinion, 3 May 1828; Warburton to Gregory, 26 May 1828 (P.R.O., H.O. 100/221).

[63] Tipperary outrages, May 1828 (P.R.O., H.O. 100/221).

[64] Ibid.

[65] Case and opinion, 3 May 1828 (P.R.O., H.O. 100/221).

[66] Anglesey to Col. Maxwell, 15 Feb. 1828 (P.R.O., H.O. 100/224).

the lord lieutenant believed he saw indications that the catholic soldiers had been 'won over' by O'Connell and his followers.[67] By early 1828 there was serious concern in the upper reaches of government about the effectiveness of the army if called upon to suppress a catholic uprising.

Traditionally, higher ranking officers tended to view the role of the army in Irish affairs with some dissatisfaction. As the commander of the forces, Sir George Murray, complained in 1825, he was unable to consider the army in Ireland 'with reference to its power as a military body, but rather with reference to its capacity for meeting all the demands that the civil government have been in the habit of making upon it'.[68] The use of soldiers as policemen interfered with the main mission of the army, the defence of Ireland, and caused numerous annoyances ranging from additional problems of discipline to involvement in politics.[69] The response of the military was what might have been expected – strict observance of general regulations and neutrality in Irish affairs. According to Murray, the army was not to 'give the slightest indication of party feeling or give offence to any party'.[70] But with the emancipation question growing ever more pressing, neutrality became difficult to maintain. Murray continued to insist that 'military men should keep . . . separated from all party feelings connected with that subject',[71] but by the time the months of crisis arrived in 1828–9, entire units had declared themselves on the issue of catholic emancipation.

Official concern over the possible influence of the Association among the Irish catholic soldiers had appeared as early as October 1826. Ireland had been for years the most fertile recruiting ground for the British army, and many of the regiments had a high proportion of Irish catholics in their ranks. As Goulburn wrote, 'It is not easy to pronounce beforehand that this religious excitement will not operate on Roman catholic soldiers, in a disturbance which, if it arises, will assume

[67] Anglesey to Peel, 25 Mar. 1828 (P.R.O., H.O. 100/224).
[68] Murray to Taylor, 10 Oct. 1825 (P.R.O., W.O. 80/1).
[69] In 1826 a magistrate had a military detachment arrested following a clash with local moonshiners. Col. Wedderburn to C. R. Trefuses, 14 Feb. 1826 (P.R.O., W.O. 80/6).
[70] Wedderburn to Col. Hancox, 19 July 1826 (P.R.O., W.O. 80/6).
[71] Murray to Gen. Bingham, 13 July 1826 (P.R.O., W.O. 80/6).

the character of a crusade.' But the chief secretary immediately qualified this statement, adding, 'Do not suppose that I have at present the least doubt as to the fidelity of the army. I am merely adverting to what may hereafter be the case.'[72] Sir Herbert Taylor warned Murray that religious controversy might have a dangerous influence on catholic soldiers.[73] Whether the reliability of the catholics in the army was actually undermined by the efforts of the Association and the priests it is impossible to say. During 1827–8, a considerable number of reports reached the authorities concerning efforts to subvert the soldiers and warning of possible mutiny.[74] But most of the reports had a familiar ring: as with so many reports from the rural areas in the past, they paraded the fears of the author, but provided little information of sufficient reliability to justify action by the authorities. Priests were haranguing the soldiers, some of whom were contributing to the catholic rent. A Captain Masterson was accused by a 'red-hot protestant' of attending Association meetings and distributing 'seditious papers'; a sergeant was reported as being 'upon rather too intimate terms with the people of the country'.[75] Given the excitement engendered by the final drive for emancipation, the emotional involvement of numbers of catholic soldiers with the cause is not surprising. But despite warnings from some field commanders, the military leaders in Dublin refused to be stampeded and continued to hold to Murray's policy of keeping emancipation an 'open question' within the army.

Of added concern to the authorities were the activities of some of the protestant soldiers. The appearance of the Orange-decorated soldiers in Tipperary on 12 July 1827 was an example; the previous year, a detachment of the Seventh Dragoon Guards had taken part in an Orange celebration, and their drinking and 'obnoxious songs' had attracted the attention of the press.[76] The letters and reports amassed during the investigation of the Tipperary affair testify to the government's concern.[77] Not only

[72] Goulburn to Peel, 31 Oct. 1826 (Peel papers, B.M., Add. MS 40332).
[73] Taylor to Murray, 24 Dec. 1826 (P.R.O., W.O. 80/1).
[74] For examples, see P.R.O., H.O. 100/220–2.
[75] Wedderburn to Taylor; Wedderburn to Maj. Eeles, 7 Mar. 1827 (P.R.O., W.O. 80/6).
[76] Wedderburn to Hancox, 19 July 1826 (P.R.O., W.O. 80/6).
[77] P.R.O., H.O. 100/220.

was the reliability of the catholic soldiers in doubt, but it was also possible that the army itself might become divided into hostile religious factions. And added to this gloomy prospect was the possibility of clashes between protestant soldiers and catholic civilians, to the detriment of the uneasy truce then prevailing in the countryside. But the investigation of the Tipperary incident led only to the punishment of several of the soldiers and the transfer of the regiment from Ireland to a much warmer climate.

By mid-1828 the lord lieutenant and the prime minister were both convinced that the army would not be fully reliable. Wellington viewed with suspicion the presence of large numbers of catholics in the ranks and wrote of 'precautions taken respecting Roman catholic soldiers'. Anglesey was convinced that the catholic soldiers were under the domination of the Association and the priests. At least one regiment, he reported, was split into protestant and catholic factions, bitterly hostile to each other, and he suggested that it might be necessary to replace some of the Irish troops with men recruited in other parts of the British Isles.[78] Apparently the military authorities attempted to lessen the chances of catholic contagion among the troops by leaving reinforcements intended for Ireland in west England, to be transported to Ireland should the need arise. Here they would be safe from the influence of the Association and the priests, but readily available to cross the Irish Sea. By early autumn, 1828, all available forces in England were camped on the English west coast, while the Irish establishment itself was increased only slightly.[79] In a gloomy letter dated 24 September 1828 the chief secretary informed Peel that 'on this side everything is in readiness to meet [any] contingency, as far as our means allow'.[80]

As tension mounted in Ireland and fear began to grow that the army might not be reliable, the Constabulary assumed a position of even greater importance.[81] By 1827, the Constabu-

[78] Wellington to Peel, 21 July 1828 (Peel papers, B.M., Add. MS 40307); Anglesey to Peel, 20 July, 27 July 1828, in Peel, *Memoirs*, i, 158–9, 164.

[79] See Wellington to Peel, 20 October 1828 (Peel papers, B.M., Add. MS 40308).

[80] Leveson Gower to Peel, 24 Sept. 1828 (P.R.O., H.O. 100/223).

[81] Miller to Lamb, 14 Dec. 1827 (P.R.O., H.O. 100/220).

lary had been installed in all the counties, and totalled 5,244 officers and men.[82] Although the personnel of the Constabulary were in part catholic, the Castle seems to have been confident of their loyalty and, perhaps because they were singled out by O'Connell as objects of vilification,[83] the propaganda of the Association seems to have had little effect upon the catholic sub-constables. Also, as Goulburn had suggested in 1826, the police were 'too roughly handled by the mob to be friendly to them'.[84] But, while Goulburn was convinced that the Constabulary was trustworthy, Peel had doubts. A sizeable portion of the organization were catholic and thus suspect to the home secretary, who could not free himself from the fear that loyalty to their religion might undermine the reliability of the police should revolution occur.[85] Commenting on what has been described as 'one of the most foreboding aspects of the crisis',[86] Peel wrote to Sir Walter Scott in 1829,

We were watching the movements of tens of thousands of disciplined fanatics – abstaining from every excess and every indulgence, and concentrating every passion and feeling on the single object – with hundreds of police and of soldiers, half of whom were Roman catholics. That half, faithful and prepared, I have no doubt, to do their duty, but is it consistent with common prudence and common sense to expect such scenes and to incur such risk of contagion?[87]

But whether or not the catholic policemen were reliable, a major flaw in the police system was increasingly apparent in another direction. As long as the control of the Constabulary was shared between the government and the magistrates, the inefficient and obstructive country gentlemen could greatly limit the effectiveness of this instrument. In Tipperary in 1827 the magistrates continued to press for a return to the insurrection act, and sulked and refused to co-operate with the Castle when their request was refused.[88] It took over four months to get the

[82] *Return of the number of chief constables, constables and sub-constables in the several counties in Ireland*, H.C. 1826–7 (409), xx, 27–9.

[83] See Reynolds, *Catholic emancipation*, p. 109.

[84] Goulburn to Peel, 31 Oct. 1826 (Peel papers, B.M., Add. MS 40332).

[85] Peel to Goulburn, 29 May 1828 (P.R.O., H.O. 100/222).

[86] Gash, *Peel*, p. 524.

[87] Peel to Sir W. Scott, 3 Apr. 1829 (Peel papers, B.M., Add. MS 40399).

[88] Gregory to G. Hutchinson, 4 Apr. 1827 (P.R.O., H.O. 100/217); Lamb to Lansdowne, 18 Oct. 1827 (P.R.O., H.O. 100/218).

Tipperary magistrates to agree to increase the strength of the Constabulary detachments in seven baronies in the western half of the county.[89] From Connaught, Inspector Powell wrote of the split in the magistracy over the religious question, which made it difficult for them to work together.[90] Thus the major instruments of the Irish government for suppressing disorder and possibly revolution were showing signs of serious weakness at the moment when the long struggle for catholic emancipation was reaching its climax, the Clare election of 1828.

The story of this famous election has been told many times. Vesey Fitzgerald, member for Clare, was appointed to the presidency of the board of trade and thus forced to vacate his seat and stand for re-election. O'Connell was persuaded to contest the seat, although as a catholic he could not sit in the house of commons. The Waterford election of 1826 had been a portent of what was to happen in Clare in 1828. On 5 July, after five days of polling, Fitzgerald withdrew from the contest. The effect of O'Connell's victory was quite clear. As Professor Gash observes, 'The 1826 election had shown that the Irish representative system could be captured; Co. Clare in 1828 showed that it could be destroyed.'[91] What had happened in Clare was certain to be repeated in an increasing number of Irish constituencies, but a catholic, legally elected to parliament, was debarred by law from membership.

If O'Connell were refused his seat in parliament, civil war might follow, a war which the government was ill-equipped to handle. But the widely repeated assertion that Wellington 'surrendered' in mid-1828 and accepted emancipation as the alternative to revolution needs qualification. In a recent study of the emancipation controversy in England, G. I. T. Machin suggests that Wellington conducted a strategic withdrawal rather than a surrender: the duke saw concession as a means whereby he could strengthen his efforts to restore order. Emancipation, passed into law with proper safeguards, would

---

[89] F. Prittie to Wellesley, 26 Jan. 1827 (P.R.O., H.O. 100/217); Gregory to Hutchinson, 4 Apr. 1827 (P.R.O., H.O. 100/217).

[90] Powell to Lamb, 26 Oct. 1827 (P.R.O., H.O. 100/218); see correspondence between Wellington and Anglesey, 1829 (Durham University, Grey papers, box 4).

[91] Gash, *Peel*, p. 523.

check the insidious growth of democracy in Ireland, strengthen the ministry by rallying the English 'catholics' to it, and thus enable Wellington to get the support from parliament necessary to halt agitation and deal with possible revolution.[92] In a sense, the duke was hoping not only to restore order to the countryside, but also to restore the pre-Association political order. Both Wellington and Peel abhorred the idea of a civil war, but if rebellion came despite their efforts the government was determined to crush it. There was general agreement among the official policy-makers that the Association did not want an uprising, but there was doubt that the catholic leaders could keep their followers in check. As Peel wrote to Anglesey late in July, 'Whatever are our hopes that there will be no actual collision, it is true policy and true mercy to be well prepared. All parties will agree that any attempt at insurrection must be promptly and effectively put down. The more promptly and the more decisively, the less would be the ultimate evil.'[93]

Before the emancipation bill could be introduced in parliament the stubborn opposition of the king had to be overcome, and until the royal permission was granted Wellington's proposal had to be kept secret. As the tension in Ireland increased, following the Clare election, catholic processions and mass meetings began to occur, and there was again the question of the Association's power to control the peasants and keep religious animosity in check until emancipation could be granted.

The discipline exercised over the Irish peasantry by the Association and the priests had never been more apparent than during the Clare election. It has been estimated that between 40,000 and 50,000 peasants assembled in Ennis at this time, but violence was so rare as to be almost unknown. One observer stated that 40,000 of the peasants went so far as to renounce all forms of alcohol for these days, and the large masses of peasants moved in and out of town in military formation, led by 'officers'.[94] During the weeks following the election, the

[92] G. I. T. Machin, *The catholic question in English politics, 1820–1830* (Oxford, 1964), pp 123–4; Wellington to Peel, 12 Sept. 1828 (Peel papers, B.M., Add. MS 40307); Harriet Arbuthnot, *The journal of Mrs Arbuthnot 1820–1832*, ed. F. Bamford and the duke of Wellington (London, 1950), ii, 107–99.

[93] Peel to Anglesey, 23 July 1828 (Peel papers, B.M., Add. MS 40325).

[94] Reynolds, *Catholic emancipation*, pp 157–8.

discipline of the lower classes continued. There were exceptions in mid-July, when many of the rural towns and villages 'illuminated' to celebrate O'Connell's victory and some of the protestants who refused to place candles in their windows were attacked by catholics, but such incidents were infrequent. It was reported to the Castle that the priests were doing everything possible to keep their parishioners from drinking and fighting at the fairs, and that the population was 'under the most absolute control of the priests'.[95]

There is no evidence of any overt activity by the agrarian secret societies during the crucial months following the Clare election. If the evidence provided by police officials and the chief secretary's office is at all reliable, in 1826–7 and in early 1828 banditti leadership prevailed over the leadership of the Association in several of the traditional trouble-spots of the countryside. But during the months of crisis, and despite nearly ideal conditions for their activity, the banditti were conspicuous only by their lack of action. Apparently the secret societies finally had found leadership of a 'higher order' – O'Connell and the Association; if this happened, and it is logical to assume that it did, banditti acceptance of outside leadership may have been of vital importance in the final drive for emancipation.

But there were signs of increasing restlessness among the catholic lower classes. Chafing under the restraints imposed by their leaders, the peasants showed a marked tendency to fight among themselves. During July and August, reports were received from Tipperary, Limerick, and Monaghan of serious clashes between catholic factions.[96] The catholic leaders immediately turned their attention to this threat to the unity of the movement, and wherever factions were causing trouble meetings were called by the Association, which had some success in effecting agreements between the groups.[97] In Tipperary, the 'three-year-olds' and the 'four-year-olds', bitter enemies for years, met and arranged a truce. They then marched in formation to the house of the local priest, gave a cheer for 'O'Connell and independence', and planted a tree in the

[95] A. Hill to Gregory, 21 July 1828 (P.R.O., H.O. 100/222).

[96] Abstract of reports of outrages, Aug. 1828 (P.R.O., H.O. 100/222).

[97] Reynolds, *Catholic emancipation*, p. 149.

fairgrounds as a symbol of unity.[98] At Eliogarty, the local
schoolmaster and agent of the Association assembled 'between
five and six thousand' of the local inhabitants and informed
them that catholic emancipation was close and that they must
unite to stop fighting at the fairs. They were instructed to return
to their homes peacefully, 'and on no account to assemble as
they were now'.[99] In Kilferman, the members of two factions
were assembled at the chapel to settle their difficulties. An
agreement was reached, but not until a final fight had taken
place, ending with the 'most riotous taken away by friends'.[100]

But this practice of calling large groups together to settle their
differences had an unforeseen effect that alarmed the catholic
leaders. O'Connell's rural followers began to meet without
receiving instructions from their leaders. In August, an estimated
10,000 men in three distinct formations marched into Cappagh-
white to the sound of drums and fifes, merely to celebrate the
reconciliation of the factions.[101] From Thurles, Wilson reported
that formations of 4,000 or 5,000 men were 'parading' on
Sundays,[102] and at Bonisoleigh a formation of 2,000 men in
makeshift uniforms marched through the town.[103] At Cashel in
early September, '394 mounted and 756 foot in array quite
military' paraded in the town, which had been decorated with
green boughs and was illuminated at night.[104]

Both the catholic leaders and the Irish government were
thoroughly alarmed at this independent action by the peasants.
The danger was real, and the reaction of the prime minister was
an angry determination to halt the processions and mass-
meetings of the catholics: 'I am for the prosecution of everybody that can be prosecuted.'[105] Strong action by the government was certain to make it even more difficult for the catholic
leaders to maintain order. The catholic clergymen had particular

[98] Chief-constable Donlan to Miller, 20 July 1828 (P.R.O., H.O.
100/222).
[99] Tipperary outrages, 31 Aug. 1828 (P.R.O., H.O. 100/222).
[100] Ibid.
[101] Abstract of reports of outrages, Aug. 1828 (P.R.O., H.O. 100/222).
[102] Wilson to Gregory, 2 Sept. 1828 (P.R.O., H.O. 100/222).
[103] Reports of outrages since 23 September (1828) (P.R.O., H.O. 100/
222).
[104] Carter to Gregory, 7 Sept. 1828 (P.R.O., H.O. 100/222).
[105] Wellington to Peel, 14 Oct. 1828 (Peel papers, B.M., Add. MS 40308).

reasons for concern; in several instances when the priests attempted to stop unauthorized meetings and parades, their parishioners refused to listen to them. The Association doubled its efforts to regain control over the peasant groups,[106] who were warned that their assemblies had caused alarm in government circles, and that trouble resulting from their actions might fatally damage hopes for catholic emancipation.[107] The Association sent 'pacificators' to southern Ireland in an attempt to persuade the local groups to discontinue these meetings, for the Association realized that if the Irish government attempted to break up the assemblies the results might be tragic, and catholic emancipation, which was about to be won, might be lost. Moreover, there was always the possibility of a clash between the catholic groups and the protestants, to be avoided at all costs.[108] It was the threat of revolution, not revolution itself, that would force the British government to grant emancipation. The Castle 'proclaimed' the processions and assemblies illegal, but it was the activities of the 'pacificators' that ended the meetings. By November 1828 the authority of the Association seemed to be re-established over the catholic 'armies'.[109] But if the meetings of the catholics ceased to be of pressing concern after November, both the Association and the Castle now found themselves faced with a new and equally serious problem – the appearance in Ireland of a militant, ultra-protestant organization known as the 'Brunswick clubs'.

The Brunswick clubs, which first appeared late in the summer of 1828, were conceived as ascendancy counterparts of the Catholic Association, complete with a 'protestant rent' and dedicated to the idea that only by joining together could the Irish protestants hope to protect their interests. Peel attempted to explain the establishment of these 'protestant action' clubs by stating that the 'Brunswickers have risen because they think the government has deserted them',[110] but the lord lieutenant was contemptuous of them:

[106] Reynolds, *Catholic emancipation*, pp 152–3.

[107] Address to the Roman catholics of Tipperary, 25 Sept. 1828 (P.R.O., H.O. 100/223).

[108] Reynolds, *Catholic emancipation*, pp 152–3.

[109] See Miller to Leveson Gower, 7 Nov. 1828; Statement of outrages in Tipperary, Nov. 1828 (P.R.O., H.O. 100/223).

[110] Peel to Anglesey, 22 Sept. 1828 (Peel papers, B.M., Add. MS 40326).

. . . the Orangemen, or I suppose I am now to call them the Brunswickers, are rivalling the Association both in violence and in rent.
Two associations and two rents is rather formidable. . . . The
[Brunswickers are] certainly not very flattering either to the king or
to his ministers, . . . or to his army, since they deem it necessary to
take the whole under their special protection.[111]

According to Anglesey, the catholic leaders were certain that
the Brunswick clubs had been formed for the purpose of causing
a serious clash between the two religions, thus ruining the
chances of emancipation.[112] If this was the purpose of the
organization, it soon appeared that it might succeed. The mere
presence of the clubs among the catholics of the south was
enough to infuriate them, but added to this was the rumour
that the 'protestant rent' was being used to purchase arms for
use against the catholics.[113] Wherever a club was established,
trouble was apt to follow.

A club was formed at Mount Shannon in Clare in October,
and by 1 November it was reported that 'a protestant cannot
go a mile from his home and hope to get back'. The rumour
spread from Mount Shannon into Tipperary that the priest in
this town had been beaten by the protestant clergyman and was
dying. The catholics in north-west Tipperary were planning to
attack Mount Shannon and burn it in retaliation when this
scheme was discovered by the Constabulary.[114] From Mount
Shannon, rumours reached Tomgrany, where the Constabulary
barracks and the houses of the protestant inhabitants were
smeared with blood,[115] and at Clonland, catholic labourers
refused to work for protestants. Signal fires burned at night, and
the local authorities believed an uprising to be imminent.[116]
The religious conflict continued to spread, until, about six days
after the incident at Mount Shannon, it covered an area extending from Limerick City to Roscrea, created by the 'ultra zeal
of the clubbists'.[117] But here it stopped, perhaps because the

---

[111] Anglesey to Peel, Sept. 1828 (Peel papers, B.M., Add. MS 40326).
[112] Ibid.
[113] See *Annual Reg., 1828*, p. 138.
[114] W. Coffey to Leveson Gower, 1 Nov. 1828 (P.R.O., H.O. 100/223).
[115] Warburton to Leveson Gower, 6 Nov. 1828 (P.R.O., H.O. 100/223).
[116] J. Beirdon to Warburton, 4 Nov. 1828 (P.R.O., H.O. 100/223).
[117] Miller to Leveson Gower, 7 Nov. 1828 (P.R.O., H.O. 100/223).

Association quickly sent agents into the area to re-establish discipline.[118]

In Longford, a similar situation developed. A Brunswick club was established at Eyrecourt, and certain catholics of the area informed the members, by posting a notice,

. . . that there shall be no Brunswick meeting allowed here this week or at any other time. We shall if in our power prevent any such meeting – or if any of the Killaltanagh [a neighbouring town] prejudiced ruffians attempt to come here, we shall with the utmost exertions stone them to death.[119]

Presumably this threat had the desired effect, and Eyrecourt remained undisturbed.

In general, the fear that the protestant areas of the south, excited by a revival of militant protestantism as preached by the Brunswickers, might be turned into centres of conflict, proved unwarranted. Perhaps it was because of the overwhelming strength and the organization of the catholics, or it may have been due to the attitude of many of the protestants 'who have an interest in the security of the state [and] are anxious for the settlement of the question . . .'.[120] Late in 1828, the Munster inspector-general reported with surprise that throughout most of his area the two religions existed together with no trouble whatever.[121]

But the place to expect trouble between protestants and catholics was in the north. Throughout 1828, Ulster had been relatively quiet, but by the end of the year signs of serious disturbances were beginning to appear. In September, 'Radical Jack' Lawless, 'the Don Quixote of the Association',[122] had invaded this portion of Ireland on a speaking tour that seemed calculated to create trouble. As he described it, he 'galloped up the hills followed by fifty thousand people, and all the clergy', determined to visit 'all the strongholds of the Orangemen'.[123] At Armagh he was met by an armed body of protestants gathered from the entire county, and was forced to retreat.

[118] J. Gleason to W. Burke, 9 Nov. 1828 (P.R.O., H.O. 100/223).
[119] Dated Eyrecourt, 16 Dec. 1828 (P.R.O., 100/226).
[120] *Annual Reg.*, *1828*, p. 141.
[121] Miller to Leveson Gower, 7 Nov. 1828 (P.R.O., H.O. 100/223).
[122] Reynolds, *Catholic emancipation*, p. 33.
[123] *Annual Reg.*, *1828*, p. 139.

The same thing happened at Ballyboy, and Lawless ended his tour without making good his threat to 'exterminate the "Orange reptiles" and whip the Brunswickers into the walls of Derry'.[124] Following the 'invasion', Ulster was for a time deceptively quiet, but the actions of Lawless had made a protestant reaction inevitable.

Late in December the tension between the two religions in Ulster broke into violence. On 23 December, following a fair in Tyrone, a body estimated at 500 men invaded the protestant town of Augher, shouting 'Augher is our own!' The townspeople rushed from their homes to dispute this claim, and a pitched battle followed with both sides reinforced by their co-religionists from the countryside. The parties fought until forced by sheer exhaustion to end the affray, and the town was nearly destroyed.[125] Several days later, at Balleymena, Orangemen marched in procession through the town, singing party songs, firing shots, and 'calling out for the face of a papist'. The Constabulary were able to stop the clash, and on the same day they were able to break up an attack on the home of a catholic in Armagh and arrest eleven of those involved.[126] On 28 December an Orangeman was beaten to death by a mob at Poyntz Pass in Armagh. When the Constabulary attempted to intervene, they were 'beaten into their barracks', but finally regained control and arrested five of the attackers.[127] Throughout January 1829, reports of similar incidents reached the Castle in increasing numbers, and to the consternation of Constabulary officials in Ulster, the high sheriff of Fermanagh announced plans to hold a 'vast meeting of protestants' in Ulster to petition parliament against catholic emancipation.[128]

But the meeting was never held, for on 5 February 1829, George IV, in the speech from the throne, proposed the revision of the laws imposing civil disabilities on His Majesty's catholic subjects. The Wellington government and the Association had won the race against time, and lower-class Ireland under 'leadership of a higher order' had won an astonishing victory.

---

[124] Reynolds, *Catholic emancipation*, p. 150.
[125] W. Henry to D'Arcy, 23 Dec. 1828 (P.R.O., H.O. 100/226).
[126] J. Clarke to D'Arcy, 27 Dec. 1828 (P.R.O., H.O. 100/226).
[127] P. Brennan to D'Arcy, 28 Dec. 1828 (P.R.O., H.O. 100/226).
[128] D'Arcy to Leveson Gower, 12 Jan. 1829 (P.R.O., H.O. 100/226).

Before many months had passed, the 'new' Ireland created by emancipation seemed to be showing all the unpleasant traits of the old. The peasants, freed from the discipline of the Association, returned to their violent ways and, as the lord lieutenant saw it,

The intemperate partisans of the recent relief bill had looked for an instant civilization as the first of its effects – The bigoted opponents of that measure have prognosticated its tendency to produce turbulence and bloodshed. Between the fears of one party and the scarcely stifled hopes of the other, truth is but little to be expected.[129]

Peel believed that he knew precisely what Ireland needed, and during the short time left to him as home secretary he attempted to put into effect his solution to the basic problem:

Call it by what name you please, police or constabulary force – this is certain – that the reduction of Ireland to peaceful habits and obedience to the law must be effected by the agency of an organized-stipendiary-civil force whose exclusive province and profession it shall be to execute the law.[130]

[129] Northumberland to Peel, 14 July 1829 (Peel papers, B.M., Add. MS 40327).

[130] Peel to Leveson Gower, 14 Aug. 1829 (Peel papers, B.M., Add. MS 40337).

X

THE AFTERMATH OF
EMANCIPATION, 1829–30

~~~~~~

AND SO THE 'Brobdingnagian debate, which stretching over a quarter of a century fills hundreds of columns of Hansard',[1] had finally ended, leaving the tory party not strengthened, as Wellington had hoped, but seriously weakened. The ultra-tories, furious at the surrender of their leaders, continued to attack the government.[2] Wellington and Peel, who had been thought bulwarks against catholic emancipation, became the targets of scorn and abuse; Peel even lost the privilege of representing his beloved Oxford at Westminster. But Peel and Wellington were no happier in their capitulation than their critics were; they had not been 'converted' and they remained certain that their previous opposition to emancipation had been wise and just.[3]

In February 1829, Peel set about making use of benefits that might accrue to the government once emancipation became law. The three bills involved removed the catholic disabilities, dissolved the Association, and disenfranchised the lowest level of the rural Irish electorate by raising the franchise qualification

[1] McDowell, *Public opinion & govt policy*, p. 85.
[2] For an account of the progress of the bill through parliament and the aftermath of its passage, see Machin, *Catholic question*, chapters 8, 9.
[3] See Peel to bishop of Limerick, 8 Feb. 1829 (Peel papers, B.M., Add. MS 40398).

from forty shillings to ten pounds. The logical next step was to transfer the allegiance of the peasant from the 'demagogue' to the state, and Peel warned, 'Let us beware that we do not teach them how it will be to paralyse the government and the law'.[4] Emancipation might make the government's task easier; it would lessen Irish discontent and, of greater importance, it might

enable us to command the assent of a great majority in parliament to measures calculated not merely to repress casual outrages and insurrectionary movements, but to habituate the people to a vigorous unsparing enforcement and administration of the law, criminal and civil.[5]

The Irish policy of the Wellington government in 1829 was essentially an extension of the programme of the Liverpool government, aimed at restoring law and order and effecting a programme of reforms to provide 'a system of measures for the permanent civilization of Ireland'.[6] The home secretary was convinced that the first step lay in restoring rule by law, without which no further measures toward improvement could succeed:

I postpone the consideration of extensive schemes for the employment, and education, and improvement of the people, and address myself to the discussion of two measures which are indispensable to the success of all such schemes – the constitution of a thoroughly efficient police, and the punishment of crime. . . .[7]

As in the past, Peel envisioned an efficient police as a step towards the betterment of Ireland, not as a means of repression, and 'ten years' experience of the advantage of obedience will induce a country to be obedient without much extraordinary compulsion'.[8] A cabinet committee (Peel, Goulburn, and Vesey Fitzgerald) was formed to consider Irish measures, and the first to be considered was a revision of the Constabulary: 'The first duty of the government is to maintain public peace, and there is ample evidence that it is endangered.'[9]

After the emancipation bill had received the royal assent on

[4] Ibid.
[5] Peel to Leveson Gower, 30 July 1829 (Peel papers, B.M., Add. MS 40337).
[6] Ibid.   [7] Ibid.   [8] Ibid.
[9] Peel to Leveson Gower, 20 July 1829 (P.R.O., H.O. 100/227).

12 April 1829, the Irish government braced itself for the wave of violence expected to greet the news in rural Ireland. But, although the news was the cause of widespread celebration, the Castle found instead of violence 'the enjoyment of tranquillity far surpassing the most sanguine expectations of those who anxiously contemplated this peculiar crisis'.[10] As so often before, however, official optimism was to prove premature. With emancipation a reality, the Association ceased to exist; O'Connell was determined to push for repeal of the union, but many of his associates had no interest in such a campaign.[11] His tremendous influence over the peasants continued, but the powerful organization that he and his associates had created was gone, and with it had gone the discipline that had been exercised over the lower classes. To the discomfort of the Castle, even the influence of the priests over their parishioners seemed to be slipping away,[12] and by mid-1829 the restlessness of rural Ireland was making itself increasingly felt.

Perhaps the return of the peasant to his violent ways was aided by the disillusionment sure to follow from his imperfect understanding of the meaning of emancipation. Lady Gregory relates a conversation she had many years later with an old farmer who remembered the events of 1829:

When the bill passed, there were bonfires lit all about the village, and on top of the hill, and the greatest excitement that ever was. The people didn't know exactly what it was about. They thought O'Connell and Sheil would stream gold into their pockets, and I know some what wouldn't sow a crop in those years because they had been told the millennium was coming.[13]

At the same time, some of the Irish landlords were doing their part in inciting the peasants to violence. Minor eviction campaigns had been under way on a limited scale since the Clare election of 1826,[14] and following emancipation the evictions seem to have increased considerably. One John Dillon was reported in May 1829 to be dispossessing his tenants at the rate of

[10] Northumberland to Peel, 4 May 1829 (P.R.O., H.O. 100/226).
[11] McDowell, *Public opinion & govt policy*, p. 139.
[12] See Carter to Leveson Gower, 7 July 1829 (P.R.O., H.O. 100/227).
[13] Gregory, *Letter-box*, p. 267.
[14] Northumberland to Peel, 4 May 1829 (P.R.O., H.O. 100/226).

seventy a day, assisted by a large body of police from several stations.[15]

But the immediate cause of violence in July was to be found once more in the activities of the Orangemen (the act that had dissolved the organization had expired in 1828). Although the Brunswick clubs had gradually faded after emancipation, the lodges found new inspiration in the exertions of the duke of Cumberland, the most repulsive of the royal dukes and a Brunswick leader. As grand master of the Orangemen, he advised his followers that their organization was necessary to the survival of the protestant religion in Ireland and that they should remain organized and disciplined, but should avoid breaking the peace.[16] Wellington saw in Cumberland's statement a deliberate attempt to cause trouble, and the charge was made too often to be ignored, that the Orangemen were determined to cause enough disturbances to prove their case against emancipation.[17] If the lodges were set on creating difficulties for the government, they were successful; from late June to the end of August, Constabulary officers' reports devoted much attention to the clashes between groups representing the two religions.[18] And, as if to prove the case for the die-hard 'protestants', the by-election in Waterford in February 1830 seemed to support the frequently stated claim that emancipation would make parliamentary government impossible in Ireland. In Dungavan, the mob drove the Constabulary into the post office, then chased Lord George Beresford's supporters out of town. Near Clashmore, a carriage containing a group of military officers and 'gentlemen' was stopped, and when the occupants could not show a 'pass', they were accused of supporting Lord George, and their carriage was thrown into the river. Similar occurrences were reported in Tallow, where the house of a known supporter of Lord George was severely damaged.[19]

Thus Ireland seemed on its way to the violence-ridden state of affairs so characteristic of its past history. Agrarian secret

---

[15] J. Ireland to Warburton, 4 May 1829 (P.R.O., H.O. 100/226).

[16] Wellington to Peel, 23 July 1829. in Peel, *Private papers*, ii, 117–18.

[17] Peel to Wellington, 24 July 1829, in Peel, *Private papers*, ii, 118; 30 July 1829 (Peel papers, B.M., Add. MS 40308); Greville, *Memoirs*, i, 303.

[18] See P.R.O., H.O. 100/227–8.

[19] Munster outrages, Feb. 1830 (P.R.O., H.O. 100/232).

societies, usually referred to as 'Rockites', began to raid for arms; in Connaught in March 1830, agitation appeared against the payments to priests.[20] In the past, robbery for personal gain had been the exception, but early in 1830 crimes with this motive became frequent. One police official saw the approaching assize in his district as the reason for these robberies; friends of the prisoners were attempting to raise money for their defence.[21] But there was one significant difference between conditions in the rural areas in 1830 and those of earlier periods of growing unrest. From about 1829 on, an increasing number of the clashes between the peasants and the Constabulary were unorganized mob actions; the outbreaks often occurred in daylight, and the participants made little attempt to hide their identity. These clashes seem to have been spur-of-the-moment affairs, often involving women as well as men, and they usually occurred when the Constabulary arrived to perform some function not to the liking of the local peasants. By 1829, the Irish peasantry had lost much of its fear of authority, for O'Connell had shown them the strength they possessed in the sheer weight of their numbers, and the nearest, most available symbol of authority was the police.

Some animosity between the Constabulary and the Irish peasantry was to be expected, but by 1829 the attitude of the two groups towards each other can only be described as hatred. When a group of peasants and a detachment of Constabulary came together, the result was almost inevitably a clash. Much of the peasants' hatred can be blamed on O'Connell and his associates, who whenever possible made it a point to castigate the police as agents of reaction – a practice that continued even after emancipation. In a speech made during the general election of 1830, one of O'Connell's associates promised:

I shall be ready to assist you by all lawful means for the recovery of your lawful rights – from the . . . ruffian magistrate who robs you, and then tramples on you, or from the *Gens d'armerie* you pay for, tho' instituted for the support of a faction against a nation.[22]

[20] Singleton to Leveson Gower, 13 Feb. 1830; Connaught outrages, Mar. 1830 (P.R.O., H.O. 100/232).

[21] Carter to Gregory, 4 Feb. 1830 (P.R.O., H.O. 100/232).

[22] Robert Osway Cave to the electors of the county of Tipperary, 2 Aug. 1830 (Peel papers, B.M., Add. MS 40313).

Among many examples of the hatred felt by the lower classes for the Constabulary, few are more eloquent than the reaction in Dungarvan on 7 February 1829 to the funeral of Sub-constable James Hurst. The funeral procession was met by a mob 'shouting and hissing and calling out "away with the bloody Orange Peeler, the heretic, hellhound"'. During the service in the churchyard, the mob called, 'Keep on your hats boys 'tis a protestant funeral', and began to throw clods of dirt at the clergyman reading the service. At the end of the report of this incident, Inspector Miller added that 'the conduct of some of the constables was far from good'.[23]

Relations between some of the Constabulary and some of the Irish protestants were not much better. After 1828, when the ultra-protestant groups had begun their trouble-making activities, the Constabulary units had frequently found themselves between the two hostile forces. Evidently they acted impartially in most instances,[24] and thus incurred the enmity of protestants as well as catholics. At a later date, an official of the Leinster Constabulary recalled how the police in County Down had been 'hooted' by the protestants, and could hardly show their faces in some areas because 'they did their duty', and how one of the chief constables had been called 'Papist Duff', although he was a protestant.[25]

But in spite of the hatred and derision directed against them, the members of the Constabulary continued to perform their duties with a marked degree of courage and determination. The various reports reaching the Castle from 1828 to 1830 contain an impressive array of instances in which small detachments, often of no more than four or five men, attempted to disarm and disperse 'mobs' of perhaps twenty times their numbers. A few examples from the many will suffice: In Kerry, during May 1830, four constables dispersed a procession of forty men and managed to take five prisoners.[26] On 19 February 1829, five constables found themselves between hostile protestant and

[23] Miller to Gregory, 13 Feb. 1829; Croker to Miller, 16 Feb. 1829 (P.R.O., H.O. 100/230).

[24] See John Joyce to Gregory, 19 Feb. 1829 (P.R.O., H.O. 100/226).

[25] Testimony of Sir F. Sloven, *Report of the select committee appointed to inquire into the nature, character, extent, and tendency of the Orange lodges, associations, or societies in Ireland*, H.L. 1835 (225), xxiii, 319–20.

[26] Précis, Munster, May 1830 (P.R.O., H.O. 100/232).

catholic groups who were determined to fight it out. The catholic group, one hundred strong, was armed with pitchforks, clubs, and one musket, but the constables managed to disarm a number of the men, then broke up the formation and scattered the members. The protestant group of seventy men proved more difficult to handle, for they were 'well armed with firearms', which the constables could not take from them, but the group was finally dispersed. On the way back to the Constabulary barracks, the constables encountered a forty-man group of catholic reinforcements; in the resulting skirmish, the constables seized a musket, a bayonet, and two pitchforks from the group, and turned them back.[27]

The constables were not always so successful. Between 1826 and 1830, eighty-four people were killed and 112 wounded in clashes with the Constabulary, while twelve constables were killed and 449 wounded.[28] By 1831, the pension rolls for the organization listed the names of about 183 men, in numerous instances disabled by wounds, beatings and other injuries received in the line of duty.[29] Membership in the Constabulary was somewhat risky even during peaceful intervals: in August 1829, the chief secretary was informed that Chief Constable Urquhardt had 'sustained bodily injury' when 'the police station fell on him'.[30]

Writing in May 1829, the lord lieutenant stated that he believed the police system to be good, but warned Peel not 'to let decay set in, as so often happens in Ireland'.[31] Goulburn also commented: 'I know the tendency of every establishment in Ireland to become inefficient and corrupt as it advances in age and my parental affection for the police is not so strong as to make me think it is exempt from this liability'.[32]

From its first appearance in 1822, the County Constabulary had operated under several notable handicaps. Too small to

[27] Joyce to Gregory, 19 Feb. 1829 (P.R.O., H.O. 100/226).
[28] *Return of persons killed or wounded in affrays with the Constabulary force in Ireland*, H.C. 1830–1 (67), viii, 403.
[29] *Return of all superannuations granted to constables and sub-constables of police in Ireland*, H.C. 1831–2 (339), xxvi, 465–7.
[30] Sir John Harvey to Leveson Gower, 6 Aug. 1829 (P.R.O., H.O. 100/228).
[31] Northumberland to Peel, 4 May 1829 (P.R.O., H.O. 100/226).
[32] Goulburn to Peel, 30 Dec. 1829 (Peel papers, B.M., Add. MS 40333).

cope efficiently with the mobs, and further weakened by the practice of splitting the force into smaller detachments to guard the homes of the gentry, the men of the Constabulary seem to have resorted upon occasion to 'police brutality'. Frequent charges to this effect appeared in the opposition press, but Castle investigations of such charges tended to be cursory and one-sided, often taking the form of letters to police officials and magistrates, asking whether or not their detachments had misbehaved. Equally important was the handicap of weak leadership. The Irish executive had been so dissatisfied with the constables act of 1822 in its amended form that they had considered withdrawing it; to Wellesley and others, any police system that allowed the magistrates an important role was doomed to failure, and it was only after the magistracy was 'reformed' and the Constabulary had proved itself in operations against the banditti that the Castle accepted the new arrangements. While initial doubts of the Constabulary's worth had been exaggerated, they had not been completely unfounded; even before 1829 signs of the decay and corruption Northumberland and Goulburn had feared were already appearing.

A major problem was the appointment of the chief constables who led the detachments. By the terms of the act of 1822, the Castle appointed the police officials and the magistrates the men, but by around 1825 this arrangement was under attack. In 1814, Peel had warned of making a 'job' of police appointments and thus 'shamefully sacrificing the best interests of the country to the worst',[33] but the position of chief constable was attractive enough to make it a sure target for the patronage-mongers. A judge warned in 1825 that the position was too well-paid; it attracted men of good family who went 'about as private gentlemen in coloured clothes'. It was also pointed out that such men did not take orders well from magistrates who were their social and economic inferiors.[34] Initially the Castle seems to have resisted the importuning of the job-seekers, but with diminishing strength; in 1825, Goulburn warned that the decision to establish the Constabulary in Down and Louth would be a 'signal for war on the part of Lord Donohue and

[33] Peel to Saurin, 5 July 1814 (Peel papers, B.M., Add. MS 40287).
[34] Maxwell Blacker to Gregory, 10 June 1825 (S.P.O., C.S.O., Official papers, ser. 2, 588^AA/825/22).

perhaps Lord Londonderry, in the one case, and Lord Fingall
in the other', adding that he was 'persecuted to death with
demands for chief constables' and that he might submit the
names of the 'most deserving' to Wellesley before the news
made 'everybody an applicant'.[35] And, of course, members of
the Castle hierarchy were interested in providing for their own
associates: '. . . if you wish to appoint Major Mahoney's son,
there is a vacancy in Warburton's district in consequence of one
of his chief constables, and also pay clerk . . . having absconded
with £300 of the public money', wrote Gregory.[36] Willcocks's
successor in Munster was recommended by Wellesley as being
'particularly known to Sir George Murray'.[37] Thus over a
period of years, as the result of erosion rather than reversal of
policy, the County Constabulary became deeply involved
in the patronage system. When Peel was informed of the
situation by Leveson Gower in 1829, he expressed deep concern
in a letter to Goulburn: '. . . a great mistake has been committed
in making the office of chief constable an office of patronage and
placing distressed gentlemen in it. I had no conception there
was such a number of chief constables. . . .'[38] Surprisingly,
Goulburn (now chancellor of the exchequer) denied that
patronage had entered into the appointments of chief constables
made while he had been chief secretary.[39]

In 1829, Peel completed the legislation that would give him
more lasting fame than any other single accomplishment of his
career, the establishment of the London Metropolitan Police.
With this task accomplished, he turned to the Irish County
Constabulary, and in a series of letters outlined the reforms he
thought necessary in the police system. He wrote to Wellington
in July:

The police is very unpopular, chiefly for two reasons – because it is
expensive and because it does its duty. But for every purpose

[35] Goulburn to Gregory, 21 Junr 1825 (Surrey record office, Goulburn
papers, box C, pt 2).
[36] Gregory to Goulburn, 4 Mar. 1826 (Surrey record office, Goulburn
papers, box C, pt 2).
[37] Wellesley to Lansdowne, 18 Nov. 1827 (P.R.O., H.O. 100/220).
[38] Peel to Goulburn, 25 Dec. 1829 (Surrey record office, Goulburn
papers, II/17).
[39] Goulburn to Peel, 30 Dec. 1829 (Peel papers, B.M., Add. MS 40333).

excepting the resistance to physical force or the actual dispersion of organized assemblies the police is much more efficient I conceive than the military. Whatever laws of coercion we may pass we must I conceive trust to their effectual execution for many years to come to an armed stipendiary police, acting in most cases under stipendiary magistrates. If the people overpower this police by their superior numbers, I see no alternative but making that police strong enough by establishing stations [detachments] where necessary.

Why should England pay the charge of civilizing Ireland, either by direct pecuniary advances or indirectly by maintaining a great military force? My impression still is that we may dispose with a great military force in Ireland for the purpose of defending her against military aggression – that the foreign powers which might have taken part with the whole Roman catholic population discontented on account of exclusion and disabilities, will not take part with a set of lawless ruffians who set all control at defiance.[40]

Thus the control of Constabulary operations should be taken from the magistrates and placed in the hands of the Irish government. Peel envisioned a 'stipendiary police acting in most cases under stipendiary magistrates', who would be the superiors of the local magistrates.[41] But both Peel and Wellington realized that the police could not yet assume complete responsibility for law and order. The police would be strengthened and the military establishment reduced, but not eliminated, for until Ireland was at peace troops would be needed to protect the police.[42] In Peel's discussion of the financial provisions for the reformed Constabulary, there appears a strong echo of the punitive provisions of the peace preservation act: 'That [crime] must be repressed there can be no doubt, and let Ireland, as it is just, pay the charge of suppressing her own disorders, and have therefore an inducement to keep the peace.'[43]

The home secretary next turned to the problem of obtaining

[40] Peel to Wellington, 27 July 1829 (Peel papers, B.M., Add. MS 40308).
[41] The stipendiary or chief magistrates created by the peace preservation act were the superiors of the local magistrates. The resident magistrates provided for by the Irish constables bill were the equals of the local magistrates.
[42] Wellington to Peel, 31 July 1829 (Peel papers, B.M., Add. MS 40308).
[43] Peel to Wellington, 27 July 1829 (Peel papers, B.M., Add. MS 40308).

proper men for the police, and in a letter to Leveson Gower, he made the following suggestions:

I would advise you, therefore, to consider in the first place what would be the constitution of the police which would render it most efficient. I would disregard all local interests, all desire on the part of magistrates to recommend constables – all clamour in the house of commons about patronage – and if, as I strongly suspect – the best plan will be to take the nominations to all offices high and low in the police directly into the hands of the lord lieutenant, I would take them.[44]

Thus the local magistrates would be deprived of their patronage privileges as well as their control over the operations of the Constabulary. These steps alone would certainly have improved the character of the police, but Peel was not content to stop here. He was determined to establish a truly neutral police, completely impartial in their dealings with the populace:

I would certainly constitute that force in such a manner as to preclude all just objections to it on the score of partiality. I presume that at the present all party distinctions in the police are forbidden, all attendance on Orange lodges and so forth, and I think that the regulations in that respect . . . cannot be too scrupulously enforced. It would be a great object to infuse into the police force an *esprit de corps* obliterating all other distinctions local or religious, but it will be greatly obstructed by the existence of any political clubs or exclusive combinations in the police itself. . . . Have a depot in Dublin, and one if necessary, in Cork, Limerick, and Belfast. Have the names of all candidates enrolled, let them be strictly examined, and their certificates of character examined also, and select those from time to time who are best suited for your purpose.[45]

By August 1829, Peel and Leveson Gower knew what must be done to turn the Constabulary into the instrument of reform that they believed so important in 'civilizing' Ireland. At all levels, the Constabulary should be under the control of the Castle, and it should be completely 'neutral' in its relations with the people. From scattered bits of information, it is possible to reconstruct an outline of the original proposal, drawn up by

[44] Peel to Leveson Gower, 30 July 1829 (Peel papers, B.M., Add. MS 40337).
[45] Peel to Leveson Gower, 14 Aug. 1829 (Peel papers, B.M., Add MS 40337).

Leveson Gower, containing the changes necessary to achieve the desired result. A new position was created, that of the sub-inspector, who was to have 'efficient and complete control' over the detachments in the county to which he was assigned. Under the existing system, there was no police official between the provincial inspector and the chief constable. The new official would strengthen the chain of command between the Castle and the police detachments in the counties and remove a weakness that had been noted as early as 1825. The proposed bill also transferred the power to appoint constables and sub-constables from the local magistrates to the lord lieutenant, who was to fill all future vacancies. A portion of the Constabulary of any province could be stationed in any part of the province, and the chief constable could be transferred from one district to another. The new sub-inspectors were to be appointed by the lord lieutenant and would be responsible to the provincial in-spectors.[46]

It is impossible to determine precisely the fate of the bill containing these provisions. In December, Peel warned Leveson Gower of strong opposition to any steps by the government to take over the 'local aspects' of law and order,[47] opposition that extended to the cabinet, where it was suggested that such action on the part of the government would weaken the interest of the gentry in local affairs.[48] In spite of this opposition, Leveson Gower introduced the bill to the house of commons on 30 March 1830. The measure was immediately challenged as an un-warranted encroachment on the rights of the country gentlemen. Spring Rice announced that he was prepared to show that 'where the authority of the magistrates was most complete the conduct of the police had been best, and that where the authority of the government had interfered, the abuses had been greatest'. Mr Trant saw in the bill 'a settled scheme on the part of the government to take into its own keeping . . . the police,

[46] Goulburn to Peel, 30 Dec. 1829 (Peel papers, B.M., Add. MS 40333); Peel to Leveson Gower, 9 Jan. 1830 (Peel papers, B.M., Add. MS 40337); see Bill of April 1830 (S.P.O., C.S.O., Official papers, ser. 2, 588BB/830c/5).

[47] Peel to Leveson Gower, 16 Dec. 1829 (Peel papers, B.M., Add. MS 40337).

[48] Peel to Leveson Gower, 9 Jan. 1830 (Peel papers, B.M., Add. MS 40337).

not only of Ireland, but of England, and not only the police but every part of the constitution of the country'.[49] At some stage of its progress through parliament, it was defeated or abandoned.

The loss of the bill was most unfortunate. For years, the obstructionism, inefficiency, and partisanship of the local magistrates had hampered attempts to establish a truly efficient police system for Ireland. By 1830, the government was prepared to take the final step in removing the only important remaining obstacle to the success of this organization. If the government had succeeded, and if Peel's instructions had been followed, the Constabulary would have become in 1830 essentially the organization created by the whig government in 1836. But any further chances of reforming the Constabulary by the tory government at this time were lost with the resignation of Wellington in November 1830, and the end of the long period of tory supremacy. The task of creating an efficient Irish police system was thus unfinished, and was passed on to the whigs. This party, traditionally opposed to strong police systems, was now faced with the problem of maintaining order in Ireland. During the next five years, the whigs were to be confronted with all the problems of agrarian violence that had plagued tory governments since 1812. They were to try many of the solutions of their predecessors, and to adopt finally, in a somewhat improved form, the solution advocated by Peel in 1830.

[49] *Hansard 2*, xxiii, 1110–13.

XI

THE WHIGS AND IRELAND,
1830–6

THE WHIG CABINET formed in 1830 represented a breadth of
political opinion that accommodated the aristocratic whig
ideals of Lord Grey at the one extreme and the radicalism of
Lord Durham at the other. United on the issue of parliamentary
reform, the cabinet was often divided over other matters, and it
was an open disagreement between the prime minister and his
colleagues over Irish problems that caused Grey to leave office
in 1834. Two of the three men closely associated with formulating Irish policy were of conservative persuasion. The home
secretary, Lord Melbourne, who had been chief secretary for
Ireland in 1827–8, seems to have been both bored by the
demands of Irish politics and angered by the endemic violence
of the countryside. But his influence on Irish matters was
less than that of his predecessor. The chief secretary, Edward
Stanley, was made a member of the cabinet in 1831, and it was
he who 'represented' Ireland in its meetings. Stanley, who as
Lord Derby was to be three times prime minister, was a
dominating figure in whig circles. His 'latent toryism', as
manifested in his staunch defence of the established church and
his support of coercive legislation to restore order in Ireland,
caused trouble for Grey, hastened Stanley's transfer to the
colonial office in 1833, and has tended to obscure the fact that

he was closely associated with a number of important but unspectacular Irish reforms.[1]

That the whigs wished Ireland well was underlined by the return of the marquess of Anglesey as lord lieutenant in 1830. 'Martyred' by Wellington in 1828, Anglesey seemed an obviously popular choice, but such was not the case. The lord lieutenant's opposition to repeal and a quarrel over the appointment of a new solicitor-general led to another clash with O'Connell. Early in 1831, the Irish leader was arrested but never brought to trial, and following the appearance of the whig parliamentary reform proposal (which O'Connell supported) the two men observed a rather noisy truce.

Anglesey continued to advocate the liberal policy that had horrified his tory associates in 1828, for he was convinced that discontent and lawlessness could best be attacked through removal of the causes: by an Irish poor law, a settlement of the tithe question, and reform of the Irish established church. In 1831, helped by Grey and several other members of the cabinet, Anglesey was able to check the attempts of Stanley and Melbourne to invoke coercive legislation. And from that date to 1833, the Irish policy of the whigs was essentially that of their predecessors – vigorous enforcement of law and order, accompanied by 'safe' reforms.

Difficulties in governing Ireland were aggravated for the whigs by several factors – the overriding demands of parliamentary reform, which left little time for the development of Irish programmes, and the activities of O'Connell and his associates. In their efforts at parliamentary reform, the whigs had found the O'Connellites willing allies, but once that momentous issue had been resolved, O'Connell turned against the government for what he saw as weak and timorous efforts at reform in Ireland. Too few in number to be more than a constant annoyance at Westminster, the O'Connellites were a more serious obstacle to the administrators in Ireland, where the violent denunciations of the union and the Irish church added new fuel to the flames of agrarian discontent, intensifying what one observer termed the 'midnight warfare of poverty against property'.[2]

[1] See McDowell, *Public opinion & govt policy*, p. 143.

[2] Sir Henry Hardinge to Peel, 15 Oct. 1830 (Peel papers, B.M., Add. MS 40313).

But beyond the irritations of the O'Connellites, the problems met by the first years of the whigs in Ireland were drearily similar to those that had vexed the tories. Agrarian unrest took its familiar forms of violence and intimidation, and the government's efforts at control met with the old obstacles: a depleted military establishment; the futility of attempting to replace troops with the long-discredited and still-unreliable yeomanry; the obstinate, timid, or simply incompetent magistracy; and finally the inadequacy of provisions for effective policing of the country. The succession of events can be summarized; to recount the story in detail would be merely to repeat the tory experience with changes in names, dates, and places. That it took the whigs but six years to recapitulate the tories' seventeen years of police experimentation may be attributed both to the severity of the crisis and to the existence of the fundamentally usable, though imperfect, County Constabulary. It might seem that Anglesey and Melbourne, with their experience in Ireland under the tories, should have realized the direction to be taken and led the government to an earlier solution of the problem. But it should be recalled that both Anglesey and Melbourne had served in Ireland during the period of the emancipation crisis, at a time when the problem of law and order rested largely, not with the government, but with the Catholic Association. Of Ireland in deep turmoil they understood, at first hand, very little.

The Irish 'tithe war' of the 1830s has been described with varying degrees of accuracy by several writers.[3] Its origins are to be found in the simultaneous appearance of a group of circumstances, any one of which could alone have produced serious unrest among the peasants. The years from 1829 to 1831 were 'famine years' in Ireland, complicated by the severe economic distress already prevailing in both England and Ireland. The summer of 1830 saw several food riots in Limerick and Leitrim.[4] By August 1831, one observer could describe the condition of the peasants as 'more wretched than I could possibly imagine had I not witnessed it'.[5]

---

[3] For a detailed but somewhat unreliable account, see R. Barry O'Brien, *Fifty years of concessions to Ireland* (London, n.d.), i, 372 ff.

[4] Fitzgerald to Gregory, 1 July 1830; Edward Blakeney to Gregory, 9 July 1830 (P.R.O., H.O. 100/233).

[5] Sir Hussey Vivian to ——, 31 Aug. 1831 (P.R.O., H.O. 100/239).

In addition, it is quite possible that the catholic clergy in Ireland decided to reassert the leadership of the peasants that they had held during the emancipation crisis. Fearing the results of prolonged distress in the rural areas, they may have decided to adopt some of the methods of the Catholic Association to provide the peasants with a purpose calculated to discourage violence. In 1830, under the leadership of Bishop Doyle,[6] the catholic clergy began a campaign against the tithe, paid by every resident of rural Ireland, protestant or catholic, for the support of the established church. A campaign of collective passive resistance against payment of the tithe appeared over a widespread area, encouraged by the parish priests and by O'Connell and his followers. As the campaign developed, the catholic peasantry set about making the collection of the tithe as difficult as possible. Tithe law provided that a defaulter's personal property could be taken by 'distress' (the seizure of personal property to enforce payment), but it also provided that personal property in the form of live-stock could be seized only between sunrise and sunset and that animals behind locked doors were immune from seizure. Thus at one level the 'tithe war' of the early 1830s was a war of manoeuvre. The live-stock of defaulters was hidden during daylight and locked up after dark. Sales of live-stock taken by distress were boycotted, and other variations of non-violent harassment appeared. At Tralee, the power-of-attorney held by Mr O'Neill to collect his father's tithes was stolen, and whenever he attempted collection the tenants asked him to produce his authority.[7] But passive resistance was a method of protest ill-suited to the peasant temperament, and trouble appeared before the movement was well under way. To many protestants, lay and clergy, tithe resistance was more than an attack on the church; it was also a violation of the rights of property. There followed appeals to authority for assistance, and Constabulary detachments, supported by troops, were sent to collect the tithes. The response to such a move was inevitable. Some of the

[6] The home office papers contain an 'intelligence report' on this famous churchman, describing him as 'clever, ingenuous, and intriguing . . . capable of doing some good, or a great deal of mischief'. Memorandum, 18 Oct. 1833 (P.R.O., H.O. 100/244).

[7] C. O'Neill to Gosset, 23 Apr. 1834 (P.R.O., H.O. 100/246).

bloodiest encounters between police and soldiers and the peasants during the entire nineteenth century occurred between 1830 and 1834.[8]

The situation was further complicated by the reappearance of widespread operations of the agrarian secret societies. In Galway and Clare particularly, there soon arose all the familiar problems of the banditti. Now known as the 'Whitefeet' and the 'Blackfeet', the secret societies concentrated upon opposition to rent increases as well as to the tithe. Their methods were the usual enforcing of oaths, raids for arms, and brutal retribution for failure to comply with their orders. Nor was the response to their activities different from that encountered so often before. Requests for the insurrection act began to reach the Castle, followed shortly by a flood of gentry who had been forced to flee from their homes. Gallant soldier though he was, Anglesey – his police and soldiers assaulted by tithe delinquents during the day and attacked by banditti at night – began to show signs of panic, and admitted, 'I am at my wit ends'.[9] O'Connell did his best to stem the tide of violence that was breaking over Ireland,[10] and Bishop Doyle 'anathemized' the banditti and those involved in the tithe affrays,[11] but neither had any apparent success. The efforts of the government were equally futile, and by 1832 the agrarian secret societies had extended their operations over all of Leinster and into extensive areas of the other provinces. As the year progressed, conditions grew steadily worse.[12] The gentry of Queen's County described an apparently typical situation when they reported to the lord lieutenant that the banditti had established a system of intimidation so complete that it was impossible to discharge a servant or labourer, employ a tradesman, or take a farm without the permission of these 'self-constituted legislators, who carry on their plans by anonymous threats and notices, which if not obeyed are carried into effect by the vengeance of daily and nightly marauders'.[13]

[8] See O'Brien, *Concessions to Ireland*, i, 383–93.

[9] Gen. Byng to Lord Fitzroy Somerset, 14 Apr. 1831 (P.R.O., H.O. 100/238); Anglesey to Melbourne, 1 Mar., 4 Mar. 1831 (P.R.O., H.O. 100/237).

[10] McDowell, *Public opinion & govt policy*, p. 144.

[11] J. Harvey to Gosset, 16 Dec. 1831 (P.R.O., H.O. 100/240).

[12] Anglesey to Hill, 24 Dec. 1832 (P.R.O., H.O. 100/243).

[13] Petition, Lent assize, 1832 (P.R.O., H.O. 100/241).

Anglesey, Melbourne, and Stanley shared a mutual horror of the crime and violence in the Irish rural areas, and in 1831 they turned to the problem of restoring peace through the 'constitutional' means at their disposal: the military establishment, the police, and the magistracy. Within less than a year, the Irish government tried most of the instruments of law and order that the tories had employed between 1812 and 1830, and in most instances the result was either a negligible success or a complete failure.

In 1830 the strength of the army in Ireland was 20,408 men; as the disturbances intensified in 1831, it dropped to 16,701; in the following year, it slowly climbed to a strength of 19,301.[14] Serious disturbances in Ireland seemed inevitably to coincide with outside factors forcing a decrease in the size of the Irish establishment: Continental entanglements, violence in Britain, or economy drives by the British government. The drop in 1831 was occasioned by widespread disorders in Britain resulting from parliamentary reform agitation and by the government's uneasiness over possible effects of the revolutions in France and the Netherlands. In spite of Anglesey's increasing concern over the unrest in Ireland, the lord lieutenant took the reduction in the establishment with good grace, agreeing that it was 'more important to have the means of at once checking serious disorder in England than here'. He did, however, make a special request for several battalions of highlanders, for 'Those petticoats have a marvellous effect on Pat'.[15] But the fluctuations in the strength of the military at this critical period underscored for the whigs what tory administrators had learned over the years in Ireland, that the army as a means of controlling agrarian disturbances and keeping the peace on a long-term basis was an undependable, cumbersome, and hazardous instrument.

As the 'tithe war' increased in intensity, doubts as to the reliability of the army in Ireland were again expressed by some officers of the establishment. The presence of Orange lodges in a number of regiments caused the military leaders some embarrassment, but their major concern was the possible subversion of Irish catholic soldiers. The adjutant-general warned that 'attempts have been made by evil disposed persons to mislead

[14] *Return of the number of troops quartered in Ireland*, H.C. 1844 (24), xxxiii, 193.
[15] Anglesey to Melbourne, 23 Feb. 1831 (P.R.O., H.O. 100/236).

the soldiers', and suggested a 'quiet but constant observation on the part of the officers towards the men'. An officer assigned to conducting catholic soldiers to church was ordered to stay outside and avoid the 'imputation of being considered a spy'. The 'house of Widow Hacket' was a potent source of rumour: soldiers of the Fifty-Ninth were reportedly 'sworn', money was collected for what were possibly subversive purposes, and it was claimed that a soldier planned to shoot his captain, 'an English bugger', if he were 'ever out on duty with me at night'.[16] But rumours of serious trouble proved to be without foundation, and by 1832 the senior officers of the establishment had decided that the reliability of the army was not seriously undermined.[17] The policy of political and religious neutrality was carefully enforced. When 180 soldiers signed a 'Protestant address to His Majesty', their commanding officer was reminded that a soldier's oath of allegiance included 'every profession of loyalty that can be required of him, and . . . any additional expression of his sentiments whereby he identifies himself with a party . . . is highly irregular and unmilitary'.[18] On at least one occasion, 'neutrality' stretched near the breaking-point: soldiers refused to help quell a St Patrick's Day riot, causing the adjutant-general to complain, 'Sir Hussey Vivian is so fearful of awakening unpleasant feelings between the different troops concerned, that he thinks it better to treat the whole business as a drunken squabble . . . rather than run the risk of laying the foundation of still more serious misunderstanding.'[19]

As the military establishment declined in numbers, the government began its search for substitute forces. In 1830-1, an involved plan was developed for calling up a large number of military pensioners for limited service.[20] Again the experience of the previous governments was discounted. For ten years, the Irish government had refused to use the yeomanry to suppress rural disorder, realizing that the lack of discipline in these units and their partisanship made them often more a liability than an

[16] D'Ajuilar to Macdonald, 18 July 1831; to Arbuthnot, 8 Feb. 1832; to O/C 59th regiment, 8 Mar. 1832; Bambrigges's report, 8 Mar. 1832; Circular to major generals, 13 Mar. 1832 (P.R.O., W.O. 35/26).
[17] D'Ajuilar to Macdonald, 19 Oct. 1832 (P.R.O., W.O. 35/26).
[18] D'Ajuilar to Arbuthnot, 8 Feb. 1832 (P.R.O., W.O. 35/26).
[19] D'Ajuilar to ——, 24 Mar. 1832 (P.R.O., W.O. 35/26).
[20] See P.R.O., W.O. 35/36.

asset. But late in 1830 it was decided to bring the yeomanry out of their retirement and use them in support of the police and military. The yeomanry had not been 'clothed' in ten years, an estimated 75 per cent of their arms were useless, and the cost of re-activation was certain to be high. But the availability of 29,000 'loyal' men,[21] eager to be enlisted in the cause of law and order, was a lure Stanley and Melbourne could not resist. Stanley hoped to modernize the yeomanry – local units were to be combined into county divisions, arms were to be stored in depots instead of in private homes, the use of yeomanry detachments by local magistrates was to be ended. But his plan does not seem to have taken effect.[22] The re-activation was completed in June 1831, and within a matter of weeks reports of 'incidents' began to reach the Castle. Clashes between yeomen on police duty and tithe-protestors were to be expected (a serious clash occurred at Newtownbarry, County Wicklow, on 18 June), but on 12 July the Belturbet corps, in Cavan, appeared marching in an Orange procession.[23] Both their appearance and the riot it occasioned were in the established tradition of the experience of the government with the yeomanry. Other incidents followed, and O'Connell, the English radicals, and the liberal press thundered at the Castle for resurrecting an organization that had been 'a curse to Ireland'.[24] In January 1832, Anglesey announced that he could no longer support the use of the yeomanry: 'The ultra-protestants are out to produce a crisis so that emancipation will be withdrawn, and the yeomanry are a good way to do this.' The lord lieutenant suggested that a substitute be found in sending English militia units to Ireland,[25] but he was told that the English units 'lacked training' and could not be sent.[26] In March 1834 the Castle withdrew the permanent staff sergeants, drummers, and buglers from the yeomanry units,[27] and, more or less cast adrift, the units slipped back into the obscurity of the previous decade. In

[21] Memorandum, 12 Jan. 1831 (P.R.O., H.O. 100/236).

[22] Stanley's memoranda, 1831 (Durham University, Grey papers, box 65); Gosset to Stanley, 14 July 1831 (P.R.O., H.O. 100/239).

[23] Gosset to Stanley, 14 July 1831 (P.R.O., H.O. 100/239).

[24] *Hansard 3*, iv, 380–1.

[25] Anglesey to Stanley, 14 Jan. 1832 (P.R.O., H.O. 100/241).

[26] Minute by the duke of Richmond, n.d. (P.R.O., H.O. 100/241).

[27] Wellesley to Melbourne, 7 Mar. 1834 (P.R.O., H.O. 100/245).

attempting to use the yeomanry, and incidentally in the request for English militia units, the whig government had repeated one more of the unsuccessful experiments of its predecessors.

As the activity of the agrarian secret societies brought banditti violence to alarming proportions, the Irish magistracy wasted no time in proving to the whig government that they left much to be desired as the mainstay of the system of law and order. Almost from his arrival in Ireland, Anglesey had been receiving complaints of 'a want of decision on the part of the magistrates' and charges that they were being intimidated by the banditti.[28] Early in March 1831 the Castle learned that the magistrates of Meath had released without trial forty-five prisoners who had been arrested for committing outrages.[29] This incident, added to the growing list of complaints against the magistrates from the Constabulary officers, was more than Anglesey's patience could endure. Late March and early April found him touring Ireland, alternately threatening the magistrates and pleading with them to attend to their duties.[30] But the exertions of the lord lieutenant brought meagre results: two years later, he recalled that

Unhappily they did not act upon the suggestions. Their jealousy of the government was such, that they neglected their obvious duties rather than support it, and by their supineness and disaffection, they gave time (and almost countenance) to a general combination which in the end proved too powerful for the law.[31]

The measure of control that the magistrates exerted upon the Constabulary continued to hamper effective use of that body. As they had done in earlier times of unrest, some magistrates now refused to use the detachments to combat crime, preferring to assign the constables to guard duty at the homes of the gentry and to leave the rest of the barony open to the depredations of the banditti.[32] In other instances, magistrates refused to allow

[28] Anglesey to Stanley, 26 Jan. 1831; Chief Constable Frinan to Gosset, 5 Feb. 1831 (P.R.O., H.O. 100/236).

[29] J. Smart to Warburton, 26 Feb. 1831 (P.R.O., H.O. 100/236); Gosset to Stanley, 21 Mar. 1831 (P.R.O., H.O. 100/237).

[30] See T. Arbuthnot to Byng, 4 Apr. 1831; Byng to Fitzroy Somerset, 11 Apr. 1831 (P.R.O., H.O. 100/238).

[31] Anglesey to Hobhouse, 25 Apr. 1833 (Broughton papers, B.M., Add. MS 36467).

[32] Byng to Fitzroy Somerset, 15 Mar. 1831 (P.R.O., H.O. 100/237).

the units to be strengthened, insisting that the Castle send soldiers to restore order to their areas.[33] When magistrates did attempt to direct the activities of the police, their leadership was often characterized as 'inefficient', and was blamed for the high proportion of casualties sustained by the Constabulary in clashes with banditti or tithe defaulters.[34]

Thus in a brief period of time, the magistracy of Ireland succeeded in demonstrating to the whig government most of the means by which the venerable institution had thwarted, circumvented, and defied the workings of law and order in Ireland over the previous decades. It was impossible that the whigs should take action against the magistrates at so early a stage of their term in office, for they had long been loud in protest at the tories' 'unconstitutional' attempts to limit the powers of the magistracy. The only possibility at this point was to find a means of circumventing the magistracy in the enforcement of law and order.

Such a means Stanley believed he had discovered in the existence of the Peace Preservation Force, an organization 'more expensive than the Constabulary and under different regulations', but completely at the disposal of the Castle and free from the influence of the country gentlemen.[35] Between March 1831 and February 1833, the number of stipendiary magistrates was increased considerably;[36] counties and portions of counties were proclaimed, and received detachments of the Peace Preservation Force. In 1833 detachments were operating in Clare, Galway, Louth, Limerick, Kilkenny, Queen's County, Tipperary, Wicklow, and Cork.[37] In 1832 the Castle announced that in three months' time a detachment of the Peace Preservation Force had tranquillized Queen's County in a 'most satisfactory' manner by the use of 'energetic measures'. This success was characterized as 'a specimen of the proceedings which restored Clare, Galway, and Limerick last year'.[38]

[33] Draught to Gosset, 27 Apr. 1831 (P.R.O., H.O. 100/238).

[34] See C. H. Tuckey to Gosset, 15 Dec. 1831 (P.R.O., H.O. 100/240).

[35] Gosset to Stanley, 19 Mar. 1831 (P.R.O., H.O. 100/237).

[36] *An account of the stipendiary magistrates*, H.C. 1833 (518), xxxii, 453.

[37] *Return of the Peace Preservation Force in Ireland during each of the last three years*, H.C. 1834 (201), xlvii, 399.

[38] Gosset to Melbourne, 16 June 1832 (P.R.O., H.O. 100/241).

Evidently the Force met with little opposition from the magistrates;[39] but, considering that one detachment, 103 strong, cost Clare £3,340 in 1836,[40] it would have been most unlikely that the Force could operate for long in an area without occasioning complaints of the burden of maintaining two police establishments. Two things, however, are certain: the 'new administration' in the Castle was greatly impressed by the efficiency of the Peace Preservation Force, controlled by the Irish government and operating under the orders of a 'professional' police officer, and agrarian outrages did decrease in the areas covered by the Force. Like their predecessors, the whigs had learned the value of the 'professional' policeman over the army or the amateur leadership of the magistracy in maintaining law and order.

But the whigs found too that the Force was not a completely satisfactory answer to their problem. By the end of 1832, the momentary relief at the abatement of banditti activity had melted away. There developed in Clare what would appear to have been a jurisdictional quarrel between the Force and the Constabulary which limited the effectiveness of both organizations. To complicate matters further, on 15 January 1833 in one of the rural towns, a constable arrested a drunken soldier. To the delight of the assembled townspeople, there followed an engagement between soldiers and policemen, ending in the soldiers chasing the constables out of town.[41]

Meanwhile the 'tithe war' continued. When the Constabulary was used to enforce the law against the tithe delinquents, the tasks assigned them were frequently of such magnitude that even large detachments ran the risk of destruction if they attempted to do their duty. The danger was demonstrated at Carrickshock, County Kilkenny in December 1831 when a forty-man detachment on 'tithe duty' encountered a mob estimated at two thousand. The chief constable and sixteen of his men were killed, and seven were seriously wounded.[42]

[39] See Lord Sligo to Gosset, 22 Jan. 1833 (P.R.O., H.O. 100/244).

[40] *Peace preservation police*, H.C. 1836 (527), xii, 161.

[41] Miller to Gosset, 13 Dec. 1832 (P.R.O., H.O. 100/243); Dublin *Evening Post*, 15 Jan. 1833.

[42] Tuckey to Gosset, 15 Dec. 1831 (P.R.O., H.O. 100/240). The number of dead varies from one account to another.

By 1832 it was becoming increasingly apparent, both in Dublin and at Westminster, that the combined strength of the Irish military establishment and the police could not force the Irish peasant to pay the tithe against his wishes, and that further attempts to collect by force could lead only to additional bloodshed.[43] But the government of Lord Grey remained unconvinced. In 1832, legislation was passed enabling the government to advance to the clergy of the established church the amount due them in tithes for the year 1831, and empowering the government to collect the amount advanced from the tithe-payers. It was also stated that a measure amending the tithe laws would be introduced in the future. In August, a bill was passed making the provisions of the tithe composition act of 1823 compulsory, but this feeble gesture accomplished nothing since it stopped short of any genuine solution of the problem, although it did manage further to antagonize the O'Connellites. The 'tithe war' continued, with the lord lieutenant now firmly established, in O'Connell's words, as 'tithe-proctor-general of all Ireland'.[44] But the law authorizing the Castle to collect the tithe arrears was little more than an added sanction to a practice the government had been using for some time, and of the £104,000 outstanding in unpaid tithes, only £12,000 was recovered.[45] O'Connell toured Ireland, encouraging his countrymen to persist in their opposition, and the chief secretary was informed that those who wished to pay the tithe were prevented by fear of vengeance from their neighbours.[46] As a final burden, after an absence of several years, faction fights reappeared to harass the already over-worked police.

By 1833 the Grey government had yet to try the one remaining 'traditional' measure for the suppression of widespread violence – coercive legislation. In February this last step was taken with the introduction of the church temporality bill and the peace preservation bill, both drawn up by Stanley. The

[43] See *Correspondence relative to the collection and payment of tithe and resistance offered thereto*, H.C. 1831–2 (663), xxii.

[44] 2 Will. IV, c. 41, 1 June 1832; 2 and 3 Will. IV, c. 119, 16 Aug. 1832; O'Brien, *Concessions to Ireland*, p. 394.

[45] *Hansard 3*, xx, 342.

[46] Miller to Stanley, 17 Nov. 1832 (P.R.O., H.O. 100/242); Carter to Stanley, 29 Sept. 1832 (P.R.O., H.O. 100/241).

first of these measures provided for abolishing the church cess, paid by protestant and catholic alike for the upkeep of church property and other similar expenses. The church cess was to be replaced by a tax on all clerical incomes of over £200 a year. Ten bishoprics were to be abolished, and provision was made for the suspension of appointments to parishes where no religious service had been performed for three years. Clause 147 of the bill, providing for the creation of a fund, a portion of which might be used for poor relief, educational purposes, and the payment of catholic clergy, was dropped by the cabinet.[47] Thus the measure, as finally passed, touched the Irish catholic only in the abolition of the church cess. The peace preservation act or, as it is more usually known, the coercion act, is of considerable interest. In some respects, it seems the embodiment of the frustrations at the failure of the whigs to tranquillize Ireland. The first portion of the measure empowered the lord lieutenant for a year to proclaim an area to be in a state of disturbance, and made it a breach of the law to hold meetings of any kind in the area under proclamation. In these provisions, the law was similar to the insurrection act, but its second section was in some respects more rigorous than that measure. Under the insurrection act, offenders were tried at a special session of the local court, usually without a jury; the new law provided for trial by courts-martial. The courts were to consist of not fewer than five nor more than nine officers, over twenty-one years of age and veterans of at least two years' service, assisted by a law serjeant or a king's counsel. The writ of habeas corpus was to be suspended for any prisoner until three months after his arrest.[48]

In the light of the history of attempts to establish law and order in Ireland, the coercion bill has an interest beyond its place in the list of measures invoked over the years for the control of agrarian crime. Here was 'official' recognition of the incompetence and intransigence of the magistracy in the performance of their judicial duties. Courts-martial were to be used instead of special sessions, not because they were more efficient, but because they would be completely free from reli-

---

[47] A. Macintyre, *The liberator* (London, 1965), pp 39–41.
[48] 3 and 4 Will. IV, c. 3, signed 2 Apr. 1833.

ance upon the competence and co-operation of the magistracy.[49] But the 'Instructions on the coercion act' sent to the commanders of the military districts of Ireland contain an assault upon the magistracy not mentioned in the act. Troop commanders of detachments in the disturbed areas were to be given the commission of the peace '. . . even where there is a civilian magistrate, especially if he has faction leanings', and the officers were specifically instructed not to identify themselves with the interests of any group. 'Act at all times with temper and forebearance. Show if possible an unusual degree of kindness and consideration, [and] only the wicked have anything to fear.'[50]

Thus by 1833 the troops assigned to police duty were under the control of officers who also held powers of magistrates. In 1833 the Peace Preservation Force, under stipendiary magistrates, totalled 1,514 men, approximately one-fourth of the number then in the Constabulary.[51] Only the detachments of the Constabulary were still under the control of the country gentlemen; logically, the government's next step was to complete its task by duplicating Peel's police proposal of 1830. But this move was not attempted until a reconstituted whig government took office in 1835.

The coercion act of 1833, like similar measures of the past, proved very effective against banditti activity. But the sudden collapse of the banditti forces in the early spring of 1833 involved more than the application of the act: the collapse was furthered considerably by the imaginative use of police and military power as well. In effect, the 'war' against the tithe-defaulters was reduced to secondary importance, while the bulk of the force at the disposal of the government was concentrated against the 'midnight marauders'. New tactics were developed. Patrols were instructed to vary the time and location of their activities; military officers were told to 'place parties in ambush by strategic bridges' to check the movement of banditti at night.

[49] This is at least implied in Anglesey to Hobhouse, 25 Apr. 1833 (Broughton papers, B.M., Add. MS 36467), and in Lord Duncannon to Edward Littleton, 2 Oct. 1834 (Wellesley papers, B.M., Add. MS 37307); see also McDowell, *Public opinion & govt policy*, p. 150.

[50] Gen. Vivian to Gen. Blakeney, 8 Apr. 1833 (P.R.O., H.O. 100/244).

[51] *Return of the Peace Preservation Force in Ireland*, H.C. 1834 (201), xlvii, 399.

Since the house of a suspect could not be searched without a warrant, leaders of military detachments were told to surround the house and simply wait for something to happen.[52] In April, the under-secretary wrote, 'The improvement is manifest, and such is the terror it has inspired in the offenders, that many of the worst characters have taken their departure for America or elsewhere.'[53]

But the timid efforts of parliament to reorganize the tithe system had not met with similar success. Opposition to the tithe apparently increased. The news that the church cess would no longer be levied evidently caused some of the peasants to believe that the tithe had been abolished, while others renewed their determination to oppose any measure that fell short of complete abolition of the tithe.[54] There were continued clashes between the police and military and the tithe delinquents, but these were less frequent than during the preceding two years. By mid-1833 the Castle seems to have abandoned its efforts to act as tithe-collector, and there was increasing reluctance to make extensive use of troops and police to assist the tithe-owners in their efforts at collection. Parliament, as well as the Castle, seemed to be showing signs of war-weariness. In June an act was passed which allowed tithe-owners to draw sums of money from the government against uncollected tithes. Given the hostility of the peasants and the inability of the authorities to enforce payment, the act meant in effect that tithe arrears for the past two and a half years were cancelled.[55]

Edward Littleton, who had become chief secretary upon Stanley's transfer to the colonial office in 1833, was anxious to limit the use of force in collecting tithes. He asked the cabinet for suggestions, but the reply was unenlightening:

The cabinet entirely agree with you that this is a very important question; it is also a question of some difficulty and for the determination of which it is impossible to lay down definite rules or give precise instructions beforehand, as the course which it may be prudent to pursue must depend very much on the general aspect of

[52] Vivian to Blakeney, 8 Apr. 1833 (P.R.O., H.O. 100/244).

[53] Gosset to Hobhouse, 18 Apr. 1833 (Broughton papers, B.M., Add. MS 36467).

[54] See P.R.O., H.O. 100/245.

[55] Macintyre, *Liberator*, p. 188.

affairs, and the particular circumstances of each case, which may be brought under the consideration of the Irish government.

But it was clear from the remainder of the letter that the cabinet shared Littleton's reluctance to employ force; the cabinet felt that in the final analysis it was impossible to deny 'assistance and protection', but that the circumstances of each case should be considered and every possible means used to persuade the tithe-owner to 'adopt the more moderate course'. If the owner then persisted in his request for forceful collection of the arrears, 'precautions should be taken for restoring the public peace in case it should be interrupted, but the process server or other officer should not be actually escorted either by troops or police'.[56]

To the anger of the tithe-owners, the policy outlined in this letter was that followed by the Irish government for the next two years. Upon receipt of an application for assistance, the Castle would insist that all other possible means must first be attempted, for, as the home secretary suggested in 1835, 'You must of course never positively decline assistance in preserving the authority of law, but you may with propriety suspend your decision for a time.' And even when assistance was granted to the tithe-owners, 'where no breach of the peace is imminent . . . the presence in the field of the force . . . is not necessary for the preservation of the peace . . .'.[57] Thus the tithe-proctors were forced to venture into the villages without escort; if they were threatened or attacked, they could then summon the police or military to their assistance. It is no wonder that the tithe-owners and their proctors felt themselves 'abandoned' by the Castle and that the number of tithe affrays decreased;[58] but when the peasants were determined to have a 'show-down', the Castle was forced to oblige the tithe-owners, and occasionally serious trouble did result.

Anglesey had left Ireland in disgust, following the passage of the coercion act in 1833, and Wellesley had returned as lord lieutenant, serving until January 1835. Following the break-up

[56] Melbourne to Littleton, 29 Aug. 1833 (Wellesley papers, B.M., Add. MS 37306).
[57] Russell to Lord Mulgrave, 27 May 1835 (P.R.O., Russell papers, 30/22, box 1).
[58] For letters of protest from tithe-owners, see P.R.O., H.O. 100/245–7.

of the Grey ministry in 1834, Melbourne became prime minister until the tories, under Peel, returned to office in November. Peel's first ministry was of greater significance than its brief duration and meagre legislative accomplishments would indicate, if only because it led to the Lichfield House compact between O'Connell and the whigs. The Irish leader, convinced that tory policies would be more detrimental to Ireland than those of the whigs, accepted whig leadership and an 'alliance based on an exchange of political advantages'. Peel was defeated in April 1835, the whigs returned to office under Melbourne, and the alliance continued.[59] Lord John Russell became home secretary and leader of the house of commons, Lord Mulgrave (later the marquess of Normanby) was appointed lord lieutenant, and Lord Morpeth accepted the office of chief secretary.

As political figures, Russell, Mulgrave, and Morpeth represented an interesting combination of strengths and weaknesses. Russell – stubborn, outspoken, and impetuous – championed a concept of civil liberty that owed more to the seventeenth century than to the nineteenth. Mulgrave was considered something of a buffoon by London society, but Greville ascribed to him 'courage and firmness and no want of ability'. Morpeth, perhaps the weakest of the three, was considered to have 'very fair ability of a showy kind', but doubtfully possessed of the 'strength and stolidity' required for the 'rough work which is allotted to him'.[60] Disturbed by the violence of the recent 'tithe war' and mindful of the importance of the understanding with O'Connell, the policy-makers realized that steps must be taken to lessen discontent, and perhaps even to save the union. The Irish policy of the government was to be based on the assumption that a programme of constructive reform and administrative fair play would make the union workable, and even desirable to large sections of the Irish people.[61] And from 1835 to 1840, the men who guided Irish affairs showed a refreshing willingness to try new solutions for old problems.

[59] See A. H. Graham, 'The Lichfield House compact, 1835', I.H.S., xii, no. 47 (Mar. 1961); Macintyre, *Liberator*, pp 135–46.
[60] Greville, *Memoirs*, iii, 199.
[61] McDowell, *Public opinion & govt policy*, p. 178.

Surprisingly, however, the Irish government between 1835 and 1840 appeared to be dominated by the under-secretary, Thomas Drummond. A Scot who had gained an intimate knowledge of Ireland and the Irish at first hand while working on the ordnance survey, Drummond was deeply moved by the poverty and misery of the Irish peasants. His famous reminder to the Irish landlords that 'property has its duties as well as rights' caused his property-loving superiors some embarrassment, and Morpeth wrote to Russell, 'Drummond's merits are boundless, but he may at times be wanting in considerateness.'[62] Under Mulgrave the problems of maintaining law and order became primarily the province of the under-secretary, and much of the success of the Irish government in this direction between 1835 and 1840 was the result of the abilities and hard work of Drummond.

The new approach to Ireland and Irish affairs appeared early in the steps taken to cope with agrarian violence. Among the first problems to receive the attention of the Castle, and one considered basic to the policy of reform and fairness, was the unsatisfactory condition of the County Constabulary. The major weakness of the Constabulary, according to Drummond, was the influence of the magistracy on this organization: by the pernicious exercise of their power to appoint the constables and sub-constables, the magistrates had created a force that was regarded as a partisan body.[63] Apparently Drummond and his superiors concluded that the flaws in the County Constabulary were too deeply rooted to be remedied with piecemeal reforms: if the effectiveness and the reputation of the police were to be improved, a thorough overhaul of the existing organization was necessary.

The constabulary bill, introduced to the house of commons on 10 August 1835,[64] contained the following provisions: the four provincial inspectors were to be replaced by an inspector-general, appointed by the lord lieutenant, who was to be

[62] Morpeth to Russell, 17 Mar. 1838 (P.R.O., Russell papers, 30/22, box 3).

[63] See McDowell, *Public opinion & govt policy*, p. 185.

[64] It seems that Littleton, who was chief secretary from May 1833 to Dec. 1834, drafted a bill which embodied a number of the reforms contained in the constabulary bill (see *Hansard 3*, xxx, 1189).

responsible for the entire constabulary system. He was to receive a salary of £1,000 a year and have the powers of a magistrate in every county in Ireland. He would be assisted by a deputy-inspector, paid £600 a year. There would be thirty-two county inspectors with salaries of 'not over' £300 a year; and they were to have the powers of stipendiary magistrates. Apparently these country inspectors were also to function as paymasters and storekeepers, assisted in each county by a clerk at £50. Under the county inspectors would be a number of sub-inspectors, each at the salary of a 'first-class chief-constable'; and, it is interesting to note, the sub-inspectors were also to have the powers of stipendiary magistrates. There were to be eighteen chief-constables for each county at a salary of £70 a year; the bill did not specify the size of detachments under the chief-constables. The local magistrates lost the right to appoint the constables and sub-constables. The personnel of the entire police system were to be appointed by the lord lieutenant, who also was given authority to establish the rules and regulations for the police, a right which had formerly rested in part with the local magistrates. It was also the right of the lord lieutenant to 'reduce or arrange' the police in any area as he saw fit. The only power remaining in the hands of the local magistrates was that of requesting an increase in the size of the force in their county.[65]

Like Peel's proposal of 1830, the new bill was designed to eliminate the role of the magistrates in the functioning of the Constabulary by placing the entire system in the hands of the Irish government. But the 1835 bill was a much stronger measure. The new bill placed a considerable amount of power with one man, the inspector-general; and because of the number of new positions it created, it was certain to be more expensive. These points came in for some criticism during the debate on the bill, but the loudest complaints came from those who saw it as an attack on the patronage of the magistrates. In the house of commons, Colonel Percival asked '. . . on what grounds the government attempted to degrade the unpaid and independent magistracy of Ireland by depriving them of the power of selecting the police – a duty for which no men were more competent'. Another member, Mr Shaw, contended that

[65] *House of lords, bills, public*, H. L. 1835, ii, 362–8.

'the effect of the bill would be to vest an immense power of patronage in the hands of the Irish government, and to supersede the magistracy of the country . . .'.[66]

The bill managed to pass through committee without important modifications, only to encounter serious resistance in the house of lords. Morpeth had warned of the strength of the opposition to the bill in the upper chamber, and on 25 August he wrote to Drummond,

Duncannon says the lords mean to throw out the constabulary bill, for which I shall be very sorry on all accounts, but chiefly because I think you will not be able to refrain from butchering every member of the aristocracy.[67]

True to Morpeth's prediction, the lords rejected the bill by a vote of fifty-one to thirty-nine. The earl of Roden objected to the measure because '. . . the bill would take the appointments out of the hands of the magistrates, who were a most excellent and fearless body of men'. The earl of Wicklow stated that if the bill were passed 'the magistracy of Ireland would receive it as a withdrawal of confidence from them', and the marquess of Westmeath said that he would 'be ashamed to show his face amongst his brother magistrates in Ireland if he consented to take from them that power which they had so long and so faithfully exercised'. Another reason for the rejection of the bill by the lords was indicated by Lord Duncannon when he said that 'there were some noble lords who seemed to say they would vote against everything which Mr O'Connell had supported'.[68]

In 1822, when Goulburn had faced a similar situation, he had amended his police bill to make it acceptable to its opponents, and thus insured the passage of the weaker measure. Following the defeat of the constabulary bill of 1835, Morpeth and his associates not only refused to remove or amend the portions of the bill which seemed most objectionable to the lords, but proceeded to frame a measure somewhat stronger than the original. The bill of 1836, as finally passed,[69] contained the

[66] *Hansard 3*, xxx, 656, 659.
[67] Morpeth to Drummond, 25 Aug. 1835, in R. Barry O'Brien, *Thomas Drummond, life and letters* (London, 1889), p. 200.
[68] *Hansard 3*, xxx, 1002–7.
[69] 6 and 7 Will. IV c. 13, 20 May 1836.

following provisions different from those of the 1835 bill: The salary of the inspector-general was raised from £1,000 to £1,500 a year. He was given two deputy-inspectors instead of one, each at a salary of £800 per year instead of £600. The county inspectors were reduced in number to four, one for each province, as in the existing system, at a salary now raised to £500 per year. The thirty-two sub-inspectors remained, at a salary of £250. Eighteen combined paymaster-storekeeper-clerks at £100 a year were added, and the salaries of the chief constables were raised from £70 to £150 a year. To make certain that the personnel of the police at all levels would be as impartial as possible in their dealings with the citizenry, an oath was to be administered which would exclude members of 'political or secret societies', except Masons, 'which are largely charitable'. No inspector-general, county inspector, or government magistrate could sit in parliament, and no member of the Constabulary would be allowed to vote in an election. The Peace Preservation Force was to be dissolved, but several of its desirable features were to be retained. The lord lieutenant was to have the right to proclaim an area to be in a state of disturbance and to reinforce the police in that area as he saw fit, within prescribed limits. The stipendiary magistrates were to be continued, and the lord lieutenant was given the right to install them where he believed their services were needed. Also, indicating the change taking place in Dublin Castle, it was specifically stated that the police were not to be used to 'levy tithe or to collect rent by distress'.

The bill encountered no serious opposition in the house of commons, perhaps because Morpeth had come well prepared to answer the friends of the Irish magistrates. He informed them that 'within the last three months, not fewer than ninety-six constables and sub-constables had been dismissed from the force for belonging to secret [Orange] societies'. Any remaining chance that the bill might be defeated in commons was diminished when Peel arose to make his last contribution to the long struggle to establish an efficient Irish police system. He informed the members that it was '. . . of the highest importance that the police force in Ireland should be kept perfectly free from the influence of party animosity and party excitement'. And to assure this, 'The appointment of the police . . . had better be trusted to the hands of . . . the crown than any local authority.'[70]

The bill passed the house of commons on 23 March, but the major obstacle, the house of lords, had still to be surmounted. On 12 April, during the second reading, the duke of Wellington led the attack on the measure. He dissected the financial provisions in detail, and declared that the proposed police system would cost £200,000 a year more than did the existing police. The bill passed the second reading, but the number of peers who joined Wellington in denouncing the measure[71] indicated further trouble to come. On the same day, a meeting was held at Wellington's house, evidently attended by members of the cabinet and the leaders of the opposition, where 'an altered constabulary bill' was adopted. What the alterations were is not mentioned, but possibly it was at this time that the number of county inspectors was reduced; for, as Russell wrote to the lord lieutenant, 'Your constabulary establishment seems to be too expensive. Especially the number of £500 men.'[72]

On 21 May 1836, Morpeth wrote to Drummond,

The constabulary bill has received royal assent, and whatever is in it, if this effect was to incarcerate us both for life, still at the consummation I must rejoice. . . .[73]

After twenty-three years of failures, crises, and frustrations, Ireland finally had a well-organized system of police, which had emerged by gradual evolution over a period of years, rather than by sudden change. Because the Irish Constabulary had developed in response to the challenge of agrarian violence, mobs, and banditti armies, it was a para-military organization, tailored for a purpose that could not be met by a 'civilian' police. It was a unique organization; as Lord John Russell wrote in 1838,

The force is a very peculiar one; it neither resembles the regular troops nor the militia nor the metropolitan police, but it should have one quality in common with all of them, that any ministry which may be called to advise the crown [?] should have the services and the officers and men completely and effectually at their command.[74]

[70] *Hansard 3*, xxx 534–45.
[71] *Hansard 3*, xxxii, 883–93.
[72] Russell to Mulgrave, 12 Apr. 1836 (P.R.O., H.O. 100/251).
[73] Morpeth to Drummond, 21 May 1836, in O'Brien, *Drummond*, p. 220.
[74] Russell to Mulgrave, 8 Apr. 1838 (P.R.O., Russell papers, 30/22, box 3).

Testifying before a select committee of the house of lords in 1839, Justice Arthur Moore, who had been a member of the Irish judiciary since 1814, stated that he detected in Ireland 'a tendency to a state of order and improvement which did not exist in the former periods'.[75] Moore was undoubtedly correct, for between 1835 and 1841 a 'tendency' towards a more peaceful state of affairs could be detected, abetted by the legislative and administrative efforts of the whig government. In 1835 an Irish municipal reform bill was introduced, based on the British bill of the same year and designed to remodel the corrupt and exclusively protestant machinery of borough government in Ireland. In 1838 Ireland received the benefits of a poor law, and further tithe legislation was enacted during the same year. The tithe was converted to a rent charge based on 70 per cent of the normal value of the tithe, and all arrears were cancelled.

In 1836 the efforts of the Melbourne government to 'civilize' Ireland were made somewhat easier by the voluntary dissolution of the Orange order. The re-activation of the 'Orange' yeomanry in 1831 had caused widespread criticism of Orangeism in England and in Ireland. The position of the duke of Cumberland as grand master of the order, and charges of spreading Orangeism in the British army, had caused some members of parliament to fear that the duke intended to change the succession by force. Following the report of a select committee formed to inquire into the activities of the lodges, an address was carried in the house of commons asking the crown to discourage the activities of the organization, and as a result the grand lodge of Ireland dissolved itself.

As early as December 1835, before the findings of the select committee had been presented to parliament, the king suggested that Orangemen holding positions in the Irish government should be 'eased out'.[76] Armed with the royal approval, the Castle began to remove the members of the lodges from government service, and the traces of Orangeism which had appeared in the Constabulary in recent years were quickly eliminated. Orange magistrates 'who encouraged violation of the law' were

[75] Testimony of Justice Arthur Moore, *State of Ireland in respect of crime part iii*, H.L. 1839 (20), xxi, 1240.
[76] Russell to Mulgrave, 6 Dec. 1835 (P.R.O., Russell papers, 30/22, box 1); see also Senior, *Orangeism, 1795–1836*, pp 254–73.

to be deprived of the commission of the peace.[77] As a further indication of the liberalization of the Irish government under Russell and his associates, a certain number of the higher posts in the government were, after 'caution and selection', given to catholics.[78] Three of the six Irish judges appointed between 1835 and 1841 were catholics, and during this period either the attorney-general or the solicitor-general was a catholic.[79] Russell was probably correct when he informed Mulgrave in 1837 that 'the Roman catholic clergy have more confidence in your government than they have had in any since the revolution in 1688'.[80]

Of the Irish reforms instituted by the whigs during this period, the reform of the police system was undoubtedly the most successful. Once established, the new police grew rapidly. In 1835, the rural police establishment, consisting of the Peace Preservation Force and the Constabulary, had totalled 7,319 officers and men; by 1840 it had increased to 8,590 and in 1850 had reached 12,758.[81] In many respects, the new force resembled an army more than a civilian police. The first inspector-general was Colonel Shaw Kennedy, and most of the senior officers were men with military experience. The rank and file of the Irish Constabulary lived in barracks, were armed with carbines, and were instructed in military drill.[82] The personnel of the new police were under military discipline, and Constabulary courts were established to enforce strict obedience at all levels. Under-secretary Drummond, who had served as an officer in the British army, viewed the Constabulary as a regiment, with the new head constables performing the duties of sergeant-majors and the chief constables those of ensigns.[83] With the end

[77] Russell to Mulgrave, 9 Dec. 1835 (P.R.O., Russell papers, 30/22, box 1).

[78] Russell to Mulgrave, 15 Jan. 1836 (P.R.O., Russell papers, 30/22, box 1).

[79] McDowell, *Public opinion & govt policy*, p. 129.

[80] Russell to Mulgrave, 9 Dec. 1837 (P.R.O., H.O. 100/251).

[81] *Amount of force employed in each county or city in Ireland, 1 January 1840*, H.C. 1840 (290), xlviii, 159; *Amount of force . . . 1 January 1850*, H.C. 1850 (431), li, 287.

[82] See Hargrave L. Adam, *The police encyclopedia* (London, n.d.), i, 158–68.

[83] Testimony of Thomas Drummond, *State of Ireland in respect of crime, part iii*, H.L. 1839 (20), xx, 963–4.

of the influence of the local magistrates over the police, an 'enlightened' personnel policy was adopted, similar to the one established by Peel in 1814. The lord lieutenant gave the power to appoint the personnel of the Constabulary to the inspector-general, and thus the operations and administration of the entire system were placed in his hands.[84] The Irish Constabulary was in most respects an 'Irish army', under the complete control of the civil authorities, for use in Ireland alone.

It is generally accepted that the Irish Constabulary was efficient in the performance of its duties and enjoyed at least the qualified respect of the average Irishman. It was respected both because it earned a reputation for impartiality and fairness in its relations with the peasantry and because over a period of years the personnel became predominantly catholic and of peasant origin. The success of the Constabulary was aided considerably by the removal of two important causes of rural violence – faction fights and Orange processions. The dissolution of the Orange order in 1836 served to increase the activities of the 'inferior class' membership of this organization, and the lord lieutenant announced that the first item on the agenda of the new police would be to stop the 'illegal' activities of the Orangemen.[85] The Orangemen chose 12 July 1836 as the day for a 'show of strength', and when the news reached the Castle orders were issued to arrest all who participated in the demonstrations. By the evening of 12 July over four hundred troublemakers were in jail; when the same situation arose a year later, those arrested were sentenced to imprisonment for terms ranging from one to three months. So many Orangemen were arrested in Antrim at this time that the jail could not hold them all.[86] To end the faction fights, a plan of operation was developed by the inspector-general's office and forwarded to the local police officials. All the Constabulary detachments in an area where trouble was expected were to be alerted, ready to reinforce the police assigned the task of patrolling the village or fairground in question. Any armed person entering this area

[84] Ibid.

[85] Mulgrave to Russell, 18 Jan. 1836 (P.R.O., Russell papers, 30/22, box 2).

[86] Testimony of Thomas Drummond, *State of Ireland in respect of crime, part iii*, H.L. 1839 (20), xx, 485–7.

was to be arrested immediately, and if trouble occurred in spite of these precautions every effort was to be made to arrest the rioters. Those not arrested at the time were to be 'identified' and arrested later. In an attempt to prevent faction fights, the chief constables were to be 'called to account' for any riots in their districts. According to Thomas Drummond, by 1839 faction fights had virtually ceased.[87]

[87] Ibid., pp 967–9.

XII

THE SEARCH FOR LAW
AND ORDER, 1812–36

IF THE IRISH CONSTABULARY of 1836 was, as Lord John
Russell said, a 'very peculiar' force, it was also one which few
people in Ireland really seemed to want. The peasant still saw
the policeman, however reformed, as an agent of political and
economic repression. O'Connell and his associates, though not
so overtly critical of the new force as they had been of the old
County Constabulary, seem to have accepted the 1836 police
reforms as at best a modest improvement. The loudest criticism
of the new arrangements came, of course, from the gentlemen
who manned the magisterial benches of rural Ireland. The
substance of their attack in 1836 was the same as that which
they had directed against the police reform of 1814 and had
repeated during the debates prior to the reform of 1822:
Castle-controlled police represented a dangerous usurpation of
the powers of the 'constitutional' magistrates. And the substance
of the Castle's reply was that which had been used against the
magistrates for the better part of the previous twenty-four
years: local magistrates lacked the personal qualities necessary
for the effective supervision of rural law enforcement.

But more was involved in this long and noisy dialogue than a
mere struggle for power between conflicting interest groups. A
prominent feature of nineteenth-century Irish and British
administrative history was the development of administrative

sub-systems which had the effect of spreading state intervention into areas of politics and economics traditionally dominated by local government or individual effort. It is doubtful that Peel, Goulburn, or even Drummond saw himself as part of a 'new breed' of administrative reformer, but in matters of law-enforcement the accomplishments of these men mesh neatly with the traditions of that group: the cause of efficient and impartial law-enforcement could best be served by increasing the police powers of Dublin Castle at the expense of local authority. Collectively, Peel, Goulburn, and Drummond were responsible for the first major change in the traditional division of power between local government and central government during the nineteenth century.

Imperfect as were the local magistrates, it is possible to feel a certain amount of sympathy for these much-censured gentle-men. It would have taken men of heroic stature to reach the level of magisterial efficiency demanded by Peel during the early years of his chief-secretaryship. The magistrate had a central role in the maintenance of rural law and order. His functions ranged from the supervision of local police and the direction of military units used for police purposes to participation in the judicial processes that sentenced convicted criminals to imprisonment, transportation, or death. But the system over which the magistrates presided could not function successfully without the support of the populace and the strength of effective, reliable instruments of law-enforcement. At the time of Peel's arrival in Ireland in 1812, neither public support nor effective physical force was at the disposal of the magistrates. The public – in rural Ireland, the peasants – were turning increasingly from support of the ascendancy-made law of the magistrates to support of a law of their own, based upon the will of the peasant community. The duly constituted government was unwilling or unable to deal with the major concerns of the peasants – high rents, evictions, the tithe. Thus, not only did the peasant support his own body of law, but also over a consider-able portion of Ireland he gave his assent to what was in effect his own government – government in the form of the agrarian secret societies whose political activity took the form of agrarian outrage. Ulster, where the main concerns of the peasants were religious rather than economic, was an exception to the general pattern. Improved economic conditions made existence there somewhat more certain. A protestant majority deeply involved with the ultra-protestant Orange order seemed to justify the existence of the Ribbon order for the protection of the catholic minority. In Ulster it was the clashes of the two religious organizations that turned the fairs and marketplaces into arenas and presented the north's greatest challenge to the authority of the government.

At the time of Peel's arrival, the magistrates were not in a favourable position to compel banditti obedience to ascendancy law and government. The baronial police were worthless, and the yeomanry – because of its close association with ultra-protestantism – was often more a liability than an asset when used for police purposes. The regular soldiers of the Irish military establishment were the best source of manpower available to the magistrates. For generations, soldier-policemen had been the mainstay of Irish law-enforcement, and probably would have continued to be so had not the end of the war in Europe and the economic problems of the British government forced a drastic reduction in the size of the armed forces. By 1814 it had become clear that something new had to be tried if large portions of the Irish countryside were not to be abandoned to the peasant terrorists.

It was Peel's search for 'something new' that made him the key figure in the history of Irish police reform. Disturbed by the inefficiency of existing police arrangements and angered by what he saw as cowardly incompetence in the local leaders, the chief secretary began to consider a different approach to the matter of policing Ireland. The first result was the Peace Preservation Force of 1814, an organization that made a contribution both to the Castle's efforts to cope with agrarian violence and to the political education of the future prime minister.

The Force was designed to restore local magistrates to positions of leadership, with or without their willing co-operation, by making them responsible for requesting detachments of the Force and then by making the Force's continuing assistance extremely expensive. Apart from the provision making the stipendiary magistrate in charge of a detachment the superior of local magistrates in proclaimed areas, the new police were not greatly different from other specialized police organizations operating in various parts of the British Isles. But the coercive part of the plan was unique. The proclaimed area bore the full burden of the cost of the detachment assigned to it, and the cost was made as high as possible. Once the Force had been installed, the local magistrates were powerless to remove it; they and the rest of the population of the area continued paying for its expenses until the government determined that the local magistrates were performing their duties. Only the lord lieutenant could withdraw detachments of the Force from a proclaimed area.

Castle officials did not suppose that the new and untried peace preservation act alone would enable them to control agrarian unrest. The insurrection act of 1807 was therefore requested and was re-enacted by parliament in 1814. This act was always considered an extreme measure, since it provided that certain constitutional guarantees, including trial by jury, could be suspended in an area proclaimed by the lord lieutenant. The peace preservation act was intended to be applied freely, wherever agrarian outrage was becoming a problem, while the insurrection act was for use only in instances of 'imperious necessity'. If the situation worsened in a county already proclaimed under the peace preservation act, the same county could be proclaimed under the insurrection act, and could remain under both proclamations at the discretion of the lord lieutenant.

Peel's attempts to tranquillize Ireland by widespread use of the peace preservation act alone demonstrated the futility of trying to force reform on unreceptive people and revealed another facet of magisterial character: the local leaders proved to be proud and stubborn men with powerful friends in high places. Between 1814 and 1817, banditti violence and the prideful stubbornness of the country gentlemen combined to force Peel, for all practical purposes, to abandon the coercive portion of his police act of 1814. The magistrates were very reluctant to incur the inflated costs of the Force, particularly when a proclamation under the insurrection act could assure suppression of disturbance without cost, and could by its severe restraints on peasant activity enable a handful of magistrates to perform the necessary duties at slight personal risk. Not all of the local leaders opposed the Force, and in centres of disturbance where the army garrisoned the villages and did most of the routine patrolling, the new police emerged as an effective body of 'outrage specialists' – collecting information, investigating crimes, presenting evidence at trials. A number of countries received detachments, but the widespread opposition to the Force did not subside, and Peel was forced to surrender. In 1817 an act of parliament apportioned the costs of the Force between the government and the proclaimed area.

The first serious engagement in the long struggle to 'modernize' Irish law-enforcement had ended in a draw: the magistrates had kept their traditional 'rights' and had demonstrated successfully the pressure they could bring to bear against an overly ambitious Irish administration; the Castle had retained the Peace Preservation Force which, with all its faults, still seemed to represent the 'logical' method of dealing with agrarian outrage – a body of trained policemen in mobile units, led by a stipendiary magistrate, and under the authority of the central government. The peace preservation act of 1814 was actually of greater significance than the early history of its application would seem to indicate. By 1818, the year Peel resigned as chief secretary, he had made the Irish administration 'police-conscious', and had convinced himself and others that the Force should be the model for any future country-wide system of police. The Irish Constabulary of 1836 is a clearly recognizable descendant of the Peace Preservation Force of 1814.

Between 1813 and 1816, while the Castle and the magistrates manœuvred and debated attempts at police reform, the campaign against the agrarian secret societies went forward. The fading away of secret-society activity in 1816 resulted from the insurrection act, from the pressures exerted by soldiers and policemen, and quite probably from the sheer exhaustion of the banditti. The rural areas were then relatively quiet until the Ribbon disruptions of the winter of 1819–20. Possibly the spread of Dublin Ribbonism into the countryside was meant to herald a country-wide conspiracy in all of lower-class catholic Ireland; if so, the plan failed, because the new recruits to Ribbonism became involved in the agrarian outrage that swept central, western, and south-western Ireland at this time. By the autumn of 1821 Ribbonism had been replaced as a peasant 'cause' by the more familiar and pressing programmes of the agrarian secret societies; the centre of peasant resistance to authority had returned to its traditional location, Tipperary and Limerick.

Charles Grant, the chief secretary from 1818 to late 1821, was both inexperienced and incompetent and was fated to repeat several of the more notable mistakes of 1813–16 in attempting to cope with rural violence. An advocate of the 'civilian' Peace Preservation Force as the logical weapon against rural terrorism, Grant opposed suggestions that the military establishment be strengthened, and by 1821 the army had dwindled in size until it could no longer perform the functions traditionally assigned to it. The chief secretary, a political catholic, refused to use the ultra-protestant yeomanry. The insurrection act had been allowed to expire in 1818. Thus the Castle was forced to rely on the Force, though no one in government circles – with the possible exception of Grant – believed that the special police could cope with widespread, fully-developed banditti activity. Hastily-formed detachments of the Force were assigned duties far beyond their limited resources, and the familiar argument between the Castle and the magistrates was renewed and intensified. Attempts were made to impose the Force on reluctant magistrates; when the magistrates refused, they were accused of cowardice, incompetency, and corruption. Often their response was to call for re-enactment of the insurrection act. By late 1821, Grant and the lord lieutenant, Lord Talbot, had been well and truly defeated by their opponents, and both were rather abruptly relieved of their offices.

The situation in the rural areas had deteriorated alarmingly, and the Wellesley-Goulburn administration moved quickly to deal with the 'war' in Munster. To cope with the current banditti threat and to buy time with which to lessen the causes of violence, the Castle and parliament co-operated in the re-enactment of the insurrection act, which was then kept in force by successive re-enactments until 1825. The act was not so immediately successful as it had been in earlier applications, but it did again prove to be the most effective single weapon at the Castle's disposal in dealing with banditti activity.

The appointment of Wellesley as lord lieutenant marked a modest change in the Irish policy of the British government.

The 'new' policy, based on a tacit admission that government solely in the interest of the ascendancy was no longer feasible, was aimed at encouraging the peasant to look to the government rather than to the secret societies for protection and justice. And basic to the reforms meant to give the peasant improved protection and justice was a complete overhaul of rural law-enforcement.

The Irish constables act of 1822 was the accomplishment of Henry Goulburn, chief secretary from 1821 to 1827 – advised and encouraged by his friend Robert Peel, who was home secretary during this period. Apparently Goulburn initially saw the proposed reform of rural law-enforcement as involving little more than an expansion of the Peace Preservation Force into every county on a permanent basis. Certainly Peel knew that such a massive extension of Castle authority – the entire magistracy placed under the authority of Castle magistrates – would never be acceptable to the ascendancy. Thus Goulburn began what were in effect negotiations to determine just how much centralized control would be acceptable to the magistrates and their friends. The answer was that they were willing to accept a surprising amount of control, but refused to negotiate two important 'rights': the direction of police operations and the appointment of constables and sub-constables.

In its final form the act creating the County Constabulary provided that the new police were to be established by counties, with a separate detachment for each 'division' of a county. The detachments were to 'obey' the magistrates of the county, who also appointed the constables and sub-constables. Within the upper levels, however, the authority of the Castle was complete. The four provincial inspectors, whose main function seems to have been the collection of reliable information from the countryside, were appointed by and answerable to the central government, as were the chief constables who commanded the separate detachments. Surprisingly, the Castle was given the right to discharge any member of the Constabulary, from inspector to sub-constable, for misconduct or failure to perform his duties. Finally, any seven magistrates of a county might request that a stipendiary, or 'resident', magistrate be installed where the absence or non-residence of a magistrate made one necessary. The Peace Preservation Force remained intact, with its power unchanged; evidently the Castle considered it a reserve force, over which the government retained complete control.

With less difficulty than might have been expected, the police reformers had given Ireland (on paper, at least) the most advanced police system in the British Isles. The lack of ascendancy opposition may have been due in part to the seriousness of the prolonged disorder in Munster and in part to the obvious worth of the new arrangements. But an equally strong case can be made for the assertion that the act of 1822 avoided interference with the areas of greatest magisterial sensitivity – pride and patronage. The magistrates retained the right to supervise operations of the police and the privilege of appointing the majority of the policemen. The reformers, however, were mindful of the weaknesses of the magistrates. Goulburn set about improving the quality of leadership by 'reforming' the magistracy and the quality of appointments by negotiating with the local authorities for the privilege of allowing the Castle to choose the personnel of the detachments as they were formed.

It is difficult to determine the effectiveness of the County Constabulary during the first seven years of its operation. Wellesley credited it with ending the 'war' in Munster in 1823, but it is at least equally possible that pacification came then as it had in 1816 – from the insurrection act, a strengthened military establishment, and the exhaustion of the banditti. Until 1825, the Constabulary operated under the 'protection' of the insurrection act, and from then to 1829 the maintenance of law and order in Ireland was as much the concern of the Catholic Association as of the Constabulary.

O'Connell and the Catholic Association seemed at first to be that leadership of 'a higher order' which the Castle had been dreading for years as the force which would finally unite the Irish peasantry and set them on the road to full-scale revolution. It soon became clear, however, that O'Connell's massive organization was meant to be a pressure group, exploiting to the full the threat, not the fact, of revolution. The task of preventing violence was as urgent for the Association as for the government. It was made somewhat easier with the dissolution of the Orange order in 1825 and the consequently lessened provocation for violence in the north. In 1826–7 and in early 1828, banditti leadership seems to have prevailed over the leadership of the Association and the priests in several traditional trouble-spots, and agrarian outrage followed. But during the months of crisis following the Clare election, the agrarian secret societies apparently accepted the leadership of O'Connell and his associates; the use of the threat instead of the substance of revolution was not challenged by the most violent segment of rural society. The lessons of non-violent power, however, had not been fully mastered by the peasantry.

But the peasants had learned that they need not always unduly fear authority, and the nearest symbol of authority was the police. From late 1829 on, an increasing number of the clashes between the peasantry and the Constabulary were spur-of-the-moment actions, often occurring in daylight, with the participants making little attempt to hide their identity. Ordinarily these incidents took place when the Constabulary arrived to perform some unpopular functions. The peasants' attitude towards the police was not entirely symbolic. By 1829 relations between the Constabulary and the peasantry were characterized by what can only be described as hatred. There had been frequent verbal attacks on the Constabulary by O'Connell and his associates. The police were accused of favouring protestants in clashes involving catholics and the now-revived Orange order. But the fundamental cause of peasant resentment was police brutality. The Constabulary detachments were often too small to deal with mass demonstrations without resorting to force, and the force used by frightened policemen was often excessive.

Further, in 1829 the spectre of poor police leadership had returned to haunt the Castle. The magistrates were accused of weakening the detachments by assigning men to guard the homes of the country gentlemen, but the major leadership problem lay in the inferior quality of chief constables appointed by the government. As the result of erosion rather than a change of policy, the chief constables had gradually become involved in Castle patronage. What Peel saw, however, was a general deterioration of the Constabulary, and it was this assessment of the problem that caused his abortive attempt at police reform in 1830. What was needed, he thought, was a force under the complete control of the Castle – stipendiary police under stipendiary magistrates – and completely 'neutral' in its relations with the people. But his proposal seems not to have received serious consideration in parliament.

Added to the increasing boldness of the peasants and the increasing weakness of the unpopular Constabulary was the fact that 1829–31 were famine years in Ireland, and years of general economic distress in both Ireland and England. The catholic clergy, perhaps in an attempt to discourage peasant violence by giving the people a new cause and new leadership, began a campaign of collective passive resistance to the tithe. But the issue was inflammatory, and the leadership of the Catholic Association was missing from the effort, and the country drifted into the 'tithe wars' of the early 1830s. Constabulary detachments, supported by troops, attempted to collect tithes by seizing crops and live-stock. The result was that some of the bloodiest encounters between police and soldiers and peasants during the entire century occurred between 1830 and 1834. Meanwhile the agrarian secret societies once more resumed extensive operations.

Constabulary and military officers seem to have realized early in the 'tithe war' that the agrarian secret societies were operating quite separately from the campaign against the tithe. Beginning in 1833, the police and military establishments concentrated on the banditti, attempting only to contain the disturbances caused by tithe protestors. While opposition to the tithe increased, banditti activities lessened and had virtually ceased by the spring of 1833. The collapse of the agrarian secret societies at this time remains something of a mystery; the force used against them was not overwhelming, though it was apparently applied somewhat more intelligently than had been the case in the past.

The 'tithe war' was the last occasion during which the agrarian secret societies were able to control sizeable areas of rural Ireland for considerable periods of time. Police officials claimed that by the 1840s the long-established societies in the south had ceased to exist. Probably the claim is an exaggeration: banditti 'cells' were apparently operating as late as the 1850s, and undoubtedly the traditions and techniques of the societies were passed on to future generations and may have influenced the more mature peasant organizations of the second half of the century. The 'tithe war' itself ended when the government in effect abandoned attempts at forcible collection of the tithe in 1833–4.

Disturbed by the horrors of the recent tithe war, and very much aware of the importance of the understanding with O'Connell, the whigs who directed Irish affairs from 1835 to 1840 showed a willingness to try new solutions to the old Irish problem. This willingness was demonstrated in the steps taken to cope with rural violence. During 1830–4 all the traditional methods of dealing with violence had been used to the utmost (even the yeomanry had been resurrected), and all had been found wanting. The time had arrived for another round of police reform, but modification of the existing system was not enough. The County Constabulary had been castigated so often by the O'Connellites, was so closely associated with the ascendancy, had been involved in so many tithe affrays, that the replacement of this organization was essential.

Drummond's constabulary act of 1836 contained little that was original; it was a codification of the proposals of the Castle's more knowledgeable administrators and police officials of the previous two decades. The county organizational basis was retained, the entire system – including the appointment of all personnel – was put under the control of the central government, all senior officers were made stipendiary magistrates, and a hierarchy of inspectors was created to enforce standards of performance and behaviour. There were two important differences between the Irish Constabulary and the systems of 1814 and 1822: the Constabulary of 1836 was headed by a single official, the inspector-general, who in effect took over the burden of general supervision from the chief secretary; and the new Constabulary was under regulations insuring the impartiality of the police in dealing with the citizenry. Members of the Constabulary were required to take an oath framed to exclude members of 'political' or 'secret' organizations. The Peace Preservation Force was disbanded, and with the creation of the Irish Constabulary in 1836 Drummond had completed the long search for an efficient and impartial police begun by Peel in 1814.

The development of the Irish Constabulary involved more

than the creation of a substitute army, more than the spread of state intervention into areas traditionally dominated by local government or individual effort. By 1822 the British government had come to realize that reform might succeed where coercion had failed in controlling agrarian crime. To those responsible for Irish affairs in the 1820s and 1830s it was clear that the first reforms must be those which could assure the efficient and impartial administration and enforcement of the law. All other reforms would fail unless they could be introduced into a 'moral climate' untainted by Irish sedition, violence, and crime. Thus the development of an effective, and above all an impartial, system of enforcing law and order came to be seen not only as a problem of administrative improvement, but also as one of social reform.

By 1841, when the whigs left office, the Irish Constabulary had proved itself an effective instrument to be used in the 'civilization' of Ireland. The requirements of impartiality, fairness, and efficiency were met by the new police. But the second portion of the long-range programme to tranquillize Ireland, the use of remedial legislation to remove the sources of Irish discontent, was less successful, for the basic cause of Irish discontent remained almost untouched. Neither the whigs nor the tories were willing to launch the economic revolution necessary to correct the abuses of the Irish land tenure system, or to create employment that would relieve the pressure of the increasing population on the land. Therefore extensive agrarian discontent remained, and in spite of a marked decrease after 1837 violence and crime remained at what was undoubtedly a higher level than in any other area of western Europe.

EPILOGUE: THE IRISH
CONSTABULARY

~~~~~~

DURING THE REMAINING YEARS of its existence, the Irish
Constabulary continued to grow in numbers and efficiency. In
1839 the long-needed reserve force was created, and from 1842
it was the practice to appoint cadets to be trained for the position of sub-inspector. The Constabulary played a conspicuous
role in the two minor uprisings of the mid-nineteenth century.
In 1848 a pathetic attempt at an uprising by Smith O'Brien and
his followers ended in the 'battle of Widow McCormick's potato
patch', and the Irish lord chief justice declared that the Irish
Constabulary had 'saved the country'.[1] The more serious
challenge of the Fenian uprising in 1867 put the Constabulary
to a more severe test, which they passed well. Their efforts were
rewarded by the thanks of parliament and the right to be called
the 'Royal' Irish Constabulary. With the establishment of the
Irish Free State, the Constabulary was dissolved and replaced
by the *Garda Siochana*, but the organization established in 1836
still exists in the Royal Ulster Constabulary.

The Irish Constabulary exerted a major influence upon the
development of the colonial police forces of the British Empire.
As Sir Charles Jefferies states,

. . . from the point of view of the colonies there was much attraction

[1] Adam, *Police encyclopedia*, i, 169.

in an arrangement which provided what we should now call a 'paramilitary' organization . . . armed, and trained to operate as an agent of the central government in a country where the population was predominantly rural, communications were poor, social conditions were largely primitive, and the recourse to violence by members of the public who were 'agin the government' was not infrequent.[2]

Not only did the Constabulary serve as a model for many of the colonial forces of the last century, but also as long as the parent organization existed it was a major source of recruitment for the officers of these police systems.[3] In some instances the personnel of the colonial forces were trained at the Constabulary depots in Ireland, a service still provided in the mid-twentieth century by the Royal Ulster Constabulary.[4]

[2] Sir Charles Jefferies, *The colonial police* (London, 1952), pp 30–1.
[3] Ibid., p. 31.
[4] Ibid., p. 172.

BIBLIOGRAPHY

~~~~~~

SYNOPSIS

INTRODUCTION

BY FAR THE MOST important sources of information for the history of police reform are the eighty-one bundles of letters and reports that comprise the home office series 100, collection for 1812–36. Perhaps no areas of policy were more certain to come under parliamentary attack than those involving law and order in Ireland; consequently, any information that might prepare the chief secretary to cope with these attacks was forwarded to London. Even the letters and reports of individual magistrates and minor police officials were forwarded if they seemed at all significant.

Next in importance are the papers of Robert Peel and Henry Goulburn. The Peel papers, a model of completeness and organization, reflect Peel's long-standing interest in police matters and include much information on all aspects of Irish affairs at the policy-making level. The Goulburn papers help to clarify the confused events of 1822–7 and contain important correspondence with William Gregory.

Mention must be made of the vast amount of information on all phases of Irish affairs in parliamentary papers. Some caution should be used in evaluating the testimony of witnesses before the committees and commissions whose reports appear in the papers. It would seem that a certain amount of screening was done by the Castle before witnesses were sent off to Westminster.

The sources above provide a major portion of the material used in this book. Materials in the other collections listed in the bibliography served to expand the narrative that emerged from the home office papers and to clarify matters of detail.

There are very few secondary accounts of real merit dealing with either rural violence or police reform. Cornewall Lewis's *Local disturbances in Ireland* (1836) consists of long excerpts from government reports on rural violence, tied together by the astute observations of the author. An excellent brief account of lower-class political activity appears in R. B. McDowell, *Public opinion and government policy in Ireland* (1953), and the same author's *The Irish administration* (1964) is indispensable for any student of nineteenth-century Irish history.

I SOURCES

(A) *MANUSCRIPT MATERIAL*

LONDON

British Museum

Broughton papers: Add. MS 36467
Liverpool papers: Add. MSS 38195–372
Peel papers: Add. MSS 40181–398, 40611
Wellesley papers: Add. MSS 37298–307

Public Record Office

Home Office papers: H.O. 100/165–251
Russell papers: 30/22, boxes 1–3
War Office papers: W.O. 35/25–6, 80/1, 6

KINGSTON-ON-THAMES

Surrey County Record Office

Goulburn papers: Box C, parts 1–2; II/13–14, 17, 21

DURHAM

Durham University

Grey papers: Boxes 4, 65

DUBLIN

State Paper Office

Records of the Chief Secretary's Office

Bibliography

Official papers: Series 2, boxes 581/534, 588^{AA}/825, 588^{BB}/830^c
Letter books:
Private and official correspondence, vol. 3
General private correspondence, vol. 2
Government correspondence, private; 1820–22

National Library of Ireland
Richmond papers: vols 5, 14

(B) PRINTED MATERIAL
[Place of publication London exept where otherwise stated.]

1 PARLIAMENTARY PROCEEDINGS

The parliamentary debates from the year 1803 to the present time, published under the superintendence of T. C. Hansard, vols xxvii–xli, 1812–20
The parliamentary debates . . . published under the superintendence of T. C. Hansard, new series, vols i–xx, 1820–29
Hansard's parliamentary debates, vols xxi–xxv, 1829–30
Hansard's parliamentary debates, third series, vols i–xxxii, 1830–36

2 PARLIAMENTARY PAPERS

Return of the Constabulary in Ireland, H.L. 1824 (4), xiii
Second report from the select committee on the subject of the disturbed districts in Ireland, H.C. 1825 (35), xiii
Third report from the select committee on the subject of the disturbed districts in Ireland, H.C. 1825 (36), xi
An account of proclamations issued under the provisions of the peace preservation act (54 George III, c. 131; 55 George III c. 13), H.C. 1826 (206), xx
Return of the number of chief constables, constables, and sub-constables in the several counties in Ireland appointed under the act 3 George IV c. 103, H.C. 1826–7 (409), xx
An account of the proclamations issued under the provisions of the peace preservation act, H.C. 1826–7 (206), xx
Minutes of evidence taken before the commissioners appointed to inquire into charges of malversation in the police establishment of the Leinster district, H.C. 1828 (486), xxii
Return of persons killed or wounded in affrays with the Constabulary force in Ireland, H.C. 1830–31 (67), viii
Return of all superannuations granted to constables and sub-constables of police in Ireland, H.C. 1831–2 (339), xxvi
Correspondence relative to the collection and payment of tithe, and the resistance offered thereto, H.C. 1831–2 (663), xxii
An account of the stipendiary magistrates, H.C. 1833 (518), xxxii
Return of the Peace Preservation Force in Ireland during each of the last three years, H.C. 1834 (201), xlvii

245

Bibliography

Report from the select committee appointed to inquire into the nature, character, extent and tendency of the Orange lodges, associations or societies in Ireland, H.C. 1835 (377), xv

Peace preservation police, H.C. 1836 (527), xii

State of Ireland in respect of crime, part iii, H.L. 1839 (20), xx

Return showing the number of effective troops in Ireland on the first of January each year from 1828–1839, H.L. 1839 (51), vi

Amount of force employed in each county or city in Ireland, 1 January 1840, H.C. 1840 (290), xlviii

Return respecting crimes and outrages in Co. Limerick, H.L. 1841 (40), xviii

Return of the number of troops quartered in Ireland during the following years, H.C. 1844 (24), xxxiii

Amount of force employed in each county or city in Ireland, 1 January 1850, H.C. 1850 (432), li

3 LETTERS, SPEECHES, MEMOIRS, AND DIARIES

Arbuthnot, Harriet, *The journal of Mrs Arbuthnot, 1820–1832,* ed. Francis Bamford and the duke of Wellington, 2 vols, London, 1950

Colchester, Lord Charles, *The diary and Correspondence of Charles Abbot Lord Colchester,* ed. Charles, Lord Colchester, 3 vols, London, 1861

King George IV, *The letters of King George IV, 1812–1830,* ed A. Aspinall, 3 vols, Cambridge, 1938

Gregory, William, *Mr Gregory's letter-box, 1813–1830,* ed Lady Augusta Gregory, London, 1898

Greville, Charles, *The Greville memoirs, 1814–1860,* ed. Lytton Strachey and Roger Fulford, 8 vols, London, 1938

Moore, Thomas, *Memoirs of Captain Rock,* Paris, 1824

O'Brien, R. Barry, *Thomas Drummond, life and letters,* London, 1889

Peel, Sir Robert, *Memoirs by Sir Robert Peel,* ed. Earl Stanhope and Edward Cardwell, 2 vols, London, 1857–8

Peel, Sir Robert, *The private letters of Sir Robert Peel,* ed. George Peel, London, 1920

Peel, Sir Robert, *Sir Robert Peel from his private papers,* ed. C. S. Parker, 3 vols, London, 1899

Peel, Sir Robert, *The speeches of the late right honourable Sir Robert Peel, Bart.,* 4 vols, London, 1853

Wellesley, Richard Marquess of, *Wellesley papers,* 'by the editor of the Windham papers', 2 vols, London, 1914

Wellington, Arthur Duke of, *Despatches, correspondence, and memoranda of Field Marshall Arthur, duke of Wellington, 1819–32,* ed. the duke of Wellington, 8 vols, London, 1867–80

Yonge, Charles Duke, *The life and administration of Robert Bankes Jenkinson, second earl of Liverpool,* 3 vols, London, 1868

4 NEWSPAPERS AND OTHER PERIODICALS

Annual Register, 1814–36

Dublin *Evening Post,* 1815–36

Bibliography

II LATER WORKS

Adam, Hargrave L., *The police encyclopedia*, 8 vols, London, n.d.

Anglesey, Marquess of, *One-leg*, London, 1961

Black, R. D. C., *Economic thought and the Irish question, 1817–1870*, Cambridge, 1960

Cecil, David, *Lord M*, London, 1954

Curtis, Robert, *History of the Royal Irish Constabulary*, London, 1878

Freeman, T. W., *Pre-famine Ireland*, Manchester, 1957

Froude, James Anthony, *The English in Ireland in the eighteenth century*, 3 vols, New York, 1874

Gash, Norman, *Mr Secretary Peel*, Cambridge, 1961

Graham, A. H., 'The Lichfield House compact, 1835', *Irish Historical Studies*, xii, no. 46 (Mar. 1961)

Guedalla, Phillip, *Wellington*, New York, 1931

Halevy, Elie, *The liberal awakening*, London, 1923

Holdsworth, Sir William, *A history of English law*, 14 vols, London, 1923–52

Jefferies, Sir Charles, *The colonial police*, London, 1952

Lampson, G. Locker, *A consideration of the state of Ireland in the nineteenth century*, London, 1907

Lecky, William Edward Hartpole, *A history of England in the eighteenth century*, 8 vols, London, 1890

Lecky, William Edward Hartpole, *The leaders of public opinion in Ireland*, New York, 1872

Lee, Captain W. L. Melville, *A history of police in England*, London, 1901

Lewis, Sir George Cornewall, *Local disturbances in Ireland*, London, 1836

Machin, G. I. T., *The catholic question in English politics, 1820 to 1830*, Oxford, 1964

Macintyre, Angus, *The liberator*, London, 1965

Maitland, F. W., *Justice and police*, London, 1885

McAnally, Sir Henry, *The Irish militia*, Dublin, 1949

McDowell, R. B., *The Irish administration, 1801–1914*, London, 1964

McDowell, R. B., *Public opinion and government policy in Ireland, 1801–1846*, London, 1952

O'Brien, R. Barry, *Fifty years of concessions to Ireland*, 2 vols, London, n.d.

O'Connor, Sir James, *The history of Ireland, 1789–1824*, 2 vols, New York, n.d.

O'Mahoney, Charles, *The viceroys of Ireland*, London, 1912

Petrie, Sir Charles, *Lord Liverpool and his times*, London, 1954

Reith, Charles, *A new study of police history*, London, 1956

Reynolds, James A., *The catholic emancipation crisis in Ireland, 1823–1829*, New Haven, 1954

Senior, Hereward, *Orangeism in Ireland and Britain, 1795–1836*, London, 1966

Thursfield, J. R., *Peel*, London, 1921

Trevelyan, George Macaulay, *British history in the nineteenth century and after, 1782–1919*, London, 1948

Bibliography

Walpole, Spencer, *A history of England from the conclusion of the great war in 1815*, 6 vols, London, 1902

Walpole, Spencer, *The life of Lord John Russell*, 2 vols, London, 1889

Woodward, E. L., *The age of reform, 1815–1870*, Oxford, 1938

INDEX

Date Due